THE ULTIMATE GUIDE TO

PRESERVING & CANNING

Inspiring | Educating | Creating | Entertaining

Brimming with creative inspiration, how-to projects, and useful information to enrich your everyday life, Quarto Knows is a favorite destination for those pursuing their interests and passions. Visit our site and dig deeper with our books into your area of interest: Quarto Creates, Quarto Cooks, Quarto Homes, Quarto Lives, Quarto Drives, Quarto Explores, Quarto Gifts, or Quarto Kids.

© 2020 Quarto Publishing Group USA Inc.
Text © 2009 by Lela Nargi, © 2010 by Ana Micka, © 2013 by Allison Carroll Duffy, © 2018 by Amelia Jeanroy

First Published in 2020 by The Harvard Common Press, an imprint of The Quarto Group,
100 Cummings Center, Suite 265-D, Beverly, MA 01915, USA.
T (978) 282-9590 F (978) 283-2742 QuartoKnows.com

The Harvard Common Press titles are also available at discount for retail, wholesale, promotional, and bulk purchase. For details, contact the Special Sales Manager by email at specialsales@quarto.com or by mail at The Quarto Group, Attn: Special Sales Manager, 100 Cummings Center, Suite 265-D, Beverly, MA 01915, USA.

The content in this book appeared in the following previously published titles: *The Farmer's Wife Canning & Preserving Cookbook*, Lela Nargi, editor (Harvard Common Press 2009); *The Fresh Girl's Guide to Easy Canning and Preserving* by Ana Micka (Harvard Common Press 2010); *Preserving with Pomona's Pectin* by Allison Carroll Duffy and the Partners at Pomona's Universal Pectin® (Fair Winds Press 2013); *Modern Pressure Canning* by Amelia Jeanroy (Harvard Common Press 2018).

24 23 22 21 20   1 2 3 4 5

ISBN: 978-1-55832-985-0
Digital edition published in 2020
Library of Congress Cataloging-in-Publication Data available

Cover Design: Laura McFadden
Cover Image: Grace Stufkosky
Page Layout: Megan Jones Design
Photography: Glenn Scott Photography; except pages 43, 74, 92, 94, 156, and 158 (Shutterstock)
Illustrations: Judy Love on pages 34, 35, and 38

The National Center for Home Food Preservation (NCHFP) website can be found at http://nchfp.uga.edu.

Printed in China

THE ULTIMATE GUIDE TO

PRESERVING & CANNING

Foolproof Techniques, Expert Guidance, and 110 Recipes from Traditional to Modern

BY THE EDITORS OF THE HARVARD COMMON PRESS

HARVARD
COMMON
PRESS

CONTENTS

INTRODUCTION

In recent years, we at the Harvard Common Press, along with our colleagues from other imprints of the Quarto Publishing Group, have proudly published what we think are some of the best books—full of safe and accurate advice on methods and techniques, plus delicious recipes that range from surefire classics to innovative new ideas—on various subjects in the world of canning and preserving. Each of those books tackled a specific topic in that world. In this new *Ultimate Guide to Preserving and Canning*, by contrast, we weave together material from those various topical books in order to offer you a comprehensive book on all of the major topics in preserving. In its breadth and depth, we hope this is a volume that will be both inviting and accessible for first-time preservers as well as a source of new directions for seasoned veterans. Enjoy!

Chapter 1

PRESERVING THE BEST OF THE HARVEST

Whether you are looking for the simple basics you need for getting started preserving and canning your harvest, or you're looking for invaluable advice for taking your canning to the next level, you'll find all the motivation and information you need in this chapter. You'll learn what equipment is essential to have on hand (and what is unnecessary), quick and easy precautions you can take to keep your treats safe and tasty, and troubleshooting tips that address all the common messy mistakes and storage conundrums awaiting every novice and veteran canner.

WATER BATH CANNING VS. PRESSURE CANNING

Water bath canning and pressure canning are similar in that they are both ways to preserve food in your own kitchen. The general process of putting food in jars, attaching lids, heating to seal, and storing are the same. However, there are some major differences you should know.

All foods have natural acidity levels. Many fruits and tomatoes are highly acidic. These foods can be water bath canned. Or, produce can be incorporated in a recipe that makes it safe for water bath canning, such as pickles: cucumbers (a low-acid food) are canned in an acidic pickling solution.

Water bath canning, or boiling water canning as it's sometimes called, is the method of submerging filled jars into hot water and boiling for a specific period of time. This means the internal temperature of the food in the jars is heated to 212°F (100°C). It's a great way to start canning and the most common way to make popular pantry items such as jams, jellies, and pickles. However, to get a wider range of foods in jars, you need to learn the art of pressure canning, which is discussed in detail in The Pressure Canning Process on page 50.

Pressure canning is the preserving method by which filled jars are placed into a large pot with just a few inches (7.5 to 10 cm) of water in it. A locking lid is placed on the pot and steam develops inside the pot. The jars' contents reach an internal temperature of 240°F (116°C) under a specific pressure (in pounds, see page 21), and the recipe states a specific period of time to hold that pressure. Pressure canning can be used for a wider variety of foods. You can process vegetables and fruits with low or high acidity, meats, poultry, fish, sauces, and even whole recipes—such as soups or stews. Pressure canning generally means less mess, and my jars always seem to seal when I pressure can. (I also admit some bias—I love canning meat. On the farm, we raise much of our own meat, and being able to process it myself means I can fill my pantry with healthy food that has been raised ethically.)

Pressure canning, as you might expect, is done in a *pressure canner*. A pressure canner is a large pot designed specifically for the canning process; do not confuse a pressure *canner* with a pressure *cooker*. A pressure cooker is very useful, but it's a different piece of equipment meant for general cooking. Although there is some crossover, and electric pressure cookers can be used to can a couple of jars at a time, they are two distinctly different kitchen items with similar names.

CANNING EQUIPMENT

Canning is much easier and safer if you make use of the equipment readily available in your local hardware, farm, or home supply store or online. Jars, lids, and canning-specific ingredients like pectin are available at most grocery stores.

THE CANNER

The most important piece of equipment is the canner itself. The two types of canners available are boiling water bath canners and pressure canners.

Boiling Water Bath Canner. This type of canner consists of a large pot with a canning rack and a lid. Canning pots are usually 21 or 33 quarts (about 20 or 31 liters). You can use regular pots with lids as long as they are large enough to allow for at least 2 inches (5 cm) of water over the jars.

Pressure Canner. This type of canner consists of a large aluminum pot with a twist-on, locking lid, inner sealing rim, a rack, and a pressure gauge. The most popular pressure canner sizes are 16 or 22 quarts (about 15 or 21 liters). The smaller pressure cookers, usually 4-, 6-, or 8-quart (3.8, 5.7, or 7.6 liter) sizes, are great for daily cooking but are not approved for home canning. We will discuss pressure canners in depth in Pressure Canning Basics on page 42.

ESSENTIAL CANNING EQUIPMENT

Canning Rack. Most canners come with a canning rack. The rack for boiling water bath canners has slots for the jars and handles to lift the rack in and out of the canner. Pressure canners come with flat, plate-style racks that sit at the bottom of the canner. A rack protects the jars from direct heat on the bottom of the pan and prevents them from bouncing around during processing. Make sure to use a canning rack every time you can!

OTHER ESSENTIAL EQUIPMENT

Jars: These come in a variety of sizes and your recipe will indicate the correct size for the food you are canning. Jars are typically sold by the dozen for the most common jar sizes, though higher-end, fancier jars may be sold individually. For more information on jars, see Let's Talk About Jars on page 47.

Jar Lids: The lid is critical to a well-sealed jar, not just for the covering you can see it provides but also for the seal it creates underneath. The most common type of canning jars and lids are the variety made by large manufacturers such as Ball. The lids have two pieces: the flat lid itself and a screw band that goes around the outside of the lid (see the next item in this list). If you look at the underside of one of these canning jar lids, you will see a reddish-brown ring around the edge. This ring softens during processing and forms an airtight seal as it cools. Jar lids with this sealing compound are *not* reusable; however, you can reuse the jars and screw bands. Just buy a new pack of lids before the next canning session.

Screw Bands: These bands are designed to hold the lid in place during processing. Since they can be reused, carefully inspect them for nicks, rust, and other signs the band has been weakened. As you'll read repeatedly in the recipes, the bands are screwed onto the jars until hand-tight, also called fingertip tight, and no tighter. They need to be loose enough to allow the jar lid to release air during processing. Screw bands can be removed after the jars cool completely to room temperature. Removing the band does not affect the lid seal and with no band to hide the seal it is easier to watch for any signs of leakage while the jar is in storage.

Canning Funnel: Use a canning funnel to fill your jars. You might think this would be an optional piece of equipment; however, keeping the rim of the jar clean is very important. Because you will be working with very hot foods and liquids, using a funnel will help keep your hands from getting burned as well. A canning funnel has a wide mouth and is wider than a normal funnel at the bottom to accommodate big pieces of food. They are inexpensive, and I recommend buying a few. I have both metal and plastic funnels in my canning supplies and both work equally well.

Electronic Scale: I recommend a digital scale that is reliable and that includes a tare function. (Tare means you can place your container on the scale and then set it back to 0 before weighing your ingredients.) I also prefer battery-powered scales so you don't have to deal with a cord.

Jar Lifter: This specialized item makes your canning experience much easier. You'll use the jar lifter to safely lift hot jars from the canner and protect your hands from hot water and steam. This tool has handles that stay cool, and the business end is rubber-dipped and curved to match the curvature of a jar. I have an old one and a newer model; the only difference is the newer one has plastic-covered handles and my older one has wooden handles. They both work equally well.

Wooden Chopsticks (or a similar tool): When canning, there will be times when you need a long, straight object like a chopstick or the long handle of a wooden spoon. Really, you can use almost any (nonmetal) object that can safely be poked into a jar to release trapped air bubbles and move food around as needed so it fits better. I like using chopsticks because they are cheap and effective. You can also use skewers, as long as they're wooden—you don't want to damage the glass jars. One other advantage or using chopsticks or skewers is you can use them in a pinch for other tasks, such as lifting bands out of hot water. You can also purchase a plastic tool called a bubble freer that is designed specifically for this task.

Lid Lifter: Not to be confused with a jar lifter, this little tool is a must have. Once again, it comes into play when you're handling hot items—the best way to do anything at this stage is to do it safely. Your lids will be sitting in steaming-hot water and keeping them hot while they are being placed on jars is important. A lid lifter has a small magnet on the end that lifts the lid easily, allowing for an easy transfer to the jar. Before I owned one, I had to use tongs and it was often difficult to get the lids out of the water without burning myself at least a little. Save yourself from the same experience and buy a lid lifter.

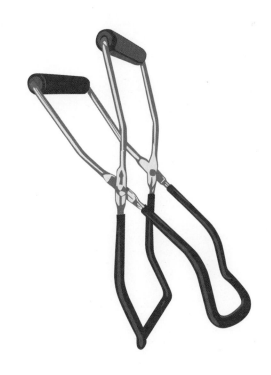

Lid Wrench: While the recipes in this book recommend hand-tightening lids before canning, there are times when lids are tough to remove after canning. If you sometimes struggle with the lids on jars, this tool will make your life easier.

Dish Towels: I can't imagine canning without a clean stack of dish towels for a variety of tasks. I use linen towels so there is no lint, but you can also use tightly woven cotton blends that have no nap. Just avoid fluffy towels that leave lint behind! Use your towels as a landing place for jars when removing them from the canner, for wiping jar rims before adding the lid, and for cleaning up spills as soon as they happen. I also use my dish towels at various other times, to protect my hands from steam, for wiping off spoon handles if needed, etc. I start my canning session with at least 6 on the counter and usually end up using every one. I recommend white towels that don't look like your everyday towels, so you keep them just for canning and bleach them as needed.

Knives: I was taught a sharp knife is safer than a dull one and I have yet to find any evidence to the contrary. Canning involves a lot of food prep, and that means a lot of cutting. Sharp knives reduce hand fatigue and help you cleanly cut uniform pieces of food. You will not need a large number of knives; a paring knife and an 8- or 10-inch (20 to 25.4 inch) chef's knife will suffice. Keep them super sharp and learn how to cut properly with each if you don't already have strong knife skills.

A little time spent learning will immediately pay you back in saved prep time.

Measuring Cups: Plastic, metal, or glass, it doesn't matter which you choose as long as the markings are clear. What is important is having more than one set of measuring cups available. Having a second (or third) set at the ready will save you from stopping to clean in the middle of canning.

Measuring Spoons: Just as with measuring cups, it's essential to have a spare set of spoons if you don't want to be caught unprepared while canning. Also, as much as I love the novelty of newer measuring spoons that slide or adjust to the measurement you need, I don't think they're as reliable for exact measurements—especially when measuring liquids. I stick to the easy-to-read, standard measuring spoons that have served cooks well for generations.

Saucepans or Stockpots: Stainless steel or enamel-surfaced pots and pans work best when preparing recipes for canning. Aluminum and copper pans are considered "reactive" and will impart a metallic taste to acidic foods.

Rubber Spatulas: While not necessary for every recipe, they are perfect for scraping out and moving sticky items such as jams and jellies. Rubber spatulas are easy to clean and they don't absorb flavors. They are also safer to use inside glass jars. I buy the type with a rubber end that can be removed from the handle for better washing and sanitizing.

Tongs: You probably have a pair of tongs in your kitchen already. They're perfect for handling hot food while keeping your hands far away—and that's true whether you're grilling or canning. I prefer the longer style that most people use for the grill, but shorter tongs will work as well.

Pot Holders: Remember that even the thickest pot holder will allow steam through the fabric, so use them with caution. Having said that, pot holders are the tool of choice for moving hot, heavy pots around your stove. They can also insulate hot jars if you need to set one down on a cool countertop. Use a pot holder in a situation like this to avoid the possibility of cracking the glass jar or damaging your counter.

Ladles: A ladle should have a long handle and although I love metal for many utensils, for ladles, plastic rules! Why? A ladle will spend quite a bit of time in boiling-hot foods when canning and a metal handle can conduct heat. The last thing you want is a ladle that's too hot to handle! I most often use a plastic ladle rated for high temperatures that measures ½ cup (120 ml) of liquid and can double as a measuring device in a pinch.

Wooden Spoons: Wooden spoons will not become soft or excessively bendable when submerged in hot liquid, unlike some cheaper plastic spoons. I use wooden spoons when cooking, and canning is no different. Actually, it just gives you the opportunity to use a wooden spoon even more—for example, you can use the handle for releasing trapped air bubbles.

NONESSENTIAL (BUT HELPFUL) EQUIPMENT

These items are not necessary for canning most recipes. However, some will make your life easier for every recipe and others are essential for a smaller group of recipes—such as jams and jellies.

Food Processor: This is definitely not a "need it" item, but once you have one it is hard to go back. I use my food processor most often for shredding; it produces even results, and it greatly speeds up the job. I also use my food processor's slicing blade to cut thin slices for pickles. If you're on the fence about buying a food processor, borrow a friend's for a weekend. You will quickly see whether the speed and convenience are worth the cost (and cleanup).

Food Mill: A food mill is designed to purée fruits and vegetables. It removes the seeds and skins as well. It's the surefire way to get silky smooth applesauce and the smooth consistency you crave in some recipes. Food mills were once hard to find, but now are sold in most big box stores. You also may get lucky and find a used model in good shape. While I don't recommend buying a crucial piece of equipment second hand, such as an old pressure canner, a used food mill is a different story. If cleaned well after every use and used carefully, this useful tool will last for many years.

Jelly Bag: A jelly bag might sound like a very specialized tool, but it can be used for much more than just jelly. It is used to strain juice from fruits and vegetables after cooking. You transfer the produce to the bag and hang it over a pot or bowl so the juice can drip out and be collected. For more information, see What is a Jelly Bag Anyway? on page 32.

Candy Thermometer: This is a cooking thermometer, inserted vertically into a mixture, with adjustable hooks or clips that allow it to be attached to the pot. It is useful when making jams and jelly to test for doneness when a specified temperature is reached.

Headspace Tool: This is a plastic tool designed to measure the headspace in the jar. It is often a combination bubble freer and headspace tool.

Timer: Yes, you can use the timer on your stove for canning. However, having a dedicated timer you can slip in your pocket is handy. Find a timer you can hear easily, and one that can get splashed without damage. (This probably means buying one with a midrange price point.) I set my timer as soon as my pressure canner reaches the correct pressure and slip it into my apron. If I get distracted (as much as I tell you not to, life does happen), I have a backup reminder that my jars are ready.

Labels: Labels are one item that may seem frivolous to beginners. After all, you can simply write the contents and date you preserved them on the metal lid. Yet, labels have their place. Good labels adhere to the glass jars, making it simple enough to identify the contents and date without handling the jars to peek at the tops. Labels are also more attractive and, thus, are a nice touch if you're making the recipes as gifts—or if your cupboard is in view from your kitchen or dining room.

I use labels on my jars and try to change them each year. This means at a glance I know the quantity that is left from a given year—helpful especially on a shelf that has many of the same things, like tomatoes. With unique year-based labels, I know quickly that there are four more quarts (946 ml) to be used up before we start eating this year's supply. So, labels are not critical to the canning process, but the more you can, the more you'll want to invest in at least simple labels.

COMMON CANNING TERMS

These terms are used throughout this book and the canning world. Once you understand the terminology, canning becomes a breeze.

Altitude: This is the elevation above sea level.

Blanch: This is the process of submerging food under boiling water for a few minutes, to loosen the skin or to stop enzymatic action in it. After blanching, the food is often placed in ice-cold water to stop the blanching process.

Boil: This is the process of heating liquid to 212°F (100°C), when bubbles break the surface.

Botulism: This is a form of food poisoning caused by ingesting the spores of *Clostridium botulinum*. The spores need an anaerobic environment (no oxygen) to survive. Botulism can be fatal.

Brine: This is a salt and water mixture used when pickling foods.

Canning Salt: This is salt that contains no iodine or noncaking agents. It is the salt used in most canning recipes.

Chutney: This is a thick recipe of sweet fruits and savory vegetables cooked with spices and vinegars.

Clear Jel: This is a modified food starch that will not break down when heated to a high temperature. It is a common thickener for canning foods.

Cold Pack (or Raw Pack): Raw food is placed in jars to be canned.

Headspace: This is the distance between the top of the food and the top of the mouth of the canning jar. Each canning recipe has a specified headspace.

High Acid: High acid refers to a food's pH of 4.6 or lower. High-acid foods include most fruits and pickled foods. Most of these foods do *not* need to be canned in a pressure canner.

Hot Pack: Hot pack is the method of heating food in hot liquid before placing it into jars.

Low Acid: These are foods with a pH higher than 4.6. Low-acid foods *must* be pressure canned.

Mason Jar: This is a glass jar designed for heating foods and liquids. Mason jars can withstand the high pressure of a canner and should not be substituted with other food jars.

Oxidation: This is the reaction that occurs when cut fruits and vegetables are exposed to the air, such as apples turning brown.

Processing: This is the length of time necessary for canned food to remain in the pressure cooker to be completely heated throughout.

Purée: This is the process of blending food to a smooth, even consistency.

Saucepan: This is a heavy pot with a broad flat bottom and deep sides. Saucepans come in many sizes.

Screw Band: This is a metal band with threads, used to attach the canning lid to the jar.

Simmer: This is the process of heating a liquid until numerous tiny bubbles rise to the surface.

Sterilize: This is a method used to kill all microorganisms.

SAFETY FIRST

This section will demystify the canning process and put to rest notions that canning is hard, complicated, or dangerous.

The four simple steps to safe canning are:

1. STERILIZE

Take a few minutes to complete these important steps at the beginning of any canning session.

BASIC STEPS:

1. Boil water. Submerge all jars, lids, and any kitchen tools you will be using for 2 minutes in boiling water.

2. Gather clean dish towels for the countertops and for wiping down the jars.

3. Clean kitchen surfaces with hot water and a touch of vinegar.

4. Make sure your hands are squeaky clean.

2. SELECT

Not all foods are canned the same way. Some use a boiling water bath canner and others require a pressure canner. It's important to know which canning method you will be using and to have the proper equipment.

Foods with a low pH (meaning they are more acidic) require the basic, boiling water bath method where the water reaches 212°F (100°C), or boiling temperature. Fruits, tomatoes with added acid, and pickles can be canned this way.

Higher pH foods (foods that are less acidic) require a pressure canner, which reaches 240°F (116°C). Higher pH foods require the increased temperature to kill off all bacteria, so it's important to follow the selection guidelines carefully. Vegetables, meats, and any stocks or soups must be processed using a pressure canner. Refer to quick reference guides on pages 20–22.

3. SEAL

Sealing occurs when a jar covered with a dome lid is processed in either a boiling water bath or a pressure canner. Ensuring you have a good, tight seal is critical to preserving your food.

Each lid has two parts—an outer ring and an inner panel with a rubber seal. Make sure both parts are sterilized and intact. The outer rings may be reused, but be sure to use new dome lids every time you can.

A FEW TIPS TO ENSURE A GOOD SEAL:

Make sure to leave the recommended amount of headspace in your jar. Headspace is the amount of room left between the top of the food and lid. Too much room, and your food will spoil on top; too little room and a vacuum seal cannot be created. Strong acid foods need ¼ inch (6 mm) of headspace; low acid foods need ½ inch (1.3 cm) of headspace.

Once jars have processed and cooled, turn upside down to check for leaks. Make sure each one is sealed by pressing slightly on the center of the dome lid. If the lid makes a hollow popping sound and moves up and down, it isn't sealed. When this happens, refrigerate the jar and eat the contents within two weeks.

4. STORE

Just two simple steps here:

First—Make sure to label your jars with the canning date and contents. Home-canned food will last up to twelve months.

Second—Store your canned jars in a cool, dark spot. Never store cans near a heat source, such as hot pipes, furnace vents or radiators, or a sunny window. This will harm the quality of your food.

I invert my canning jars for storage. This keeps the top layer of the food from drying out. Before storing jars, remove screw-top rings.

WHAT'S PH?

All cooking is chemistry—and in canning, it's the pH value of your food that matters most.

*The simplest way to remember pH is that **fruits**, **pickled foods** and **tomatoes with added vinegar or lemon juice** (high-acid foods) use a **boiling water bath canning method**. Everything else needs a **pressure canner**, which reaches 240°F (116°C) to kill off all bacteria.*

Why is this? It's because the dreaded botulism-causing bacteria don't survive in foods with a pH of 4.6 or less, so it's safe to process them in boiling water with a temperature of 212°F (100°C). Other foods require higher temperatures to be safely processed.

CHART 1: PH VALUE OF VARIOUS FOODS

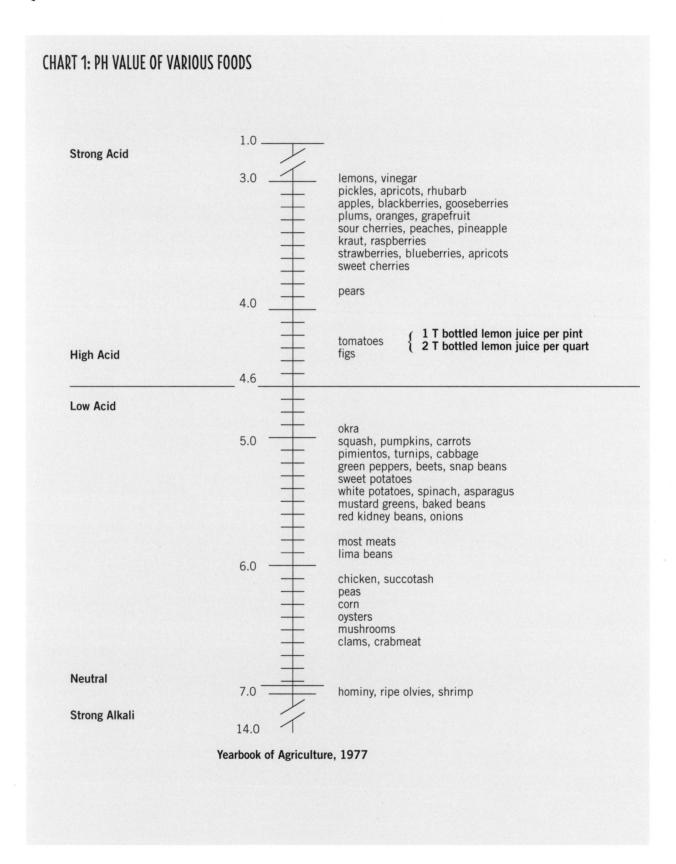

Strong Acid

1.0

3.0 — lemons, vinegar
pickles, apricots, rhubarb
apples, blackberries, gooseberries
plums, oranges, grapefruit
sour cherries, peaches, pineapple
kraut, raspberries
strawberries, blueberries, apricots
sweet cherries

pears

4.0

tomatoes   { 1 T bottled lemon juice per pint
figs   { 2 T bottled lemon juice per quart

High Acid

4.6

Low Acid

okra
5.0 — squash, pumpkins, carrots
pimientos, turnips, cabbage
green peppers, beets, snap beans
sweet potatoes
white potatoes, spinach, asparagus
mustard greens, baked beans
red kidney beans, onions

most meats
lima beans

6.0

chicken, succotash
peas
corn
oysters
mushrooms
clams, crabmeat

Neutral

7.0 — hominy, ripe olvies, shrimp

Strong Alkali

14.0

Yearbook of Agriculture, 1977

CHART 2: TEMPERATURES FOR FOOD PRESERVATION

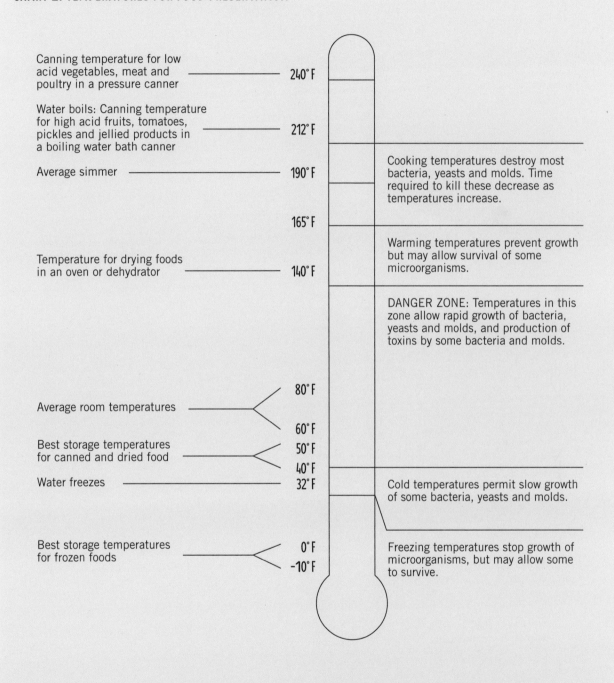

Canning temperature for low acid vegetables, meat and poultry in a pressure canner — **240° F**

Water boils: Canning temperature for high acid fruits, tomatoes, pickles and jellied products in a boiling water bath canner — **212° F**

Average simmer — **190° F**

165° F

Temperature for drying foods in an oven or dehydrator — **140° F**

Average room temperatures — **80° F** / **60° F**

Best storage temperatures for canned and dried food — **50° F** / **40° F**

Water freezes — **32° F**

Best storage temperatures for frozen foods — **0° F** / **-10° F**

Cooking temperatures destroy most bacteria, yeasts and molds. Time required to kill these decrease as temperatures increase.

Warming temperatures prevent growth but may allow survival of some microorganisms.

DANGER ZONE: Temperatures in this zone allow rapid growth of bacteria, yeasts and molds, and production of toxins by some bacteria and molds.

Cold temperatures permit slow growth of some bacteria, yeasts and molds.

Freezing temperatures stop growth of microorganisms, but may allow some to survive.

(CONTINUED)

DETERMINE CANNING METHOD

High-acid foods like fruits, pickled foods, and tomatoes

Use a Boiling Water Bath

Low-acid foods such as vegetables, meats, and soups

Use a Pressure Canner

10 pounds (68.9 kPa) pressure
kills botulism.

Remember to heat all low-acid foods before eating.

WHAT CAN I CAN?

Here's a quick summary of what we've learned so far:

In a boiling water bath you can can:

- All fruits
- Tomatoes with extra acid (lemon juice or vinegar) added
- Pickles

In a pressure cooker you can can:

- Vegetables (beets, carrots, potatoes, squash cubes)
- Beans
- Meats
- Stocks and brothy soups

Do NOT can:

- Grains and starches (including rice and pasta, even if they're in soups)
- Oils
- Dairy products
- Puréed winter squash or pumpkin (see recipe on page 85 for a solution)
- Thickeners, such as cornstarch or flour

When you can, ALWAYS:

- Use fresh ingredients. Any blemishes on produce should be cut out.
- Follow all directions and recipes to the letter.
- Know your altitude and adjust processing instructions accordingly.
- Sterilize your jars, lids, and equipment before you begin.
- Keep a journal—it's great to have as a guide for next time.
- Have fun!

PLANNING FOR CANNING

Canning is a method of food preservation that requires common sense. You can play around with ingredients, invent new recipes, and even make artistic labels that wow your friends, but *cleanliness* and *organization* are the keys to germ-free jars of food.

The most important rule for canning, and especially pressure canning, is **keep the process clean and simple**. This means keeping the work area and equipment as clean as you possibly can. You should also avoid nonstandard jars and any clutter—such as jar decorations—until after the food is ready for the pantry. You want as tidy a workspace as possible, especially as you're just getting started.

Following are other important things to consider when planning for canning:

- Start in the garden: grow what you like.

- Choose your ingredients wisely— freshest and ripest.

- Know the proper steps to canning.

- Prepare and pack the right way.

- Use reliable, tested recipes.

- Update your canning knowledge.

Let's look at each more closely.

START IN THE GARDEN

After cleanliness, my most important piece of advice as you begin your canning journey is to grow what you and your family love to eat. You may have a really tasty-sounding recipe for pickled beets, but if you're the only one in your family who enjoys beets, they probably shouldn't take up much space in the garden! It's helpful to make a list of ingredients you find yourself using most frequently in your cooking or the recipes you always rely on. Break down the recipes into ingredients and see what you might be able to grow and can yourself.

Take my family: We love tomatoes—fresh from the garden or in sauce, it matters not. My family wants to eat a tomato-based recipe every few days, so it only makes sense that I stock up on tomatoes in every form. Quart jars (946 ml) fit about one pound (455 g) of processed tomatoes, so it's easy for me to plan the quantity I need to grow or buy from a local farmer.

This past year, I asked my favorite farmer to grow 100 pounds (45.4 kg) of tomatoes for me to can. Sound like a lot? Not when you do the math for my crew. We use two quarts (1.9 L) of canned tomatoes in one meal. My plan was to have enough tomatoes for one tomato dish per week for a year. (We eat more than that, but this makes sure we don't waste tomatoes either.) You can do the same with meat, side-dish vegetables, soups, and more. By storing what you grow or buying during the season, when winter comes, your family will enjoy those summer flavors, without the sticker shock of winter shopping in the produce section.

Once you have a list of ingredients you want to can, make a general plan. Don't let that scare you. Planning for your pantry simply means thinking about the kinds of foods you will find useful to "shop" from in your own cupboards. I know my family likes soups for lunches, so I make plenty of soup bases. They also eat as much canned chicken as I can put up. Why buy tuna when you can preserve your own fish?

Canning may be simple enough, but it is work. Careful consideration about what you will preserve will keep you inspired and satisfied all year.

CHOOSE YOUR INGREDIENTS WISELY

Always start with the freshest and ripest ingredients you can. This means you should be prepared to can before you shop. Even if you don't have the specific recipe ready to go, you can have all the equipment—jars, lids, rings, jar lifter, funnel, etc.—ready before you start. At a minimum, take inventory so if you're out of something, like jars or lids, you can pick them up when you go shopping.

It might be tempting to can less-than-perfect produce. Sure, canning "ugly" vegetables is okay. Sometimes you'll find tomatoes, carrots, or other vegetables that taste great but have an odd shape or other imperfection. These are fine for canning! However, *avoid canning wilted, soft, or bruised foods*. Starting with bruised or damaged food can give decay and bad bacteria that come with it a head start. Softer vegetables will also be even softer after canning, which most often works against your recipe. Use only firm, ripe foods at their peak of freshness.

Using fresh, local produce that your family loves is the best place to start with canning.

KNOW THE STEPS TO CANNING

Successful canning means getting food quickly from the market or garden into jars. We'll cover the basic steps on page 18 and you should be familiar with them and your recipe *before* you start your work. The middle of a recipe isn't the time to look something up. Even now, at the beginning of a season, I do a dry run through the process, pretending to can. It may look silly, but many times I realize I don't have a funnel or enough dish towels. My canning kitchen looks quite different from my regular kitchen; many items on my counters are put away and I have clear access around the room.

PREPARE AND PACK THE RIGHT WAY

Even the most pristine fruits and vegetables require preparation for canning. For one, you'll want to wash off any dirt—or scrub, in the case of root vegetables. You'll also remove stems, leaves, and any part of the plant you don't want to eat (such as a tough end of a rhubarb stalk).

Beyond cleaning and cutting, you'll also be following a recipe to cold pack or hot pack your produce. Cold packing, also known as raw packing, is exactly what it sounds like: packing raw vegetables or fruit in the hot jars and pouring hot liquid over top before canning. Hot packing, on the other hand, will have you cooking your vegetables or fruit before adding them—and often the cooking liquid—to the jars. If this seems overwhelming, don't worry; your recipe will always be your guide on whether to cold or hot pack the jars.

Cutting uniformly sized pieces is key to ensuring the food in the jars cooks evenly.

USE RELIABLE, TESTED RECIPES

This can be a sensitive topic. Many cooks have emotional ties to recipes—and their historical significance—especially when it comes to something as classic as canning. The conflict comes from techniques or recipes that have since been proven unsafe. This is one area where caution rules. If you have an heirloom recipe, you can certainly find an updated version of it from a reliable source. You may also be able to troubleshoot the unsafe issue—say, by increasing the time of cooking to match modern standards. When all else fails, can the jars based on the most delicate ingredient. So, if you were to can your Great-Auntie M's famous chicken soup, use the most modern techniques for canning chicken soup you can find and can it in a pressure cooker under the correct pressure for that ingredient.

As much as I am a scratch cook who doesn't always stick to a recipe, when it comes to canning foods, following the rules is the only way. Changing things such as seasonings and how sweet you make a sugar syrup is fine, but be certain to follow canning recipes carefully and **do not experiment with time and temperature**.

UPDATE YOUR CANNING KNOWLEDGE

Each year, I review the USDA's online guidelines for safe canning techniques. While my grandmother certainly knew what she was doing, I do things a little differently, and the next generation of canners will, too. We continue to learn ways to improve techniques, safety, and recipes as the years go by. It's always a good idea to keep abreast of best practices. Recipes and techniques are often handed down through families, and it can be hard to change or give something up, but remember safety is key.

In this book, we'll be referencing the most current USDA guidelines at the time of writing in 2017. While there may be further updates or minor adjustments if a new style of pressure cooker is introduced, these guidelines will serve you well overall no matter the year.

BOILING WATER BATH CANNING

Before you begin, gather the necessary equipment. To can using the boiling water bath method, you will need a canner, canning rack, jars, lids, funnel, jar lifter, sauce or stock pans, and possibly a candy thermometer. See Canning Equipment on page 11 for details.

Follow these basic steps to make home canning simple and safe:

1. Follow the sterilization instructions on page 18.

2. Fill your boiling water bath canner two-thirds full with water and bring to a boil. You want enough water so that when you submerge the jars, the water level remains 2 inches (5 cm) above the lids. Adding vinegar (2 tablespoons [28 ml] or a good splash) helps if you have hard water. Minerals in hard water tend to form a cloudy surface on your jars. Vinegar helps keep the minerals in the water and off your jars.

3. Prepare your canning recipe, using only recipes meant for home canning. Fill your sterilized jars with the food, leaving the recommended amount of headspace. Use a nonreactive kitchen utensil, such as narrow rubber spatula or a bamboo skewer, to remove air bubbles. Air bubbles can cause uneven heating during processing and may impair the jar's ability to seal. Using a clean dish towel or paper towel, wipe the rims of the jars. This removes any spilled liquid or food, which can also prevent the jar from sealing. Place a dome lid on top of the jar and secure with a jar ring, screwing on so it's secure but not tight.

4. Submerge the jars into the canner with boiling water. Water should be 2 inches (5 cm) above the tops of the jars. ALWAYS place jars on a rack. If you don't have the rack made specifically for your canner, use a steamer basket or some other method to elevate the jars off the bottom of the canner. Jars that come into contact with direct heat through the bottom of the canning pot can crack and break.

5. Place the lid on the canning pot. Once the water returns to a boil, begin timing. Process for the number of minutes specified by the recipe, adjusting for altitude if necessary.

6. Once the processing time has elapsed, use the jar lifter to remove the jars from the boiling water. Place them on a dish towel on your countertop and let them rest until cooled. After 24 hours, test the seals by pressing slightly on the center of the dome lid. If the lid makes a hollow popping sound and moves up and down, it isn't sealed. When this happens, refrigerate the jar and eat the contents within 2 weeks. Make sure to label canned foods with the recipe name and date the item was canned. Store in a cool, dry place. Eat within a year.

ADJUST FOR ALTITUDE

Altitude matters for cooking in general and home canning in particular. Altitude affects the cooking temperature, so take a moment to look up your altitude (also called elevation) online and follow the canning instructions accordingly.

If you live in an area with an altitude above 1,000 feet (305 m), increase processing time by 2 minutes for every 1,000 (305 m) additional feet above sea level when using the boiling water bath method.

For pressure canning, you will need to increase the pressure settings for areas in higher altitudes.

BOILING WATER BATH CANNING USING POMONA'S PECTIN

A number of the recipes in this book for jams and jellies use Pomona's pectin. (For a full book of such recipes, see *Preserving with Pomona's Pectin*, 2nd edition, Fair Winds Press 2013.) For such recipes, prepare your equipment and have your recipe and ingredients on hand. Next, you'll want to make your calcium water (or confirm that you have enough left over from a previous batch). After that, you'll prepare your fruit and other ingredients before you hit the stove for the actual jamming part of the process.

PREPARING YOUR CALCIUM WATER

Every box of Pomona's Pectin contains a packet of tan pectin powder and a smaller packet of white calcium powder. The two ingredients work hand-in-hand, as the calcium activates the jelling power of the pectin.

Before making jam, use the calcium powder to make your calcium water, which you'll need for every recipe. Simply combine ½ teaspoon (1.5 g) of calcium powder and ½ cup (120 ml) of water in a small, clear jar with a lid. This makes enough calcium water for many batches of jam, so you won't have to do this step every time you make jam.

You can store extra calcium water in the refrigerator and use as needed, shaking before use. Refrigerated calcium water will keep for a number of months. Always examine your calcium water when you take it out of the refrigerator (before shaking it)—white sediment at the bottom of the jar is normal, but if you see any mold, scum, or discoloration, discard it and make more.

PREPARING YOUR FRUIT

If you're using fresh fruit, it should be as fresh as possible. Perhaps it goes without saying, but avoid any fruit that is overripe or diseased. Wash it thoroughly and then remove and discard any bruised or damaged sections. Next, prepare the fruit as directed by your recipe (peeling, pitting, chopping, and so on). If you're using frozen or canned fruit, you can obviously skip all of this—simply defrost frozen fruit or drain canned fruit (unless your recipe says otherwise), and you're good to go. How you prepare your fruit from this point on will depend in large part on whether you're making a jam, jelly, preserve, conserve, or marmalade.

If you're making a jam, conserve, or marmalade, mashing the fruit is typical, though some recipes will call for chopping or dicing. For preserves, you'll want to leave the fruits whole if they are small, such as strawberries or raspberries. If your fruits are large, such as apples or peaches, cut them into uniform pieces. Some recipes require cooking the fruit during the preparation phase, while others require only mashing or chopping raw fruit. Preparation procedures will vary based on the type of fruit, type of jelled product, and the individual recipe, so be sure to refer to your recipe for specifics.

Preparing your fruit for jelly is a little different, as you'll be extracting and using the juice of the fruit, not the fruit itself. If you're using either commercially available juice for jelly or juice that you've already made in another manner (with a juicer, for example), you can, of course, skip all of the juice-making steps. If you're starting with whole fruit, however, you'll need to prepare it and juice it. First, wash your fruit and chop it up if it's large, and then, if you prefer or if the recipe calls for it, peel, core, and de-stem the fruit. You don't really need the additional pectin found in the skin and cores because you will be adding pectin. It's more work to remove the peels and cores, of course, but I much prefer to do so, as it allows me to use the leftover fruit pulp for something else. There's not much I can do with the pulp after jelly making if I didn't remove the peels and cores ahead of time, other than compost it.

HOW RIPE IS RIPE?

All of the recipes in this book call for ripe fruit. However, fruits can be ripe to varying degrees, and some recipes are best made with fruit of a specific level of ripeness. In this book, if a recipe calls for a "fully ripe pear," for example, you'll want to use a pear that is ripe enough and soft enough to mash. On the other hand, if a recipe calls for a "ripe, firm pear," you'll want a pear that is ripe but still firm enough that you can cut the pear up and cook it as called for without it turning to mush. If a recipe simply calls for "ripe" fruit, any degree of ripeness is fine.

To extract juice from most fruits, you'll first need to cook the prepared fruit lightly with a small amount of water to make it soft enough for the juices to start flowing. Hard fruit such as apples may need as much as 1 cup (235 ml) of water per pound (455 g) of fruit, while soft, ripe fruit will need less. Juicy berries can simply be crushed to get the juices flowing. If you do choose to cook them, ⅛ cup (28 ml) of water per pound (455 g) should be plenty—and sometimes you'll need even less. Knowing exactly how much water to cook fruit with can be a little tricky because, depending on the type of fruit and the degree of ripeness, natural juiciness will vary. Ideally, you want to add just enough water so the fruit will yield the required amount of juice for your recipe. The more water you add to the fruit, the more diluted your juice (and the jelly you make from it) will be, yet adding some amount of water is essential for most fruits. Although it's never an exact science, the recipes in this book specify water quantities and cooking times that will yield pretty close to the correct quantity of juice for your jelly, so always refer to your recipe.

After you've cooked your fruit (if necessary) to make it soft, mash it and transfer it to a damp jelly bag or layered cheesecloth. (For more on using jelly bags and cheesecloth, see opposite page.) Hang the bag over a bowl and allow the juice to drip into the bowl until the dripping stops—at least two hours and often longer.

WHAT'S A JELLY BAG, ANYWAY?

Jelly is made from the juice of the fruit (or, in some cases, flower or herb-infused liquid), so to make jelly you need a way to extract the juice or liquid from the fruit or plant. A jelly bag—which is essentially a cloth bag—makes this process convenient. To use it, simply dampen the bag and pour your crushed fruit or plant matter, plus any infused liquid, into it. Then, suspend the bag over a bowl, allowing the liquid to drip out of the bag into the bowl. Discard the contents of the bag (or use them for another purpose) after draining, reserving the juice or liquid for your jelly. For added convenience, you can buy a ring stand, which is a simple metal stand designed to hold the jelly bag while it's dripping.

For a less expensive and equally effective alternative, use a large piece of cheesecloth, folded over itself a few times, to fashion your own jelly bag. Simply place your fruit on the dampened, layered cloth, gather the cloth up around the fruit, tie it at the top or secure it with an elastic band, and hang it up to drip with a bowl underneath. After you're done, wash your cheesecloth well, let it air-dry, fold it up, and store it in a clean, dry place, and use it again next time you make jelly.

If you are making a jelly with flowers or herbs, you'll steep the flowers or herbs in hot water or another hot liquid and then strain them with a jelly bag, cheesecloth, or a fine mesh strainer, discarding the flowers and herbs and reserving the infused liquid. As always, remember to refer to your recipe for specific ingredient prep requirements.

MEASURING UP!

Because individual fruits of the same kind can vary so much in size, for the sake of accuracy, most of the recipes in this book call for fruit by weight. If you're planning to do a lot of jam making, a digital kitchen scale is an excellent investment. There are relatively inexpensive models available (around twenty dollars), and with a scale at your disposal, you'll know you're using the correct amount of fruit in your recipe. If you don't have a scale at home, weighing your fruit when you purchase it at the grocery store or farmers' market is another good option.

That said, there are times when weighing just isn't an option. If you're itching to make jam but don't have a scale handy, the following chart will help you determine how much fruit you'll need for different recipes in this book. Keep in mind the quantities are approximate, and may vary based on the size of the fruit.

FRUIT (FRESH)	WEIGHT	UNIT OR VOLUME EQUIVALENT
Apples	1 pound (455 g)	3 medium apples
Apricots	1 pound (455 g)	5 to 8 medium apricots
Blackberries	1 pound (455 g)	3½ cups (508 g) whole blackberries
Blueberries	1 pound (455 g)	4 cups (580 g) blueberries
Cherries (sweet)	1 pound (455 g)	3 cups (465 g) whole cherries
Figs	1 pound (455 g)	13 to 14 small to medium figs
Grapes (sweet)	1 pound (455 g)	3 cups (450 g) whole large grapes
Grapefruits	1 pound (455 g)	1 to 2 medium grapefruits
Kiwis	1 pound (455 g)	5 to 6 medium kiwis
Lemons	1 pound (455 g)	4 to 6 medium lemons
Limes	1 pound (455 g)	5 to 8 medium limes
Mangoes	1 pound (455 g)	2 small mangoes
Nectarines	1 pound (455 g)	3 medium nectarines
Oranges	1 pound (455 g)	2 to 3 medium oranges
Peaches	1 pound (455 g)	3 medium peaches
Pears	1 pound (455 g)	3 small to medium pears
Plums (sweet)	1 pound (455 g)	4 to 6 medium plums
Raspberries	1 pound (455 g)	2 (level) pints (473 ml each)
Rhubarb trimmed	1 pound (455 g)	4 to 8 stalks, or 3½ to 4 cups (427 to 488 g) medium dice
Strawberries	1 pound (455 g)	1 (level) quart (946 ml), whole

PREPARING ADDITIONAL INGREDIENTS

Along with a recipe's primary ingredients, many recipes include additional, supporting ingredients such as herbs, spices, vegetables, nuts, or dried fruit. These ingredients may be prepared in a variety of ways, so refer to your recipe for specifics.

COOK YOUR JAM

Once you've prepared your fruit, you're ready to hit the stove—almost. Before you do, make sure you're working with the correct amount of prepared fruit. After you've prepared your fruit as called for in your recipe, you will (for most recipes) need to measure out a specific quantity of prepared fruit. After measuring out the correct quantity, you may have a little bit left over, but that's normal—simply save it for another use or compost it, if you prefer. Whatever you do, be sure that you proceed with the exact quantity of prepared fruit that the recipe calls for. This is important because recipes call for specific amounts of pectin to jell specific quantities of fruit. If you use more or less fruit mixture than the recipe calls for, your jam may not jell properly. Additionally, the end product may not contain the proper level of acidity.

Now, you're ready for the last part of the process. There are a couple of different ways you can use Pomona's Pectin to make jams and jellies. The method you use will depend on the type of jam you're making.

POMONA'S PRIMARY METHOD: COOKED JAM WITH LOW SUGAR OR HONEY

The primary method used in this book is the cooked jam with low sugar or honey method. It's extremely versatile and will accommodate many different types and quantities of sweetener, including alternative natural sweeteners that measure like sugar and alternative natural sweeteners that measure like honey, as well as artificial sweeteners that measure like sugar. It's easy, too! Following is what you do.

1. Pour your prepared, measured fruit or fruit juice into a large saucepan and then add your measured amount of lemon juice (or lime juice or vinegar), if your recipe calls for it, and your measured calcium water.

Add lemon juice (if called for) and calcium water to prepared fruit.

Combine pomona's pectin powder and dry sweetener.

Combine pomona's pectin powder and liquid sweetener.

2. In a separate bowl, combine your measured amounts of sweetener and Pomona's pectin powder. Mix thoroughly and set aside.

3. Bring prepared, measured fruit mixture to a full boil (for more information, see "That's How We Roll!" on page 36).

4. Add the pectin-sweetener mixture to the boiling fruit mixture, stir well for 1 to 2 minutes to dissolve the pectin while the mixture returns to a full boil, and then remove it from the heat.

And that's it! You now have a jam or jelly that's ready for canning.

Add the pectin-sweetener mixture to the boiling fruit mixture.

POMONA'S FRUITY ALTERNATIVE: COOKED, ALL-FRUIT JAM

If you want to make jam that is even less sweet, an all-fruit jam is a great option. Jams made with this method consist entirely of fruit, sweetened only with unsweetened fruit juice concentrate such as apple juice concentrate, orange juice concentrate, or white grape juice concentrate. There are a handful of recipes in this book that use this method. The biggest difference between the primary cooked jam with low-sugar or honey method and the alternate all-fruit method is that in the primary method, you can simply mix your sweetener and the pectin together in a bowl, whereas with the all-fruit method, you have to heat up the sweetener (the fruit juice concentrate) and then use a blender or food processor to thoroughly dissolve the Pomona's pectin powder in the juice before adding it to the boiling fruit mixture. It takes an extra step or two, but it's still easy. Here's what you do:

1. Pour your prepared, measured fruit into a large saucepan and then add your measured amount of lemon juice (or lime juice), if your recipe calls for it, and your measured amount of calcium water.

2. In a separate saucepan, bring your measured amount of fruit juice concentrate to a boil.

3. Carefully pour the hot juice concentrate into a blender or food processor and then add the pectin powder. Vent the lid and blend for 1 to 2 minutes, stopping to scrape down sides as necessary, until the pectin is dissolved.

4. Bring the fruit mixture to a full boil (for more information, see "That's How We Roll!" on page 36) and then stir in the hot pectin-concentrate mixture. Continue to cook and stir for 1 minute while the mixture returns to a full boil and then remove from heat.

Now your jam is ready for canning!

THAT'S HOW WE ROLL!

*We all know what a boil is, but when it comes to jam making and canning, a **rolling** boil—or a **full** boil, as I often call it—is what really counts. A rolling boil and a full boil are essentially the same thing, but I tend to use the term **rolling boil** when I'm referring to the water in the canner, while I usually use the term **full boil** when I'm talking about the jam. So, what **is** a rolling boil or a full boil? It's not when the bubbling first starts. Rather, it's rolling in a major way, meaning that the liquid is really bubbling hard—not just a little bit. When jars are in the canner for processing or sterilizing, the water in the canner needs to be at a rolling boil before you start the sterilizing or processing time. Also, jam should be at a full boil before you add the pectin to ensure that the pectin dissolves thoroughly. If your jam's boil can be stirred down, it's not a full boil; just wait a few moments for things to really get rolling!*

CAN YOUR JAM

Once your jam is done, it's time to get it in the can—or rather, the jars. Don't worry if your jam looks a bit soupy at this point because this is normal; jam doesn't fully jell until after canning and after it's completely cool. Assuming you've followed all the previous steps, you're ready to can.

FILLING YOUR JARS

It's important that both the jam and the jars are hot when filling the jars, so once you start canning, you'll want to move promptly so they don't cool off. Follow these steps and you'll have smooth sailing:

1. Take the lid off the canner. Use a jar lifter or tongs to remove one hot, sterilized jar at a time, dumping the water out of the jar and back into the canner as you go. Place hot, empty jars on a clean dish towel or cooling rack on the counter. There's no need to dry the jars—it's okay if they are wet. Once all the jars are removed, place the lid back on the canner and crank the heat up so that the water can return to a boil while you're filling your jars.

2. Using a ladle and canning funnel, ladle hot jam into each jar, being careful not to overfill the jars. If you need to pick up or move the jars, don't forget to use a large pot holder or dish cloth—these jars are hot!

3. Stick a bubble freer (or similar tool) down into the jam all the way to the bottom of the jar, hold the bubble freer flat against the inside edge of the jar, and then gently run it all the way around the inside edge of each jar to release any trapped air bubbles.

4. Using a headspace tool, measure the headspace of each jar. The headspace is the distance between the top of the jam and the top rim of the jar. To measure it, simply hold the headspace tool very gently on the surface of the jam, against the inside rim of the jar, and measure the distance from the surface of the jam to the very top of the jar. Most jam and jelly recipes call for ¼ inch (6 mm) of headspace, though always check your recipe. Using a small spoon, add or remove jam from each jar as necessary to achieve the proper headspace, remeasuring if needed. If you don't have enough jam to completely fill your last jar, simply refrigerate that jar after cooling and enjoy right away (rather than processing it). Alternatively, you may use a plastic ruler to measure the distance between the top of the food and the rim of the jar.

5. Carefully wipe the top rim of each jar with a clean, damp cloth or paper towel to remove any jam. This is where the lid meets the jar—ensuring that it's clean will help achieve a good seal.

6. Using a lid lifter, also called a magnetic lid wand, remove the lids one at a time from the simmering water in the small pot (the lids will be wet, but there's no need to dry them) and center a lid on the top of each jar. Gently place a screw band down over each lid and screw the band onto the jar until you meet resistance—and then tighten just a tiny bit more. This is known as fingertip tight. Do not overtighten the bands, as air needs to escape from the jar during processing.

INTERIOR VIEW OF LOADED CANNER. Make sure jars are upright, not touching each other or the sides of the canner, and are covered by at least 1 to 2 inches (2.5 to 5 cm) of water.

LOADING THE CANNER

Remove the lid from the canner and using a jar lifter, gently lower each jar down into the boiling water and place it on the rack in the canner. (If the boiling water is making it hard to see, you can turn the heat down temporarily as you're placing the jars.) Ideally, you'll want to hold the jars by their bodies, not by their necks, so that you don't dislodge the lids and the screw bands. Be careful not to let the jars tip over—and if they do, right them immediately. Also, make sure the jars are not touching each other or the sides of the canner and that there is at least 1 to 2 inches (2.5 to 5 cm) of water covering all of the jars. This allows water to circulate freely and thoroughly around all

parts of every jar during processing, which will ensure that the jam is subject to the temperature necessary to kill any microorganisms. If, after you've placed your jars in the canner, you find that they are not covered sufficiently with water, add more hot water to the canner as needed.

PROCESSING YOUR JARS IN THE CANNER

After you've loaded the canner, place the lid on it, crank the heat up to high, and bring the water to a rolling boil (for more information, see "That's How We Roll!" on page 36). Once the water is at a rolling boil, you can start your processing time. Set your timer for the specific processing time indicated in your recipe—usually 10 minutes for jams and jellies, but always double-check. If you're at 1,000 feet (304.8 m) or more of elevation, you'll need to increase your processing time (see "Adjust for Altitude!" on page 29 for more information). After the processing is complete, turn off the heat and allow the canner and jars to sit—untouched—for 5 minutes. This 5-minute waiting period is important. If you remove your jars from the canner immediately, jam will sometimes seep out of them—an occurrence known as siphoning—due to the dramatic change in temperature and pressure. The 5-minute waiting period allows the jam to cool down enough before coming out of the canner that siphoning is unlikely to occur. Be sure that you don't wait longer than 5 minutes, however, as exposure to heat for too long a period may cause your jam not to jell properly.

WHAT'S ALL THAT RACKET IN THERE?

During processing, there's a lot going on in your canning pot. Boiling water circulates around the jars, heating them to the required temperature (212°F [100°C] at sea level for boiling water bath canning) and exposing the food in the jars to that temperature for the specified processing time. As the food heats up it expands, forcing air out of the jars. After processing, when the jars begin to cool, the food shrinks, and because the air was forced out of the jars during processing, when the food shrinks, the lids get sucked down. This creates a vacuum seal, which will keep out contaminants and allow the sealed jar of food to be safely stored at room temperature.

REMOVING YOUR JARS FROM THE CANNER

After the canner has cooled for 5 minutes, it's time to remove the jars. Using a jar lifter, carefully lift the jars from the canner one at a time, always keeping them upright, and place them on a dish towel or cooling rack on the counter, with space in between each jar. There will likely be a small pool of water on the top of each jar when you take it out, but don't worry about that—the water will evaporate as the jar cools. It's tempting to check out your jam, move the jars around, and handle the jars in general, but refrain! This cooling period is when your jars are in the process of sealing, and the less you handle your jars during this time, the more likely you are to get a proper seal. Allow your jars to cool, untouched, for 12 to 24 hours. You sometimes (though not always) will hear little popping noises as the jars cool—don't worry. This popping is a good thing! It's the little "button" on the top of the lid sucking down, and it's usually a good indication that a jar is in the process of sealing.

CHECKING YOUR SEALS AND STORING YOUR JARS

After your jars have cooled for at least 12 hours, you'll want to check them to ensure that each jar has sealed properly. To do this, press gently with your finger into the center of each lid. If the "button" that is in the center of each lid is already depressed, and there is no movement when you press down, then you have a proper vacuum seal. If the "button" is not depressed, and there is movement when you press on it, then your jar did not seal properly.

If a jar doesn't seal (which occasionally does happen), you have a couple of options. You may want to re-can your jam, though this is the most labor-intensive option. To do this, you'll need to dump out the jar, reheat the jam to boiling, and reprocess it in a clean, hot jar with a new lid for the recommended amount of time. I tend to go for an easier option—if I'm planning on eating it right away, I'll put it in the refrigerator. It will keep this way for about 3 weeks. Or, if I'm looking for longer-term storage, I'll freeze the jam, as it will keep in the freezer for about 6 months. Freezing it right in the jar is just fine, though make sure the jam is cool first and be sure to remove the lid and take out a couple of spoonfuls so that there is at least ½ inch (1.3 cm) of headspace before re-capping and freezing. This will allow room for the jam to expand when it freezes.

Fortunately, jars do seal properly most of the time. After you've confirmed that your jars have sealed, remove the screw bands. (You'll notice that the bands are already quite loose—this is normal!) It may seem counter-intuitive to take the bands off, but at this point, each lid is adhering to the jar because of the vacuum seal; the screw bands are no longer doing anything useful and can cause various problems during storage if left on. After removing the screw bands, wash them, thoroughly dry them, and then store them for future use. (It's helpful to keep bands nearby, so you can easily reach for one to put on after opening a jar or when giving a jar as a gift!) Then, rinse the outside of your sealed jars thoroughly to remove any jam that may have gotten on the outside of the jar during filling or processing. Dry your jars, clearly label and date them, and store them—preferably in a clean, dry, dark location between 50 and 70°F (10 to 21°C). Your sealed jars of jam will keep well this way for up to one year.

Before you open up a jar that has been stored, it's always a good idea to make sure the jar is still vacuum sealed. To do this, check that the button in the center is still depressed, and with your fingers, very gently try to pull up the lid, making sure that it doesn't budge. You'll also want to visually inspect the jam. If you notice any obvious signs of spoilage, discard immediately. If your jar was processed correctly, it should be fine, but seal failures and spoilage occasionally do occur during storage, so it's always important to check.

You may notice when you're examining your jar that the jam has separated, but don't be alarmed—this is normal for many jams and is not a sign of spoilage. When you open a jar of jam that has separated, simply mix it up well. Opening up a properly vacuum-sealed jar typically requires more than hands alone—I use a butter knife or other metal kitchen utensil to carefully pry lids off. After you open one of your jars of jam, store it in the refrigerator, capped with a lid and a screw band. It will keep this way for about three weeks.

PRESSURE CANNING BASICS

Have you ever wondered why pressure canning works? It's actually a simple concept, and, if you are a bit of a science geek like me, quite fascinating!

The goal of pressure canning is to expose food to a high temperature under a specific pressure for a specific period of time to destroy microorganisms that are harmful if eaten. Pressure canning allows food to be heated to 240°F (116°C)—the temperature necessary to destroy these microorganisms, including the botulism bacteria.

Botulism is rightfully one of the biggest fears for those new to canning or those who don't can. It is flavorless and odorless. Even worse, it cannot be destroyed by boiling or hot water bath canning, which only reaches 212°F (100°C) regardless of how long you boil the food. Botulism thrives in low-acid foods, in moist environments, and in an anaerobic (no oxygen) environment. All these conditions are present inside an *improperly* processed jar of food. Luckily, proper pressure canning creates a higher-temperature environment and can eliminate the risk of botulism in hours.

The other big fear when it comes to pressure canning is the safety of the pressure canner itself. Through the rest of this section, we'll discuss pressure canners, essential equipment, and using the pressure canner for the first time. By the end of this section, your fear should be a thing of the past, replaced by excitement to try your first recipe!

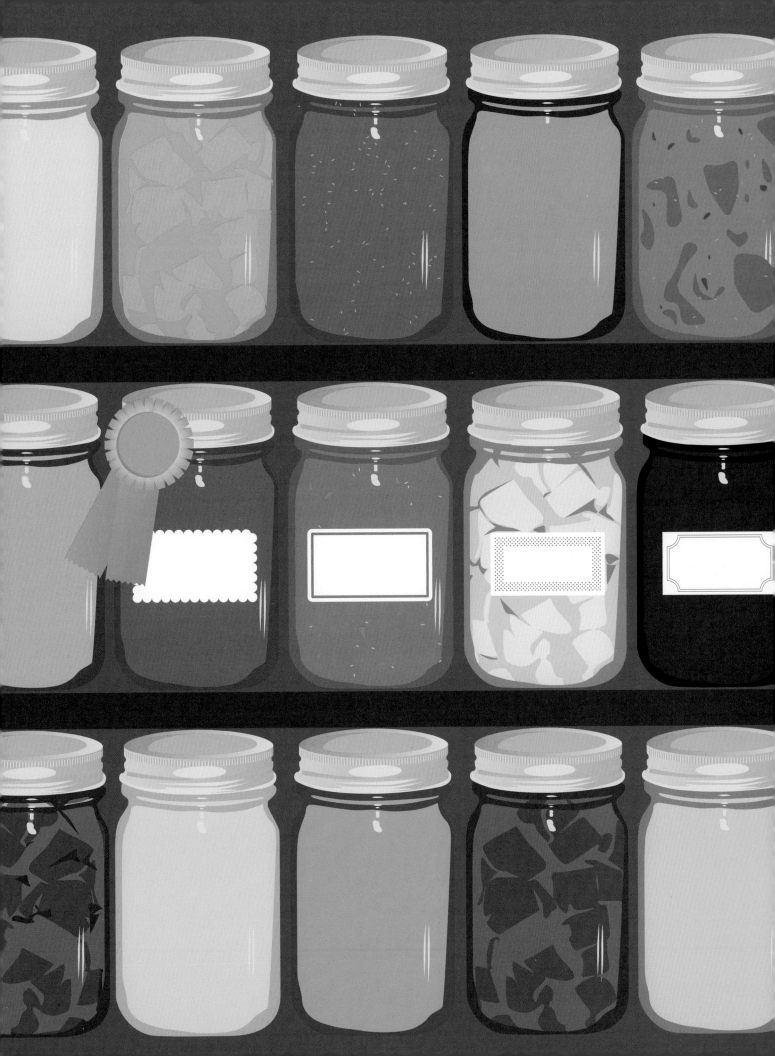

PRESSURE CANNING EQUIPMENT

When I started canning, I was a purist. I wanted to pretend my grandmother was a homesteader and she was teaching me her ways in the kitchen. I wanted to use only equipment she would have used—and everything needed to have a history. Soon, though, the reality was I needed to can large quantities to feed my growing family. There just weren't enough hours in the day to hand-shred 50 pounds (22.7 kg) of zucchini!

As I started using my food processor, a professional-quality chef's knife, and recipes with precise measurements and clear instructions, my canning became more efficient—and productive. I still have some of my old-fashioned equipment, but it has found a new home—lovingly displayed on the top of my cupboards!

That said, the equipment needed for canning is not extensive and it is affordable. If you're an avid home cook, you may already own much of what you need except, perhaps, the canner itself. See Canning Equipment on page 11. Other than the canner, jars, and lids, most items are recommended for your convenience.

THE PRESSURE CANNER

A pressure canner is, essentially, a heavy kettle designed to withstand higher pressure than a normal pot. While models vary in their features, all pressure canners offer a few common elements.

Before we get into the nuts and bolts (for some models, I mean that literally!), know this: as mentioned previously, a pressure cooker is not the same as a pressure canner. Yes, both devices use pressure and they look similar. However, pressure cookers are not designed for canning. Most models aren't large enough for cans and they don't have pressure gauges.

Pressure canners come in a wide range of models and sizes. When choosing the right model for you, consider how much you'll be canning at one time; for most people, a pressure canner in the 16- to 22-quart (15 to 21 L) range will do the trick. The other main differences will be the gauge type (dial versus weighted) and cover type (metal-to-metal or lock-on with gasket). Let's get to it.

Locking cover: All pressure canners have a locking cover that can be closed in only one correct position. There are canners with covers that lock on with a rubber gasket between the cover and kettle, and other canners that have individual locking wing nuts around the edge. I have both styles and still use them both every year. Neither one is better, objectively, but I find I reach for the model with the gasket and lock-on cover more often.

I do this because the locking process for the pots is different and I prefer the locking procedure on the cover with the gasket. Unlike a metal-to-metal cover, which requires manual tightening, lock-on covers with gaskets have a specific closing procedure with matching markings for the lid and pot and/or clamps. This means there's either a "locked" or "not locked" situation and no guessing as to the tightness of wing nuts. (Is this tight enough? Did I overtighten?)

No matter which lid type you have, always follow the manufacturer's instructions for locking the lid. Also, note that if your lid has a gasket, you'll need to clean it according to your manufacturer's instructions and use care. For example, some models may tell you to lubricate gaskets with cooking oil while others do not. Any damage to a gasket can affect the machine's ability to hold pressure correctly. Regularly inspect your gasket and replace at the first sign of wear.

Pressure gauge: Another feature that all pressure canners share is a gauge that displays the pressure inside the canner. There are two types of gauges and both work equally well. The first type of gauge is a weighted gauge. This gauge has no dial face, but instead has numbers engraved around its edges. This gauge will rattle when the correct pressure is reached; then, it will rattle faster and allow some steam to escape if the pressure gets higher than necessary. Note that it's not better to have slow or fast jiggling with this type of pressure gauge. The fact that it is moving means it is maintaining the recommended pressure. In my opinion, this gauge is more foolproof as it requires less heat adjustment than a dial gauge.

The second type, a dial gauge, is an easy-to-read, clock face–style gauge. It has a hand that moves as the pressure increases. You adjust the heat while you watch the gauge. Start the timer once the canner gauge reaches the correct pressure and adjust the heat level with the goal of keeping the pressure gauge at the correct number for the period of time specified in the recipe.

As mentioned elsewhere, it's important to check your gauge for accuracy at least annually. The start of a new canning season is a great time to do this. Your county's cooperative extension office should be able to help and some manufacturers offer this service as well

Release valve and overpressure plug: On the cover of your pressure canner, there is a release valve, which can also be referred to as a vent tube, petcock, or pipe vent in the manufacturer's manual. This release valve needs to be checked at the start of each canning session. Simply hold the cover up and make sure you can see light through the vent tube. If not, clean it with a pipe cleaner or however the manufacturer recommends. Note that this valve is where steam will come out and there are models where the weighted gauge will be on the valve.

Your pressure canner will also have an overpressure plug or safety fuse. This is a simple release that functions as a backup to the primary release valve/vent tube. The overpressure plug opens if the pressure gets too high due to the release valve being blocked. It is a safety feature not present on old-style pressure canners, and you should not use a pot that's so old it does not have this important feature. This backup release mechanism is there for your safety. You should also look for the Underwriter's Laboratory (UL) seal to ensure the device's safety.

The manufacturer of your pot may have recommendations for keeping the release valve and overpressure plug clean and operational. Always follow the best practice directions for your pot.

Canning rack: Finally, your pressure canner will come with a rack. The rack will look like a circular dish with holes in it and it's designed to sit on the bottom of the canner. Jars will sit on top of the rack; its design allows for the circulation of steam around the jars. It also helps stabilize your jars so they don't knock together or against the sides of the canner (possibly breaking them). If your canner did not come with a rack or your rack breaks, you need to buy a new one. The best place to start is the canner's manufacturer. *Don't can without a rack.*

NOTE

Weighted gauge models do not self-correct for altitude adjustments. This means at altitudes above sea level (higher than 1,000 feet [304.8 m]), the pressure you set should be adjusted upward. See the guidelines on page 50.

LET'S TALK ABOUT JARS

Jars are about to become your new best friend. There are as many styles, sizes, shapes, colors, and uses for these sturdy glass containers as there are foods to put in them. Yet despite the fact that most jars have the same purpose (food preservation), not all jars are created equal.

The canning jars I recommend are the modern-style canning jars made by Ball and similar manufacturers. They are distinguished by their sturdy glass, clearly marked volumes, and 2-piece lids.

The main alternative to this style of jar is experiencing a resurgence, though more as a dry storage jar than for canning. This alternate style of jar, called a bail-type jar, made famous by Weck, has two glass pieces—the jar and the lid—that are sealed together using a rubber gasket. Metal clips or a wire were used in conjunction to hold the lid on while canning, but the rubber seal acts like the modern seal under the lid to create the airtight environment you need to can.

While this type of jar may be used for canning, I tend to recommend it for refrigerated or dry storage instead. Weck jars with brand-new rubber seals may be used if you follow the manufacturer's instructions, but they tend to fail the beginning canner more often. Even worse, similar-looking vintage jars may not be intended for pressure canning at all. If you collect glass jars to reuse for food storage like I do, keep them in rotation only for dry goods.

So, what other options do you have within the recommended type of jars? You have a variety of sizes to choose from. Most of the recipes in this book all come with a recommended jar size. Other considerations include the size of your canner, which may not accommodate the largest jars.

The other important consideration is the size of the jar's mouth opening. Canning jars commonly come with two options:

1. **Regular-mouth jars** have a small opening, about 2⅜ inches (6 cm), but are good for liquids such as stocks or juices, and brothy soups. While many canners use only regular-mouth jars and have no trouble, keep in mind that regular-mouth jars are a little harder to clean if there is residue inside.

2. **Wide-mouth jars** are my personal favorite for a few reasons. You can easily get a utensil inside to scrape them clean. I also like wide-mouth jars because, with their opening at about 3 inches (7.5 cm), the jars are easier to fill for recipes with larger pieces. If your recipe will retain a firm texture, it's easier to remove the vegetables when serving as well.

There are many canning jar sizes, from half pints (235 ml) all the way up to gallons (liters), although these large jars are not usually used by home canners. With even grocery stores selling canning jars these days, you can easily find the right jar for the job. Most of the recipes in this book, and elsewhere, recommend a specific size. For safety reasons, use the recommended size and don't switch up sizes unless there is a corresponding recommendation for canning. Let's look at some of the jars you'll use!

- **Jelly jar:** Not just for jellies and jams, these jars come in a range of sizes from 4 ounces (120 ml) to 12 ounces (355 ml). They are the perfect size for gifting and for the little condiments you want on the table, without having to eat from the container for an extended period of time. Can you imagine a quart (946 ml) of mustard, for example? Use jelly jars for mustards, ketchups, barbecue sauce, and small-batch recipes.

  Jelly jars can also highlight a particular food. Jelly jars have wide openings so you can get out every last bite, and they are easy to clean. Due to their size, they require less processing time, which can be an advantage come canning day.

- **Half pint:** The half-pint jar gets quite a bit of mileage in my kitchen. When it comes to volume, these jars hold 8 ounces (235 ml) of food—and they also have the benefit of a wide mouth. I think it's the perfect size jar for relishes, pickles, and chunky chutneys. I use them exclusively for foods I want to use up quickly.

- **Pint:** Pint jars hold 16 ounces (473 ml) and can be used for many items. I use pints for soups I want to package as single lunches, salsas, and specialty recipes like cocktail onions. Pints are a manageable size for most recipes unless you are canning for a large family.

- **Quart:** Speaking of canning for the whole family, quart jars are my biggest workhorse. Quarts hold 2 pints (946 ml), so you can package double the soup, sauce, etc. I always use quarts to can tomatoes, family-size recipes of sides like baked beans, and soups and broths meant to serve more at once. If you are canning sweet fruits, you may want to consider quart jars. It all depends on how fast your family goes through the food—in my house, the sweets go fast!

CARING FOR YOUR CANNING GEAR

Your pressure canner is a sturdy piece of equipment with simple parts. It does require some care, however. Before the canning season, inspect your canner and all the parts for any nicks or cracks. Check the cover and make sure the overpressure plug moves freely and the vent tube is unblocked. If your pressure canner has a rubber gasket, make sure it is pliable and clean.

Every year, the dial gauge on your pressure canner should be checked for accuracy. This is usually a free or inexpensive service that can be done at your local county extension office or hardware store. Do this early, as many services require that you drop off your equipment. If you wait until the last minute, you may have to wait for the return and miss a week or two of prime produce.

Between canning sessions, a quick rinse and dry of the pot is all that is needed before storage as long as you keep it clean as a matter of course. I keep my canner in the original box once it is clean and dry. That helps keep it from gathering dust and ensures it doesn't get dinged up. It also protects the gauge from damage.

When it comes to your canning jars, they are sturdy but, at the end of the day, they are glass. Run your hand gently over the rim of each jar the day before you want to use it to find any small nicks. Also, hold each jar up to the light and look at the glass. You will be able to see small cracks if there are any.

Chips, nicks, and cracks are all signs the glass is no longer fit for canning. It is for this reason I never recommend letting your family use canning jars as drinking glasses. Something that seems as harmless as the teaspoon you stir your sweet tea with can weaken the glass. If you love the look of canning jars, buy a set just for drinking and keep the ones you use for canning stored separately.

The screw bands are the backbone of a good seal. When you purchase a box of canning jars, they come with the lid and band on each jar. The lids are not reusable, but the bands are. Once your jars cool, carefully remove the screw band and store the sealed jar. Screw bands can be reused until they become bent or corroded. Wash and dry your bands before storing them and plan to replace a few each year. I recommend keeping a box on hand for this purpose.

Likewise, keep measuring cups and spoons in good shape by keeping them clean. I like to keep all my canning supplies in the same drawer, and I like to sanitize my supplies before each canning session (see sidebar Clean is Best on page 51). This ensures my surfaces and items are as clean as possible before I start. Using plastic items means they can be sanitized without the risk of corrosion.

Every canning season should start with a visual inspection. This includes removing the lid and checking the gasket for some models.

THE PRESSURE CANNING PROCESS

No matter what food you are preserving, it requires the same steps to pressure can.

- If you're using an electric pressure canner, you will need to rely on additional instructions from the manufacturer to achieve the desired pressure for the appropriate length of time—you will not adjust it with a stovetop burner like the other models.

- Likewise, if you're using a weighted-gauge model, consult the manufacturer's instructions on setting the canning pressure and for information on how to evaluate whether the canner is maintaining pressure.

The USDA specifically calls out a serious error that can cause unsafe canning:

As mentioned previously, the **internal canning temperature drops at high altitudes**. To correct for this, adjust the pressure of your canner upward if you live above sea level. USDA guidelines recommend increases as follows for **dial gauge canners**. The recipes in this book specify dial gauge pressure for canners below 2,000 feet (610 m).

For recipes at 11 pounds (75.8 kPa):

2,001 to 3,000 feet (610 m to 914.4 m) ....11½ pounds (79.3 kPa)

3,001 to 4,000 feet (914.7 m to 1.2 km) ....12 pounds (82.7 kPa)

4,001 to 5,000 feet (1.2 km to 1.5 km) ....12½ pounds (86.2 kPa)

5,001 to 6,000 feet (1.5 km to 1.8 km) ....13 pounds (89.6 kPa)

6,001 to 7,000 feet (1.8 km to 2.1 km) ....13½ pounds (93.1 kPa)

7,001 to 8,000 feet (2.1 km to 2.4 km) ....14 pounds (96.5 kPa)

8,001 to 9,000 feet (2.4 km to 2.7 km) ....14½ pounds (100 kPa)

9,001 to 10,000 feet (2.7 km to 3 km) ....15 pounds (103.4 kPa)

For recipes at 6 pounds (14.4 kPa):

2,001 to 4,000 feet (610 m to 1.2 km) ....7 pounds (48.3 kPa)

4,001 to 6,000 feet (1.2 km to 1.8 km) ....8 pounds (55.2 kPa)

6,001 to 8,000 feet (1.8 km to 2.4 km) ....9 pounds (62.1 kPa)

8,001 to 10,000 feet (2.4 km to 3 km) ....10 pounds (68.9 kPa)

CLEAN IS BEST

We all have clutter in our kitchens. As much as things make our house our home, they also collect dust and dirt.

When you are canning, clear your kitchen counters completely of anything you aren't using for the canning process. I remove all my small appliances, jars of utensils, and my extra measuring cups and storage containers. If I am not going to touch the item for canning, it gets removed.

This may seem like extra work, but it ensures the work area can be cleaned thoroughly. It also means you won't accidentally knock into something and ruin some of your hard work. If you're wondering where to put everything, do what I do: Make your kitchen table a temporary countertop! Sure, it clutters up the kitchen table, but that's okay. You won't be using it while you can.

CLEANING

Okay, is your counter free of all clutter? Great! Now it's time to wipe down all the surfaces with hot, soapy water to remove any grease and dirt. This is the cleaning step; it will remove any small particles of food or other impurities from your countertop. Only once your counter and work surfaces are clean are you ready to move on to sanitizing.

SANITIZING

To sanitize, you can use a commercial product, such as Star San. However, most people prefer to use what they have on hand: bleach. Create a sanitizing mixture by mixing 1 tablespoon (15 ml) of food-safe bleach with 1 gallon (3.8 L) of water. This concentration of bleach in water, 200 ppm, doesn't need to be rinsed off but it does need to air-dry before the surface is considered sanitized. Do what I do and pour the mixture in a spray bottle. Once you've cleaned your counter, mist it with the sanitizing solution and wipe so you have a thin layer across the surface. Let it air-dry and you're ready to move on to canning!

For **weighted gauge canners**, as soon as you get over 1,000 feet (304.8 m) in elevation, you should switch from the 5-pound (34.5 kPa) to the 10-pound (68.9 kPa) or the 10-pound (68.9 kPa) to the 15-pound (103.4 kPa) setting for safety, depending on the recipe. The recipes in this book specify pressure for weighted gauge canners below 1,000 feet (304.8 m).

If **air is trapped in your canner**, it lowers the temperature obtained at any pressure. Take care to avoid this.

Here is a quick review of the steps we'll take:

1. Prepare the canning area.
2. Prepare the canning jars and utensils.
3. Prepare the canner.
4. Prepare the food.
5. Fill the jars to the correct level.
6. Fill the canner.
7. Follow the recipe instructions.
8. Cool the jars.
9. Check the seals; label and store the jars.

PREPARE THE CANNING AREA

If you skipped the last page (go back and read it!), preparing the area means removing whatever you don't need to pressure can from the counter: extra utensils, small appliances, daily dishes, and other items should be placed elsewhere while you focus on canning. Clean and sanitize your countertops and anything else you think will come in contact with the canning jars and lids before they go into the canner.

PREPARE THE CANNING JARS AND UTENSILS

The jars and utensils you will use should be examined beforehand to make sure nothing is chipped or broken. The jars and utensils you will use should be washed in hot, soapy water before use. The clean jars should then be placed in hot—not boiling—water. Single-use lids need to be clean. It is no longer necessary to heat Ball or Kerr brand lids, but if you choose to heat them, do not boil them.

One tip for being ready to can is to place your jars in the dishwasher and run it through a sanitizing cycle. You can leave your jars in the dishwasher until you actually need to use them. I often do this the night before so they are waiting for me first thing in the morning. Before I had a dishwasher, I would wash them the night before and place them on linen hand towels on the sideboard. In the morning, all I had to do was place them in hot water to heat while I prepped my food.

PREPARE THE CANNER

Follow the manufacturer's guidelines for filling your specific canner. You'll likely need to insert the canning rack, add 2 to 3 inches (5 to 7.5 cm) of water to the bottom of the canner, and get that water preheated.

PREPARE THE FOOD

Your recipe may require a variety of preparation techniques before you can it. Fruits or vegetables must be washed, and perhaps peeled, and cut according to the recipe guidelines. Some foods are also browned or otherwise precooked. When making broth or soup, you may cook the entire recipe before you can. In any case, your recipe will clearly provide these directions.

FILL THE JARS TO THE CORRECT LEVEL

Once your food is ready to can, the sanitized jars must be filled to the recipe's specifications. Nearly all recipes in this book provide cooking liquid or heated water to top up your jars to the proper fill level. Note that all recipes require some amount of headspace, the room between the top of the food or liquid and the rim of the jar. (Proper headspace allows the food to expand and air to be forced out during the canning process.) Once the jars are full, use a nonmetallic tool to remove any air bubbles. Wipe the rims with a clean damp cloth, carefully place the lids on, and hand-tighten the screw bands around the lids.

FILL THE CANNER

Gently place your jars in the canner on top of the canning rack, making sure they do not touch (using a jar lifter, grab the jars below the screw band). When the canner is full, double check that all jars are upright and not tilted. Place the lid on the canner and lock it according to the manufacturer's instructions.

If you accidentally prepared more food than will fit in your pressure canner, do not pack jars for the next batch and let them sit. Instead, I recommend repeating the steps here in the same order: prepare the food, prepare the canner, pack the jars, and then fill the canner once again.

Follow your manufacturer's guidelines to close and lock the pressure canner. If you're using a model with more manual controls, you typically need to secure the lid, open the petcock (vent pipe) or leave the weight off the vent port, and place the pot over high heat until steam flows continuously for about 10 minutes. At this point, it is time to close the petcock or vent port and let the canner pressurize—it should take less than 5 minutes. Again, always follow your machine's instructions as you must close and lock the lid properly to maintain pressure!

FOLLOW THE RECIPE

With your lid locked in place, use your canner's settings or a stovetop burner to get a steady stream of steam from your pressure canner for 10 minutes or according to the manufacturer's guidelines. *Only once you do this should you close the vent and start bringing the canner to the proper pressure.*

For an electric pressure canner or a weighted-gauge model, you will most likely be instructed to set the pressure now. If you're using the stovetop to supply the heat, keep the pot at a temperature that maintains the pressure at or above the recommended level for the duration of the recipe's recommended processing time.

No matter which type of pressure canner you use, *start timing your recipe once the pressure on the dial gauge is correct or when the weighted gauge moves* as described by the manufacturer. In other words, if your recipe says the pressure should be held at 11 pounds (75.8 kPa) for 30 minutes, start the timer only once the pot reaches 11 pounds (75.8 kPa), not when you first apply the heat.

PRESSURE DIP?

Did your pressure dip below the recipe's recommended pressure? *The only safe way to remedy this is to bring the pot back to the recommended pressure and restart the timer.* **Never** let the timer continue once a pot falls below the recommended pressure amount as you can no longer guarantee the safety of the canned food.

Use care not to create large drops or increases in pressure, even above the recommended range, as this could prevent some of the jars from sealing properly. (Again, if you're using a weighted gauge, the manufacturer will provide instructions on how to monitor the pressure.)

COOL THE JARS

Once your recipe is finished cooking, turn off the heat. After some of the cooling time has passed, you can safely remove the lid. The amount of time it takes before you can safely release pressure and remove the lid varies by machine. It's often about 10 minutes after the machine reaches 0 pounds (0.7 kPa) pressure.

Do not attempt to speed the cooling by putting your canner in the fridge or freezer or by placing it in a sink full of cold water. The canner needs to cool without your assistance. Trying to cool the canner faster can result in unsafe canned foods, as well as imperfect seals.

Once the lid is off, do not remove the jars immediately; let them continue to cool inside the canner for about 20 minutes. This is a good time to set up a place for the jars to rest once you remove them. I recommend setting a clean dish towel in an out-of-the way place in the kitchen, away from people who may be tempted to touch the cooling canned food and away from any drafts. You may need a spot for the cans to rest for up to 24 hours as they cool, so choose wisely!

Once you're ready to remove the jars, use a jar lifter to remove them and place them on the clean dish towel, about 1 inch (5 cm) apart. Do not disturb the jars while they cool and do not try to remove the bands yet. You will hear the jars "ping" as each lid finishes sealing during the cooling process.

CHECK THE SEALS AND LABEL AND STORE THE JARS

Once the jars cool to room temperature, remove the screw bands and check that each jar is sealed properly: Press gently on the lid. It should be concave (dip inward) if you have a good seal. It should feel firm to the touch and it should not move or dip when you push on it. Do not tip or shake the jars, but do wipe off any residue that may have escaped during the time in the canner. Label your jars and place the sealed jars in a cool, dry location. If you have any jars that did not seal properly, refrigerate them and use them within a week or two (depending on the recipe).

PRESSURE CANNING STORAGE, TROUBLESHOOTING, AND OTHER CONSIDERATIONS

You now know the basics of pressure canning. Hopefully, that also means you've purchased the equipment you need to can—maybe you even have a recipe or two under your belt.

But knowing how to can is just the beginning. Chances are you'll have ups and downs along the way. Maybe a jar or two didn't seal. Or, maybe you have a cloudy jar and are wondering if it's safe to eat. (Alert: Don't eat it!) This section covers some of the most common problems when canning, as well as how to spot unsafe food and jars.

This section also addresses a few other important issues, such as proper storage. After all, if you don't put up your canned goods with as much care as you can them, they won't last as long or taste as fresh when you open them.

AFTER YOU CAN

Let's start this section where we ended the last one—at the end of a canning session. As you already know, the last step is removing the bands from your canning jars and checking the seals by examining the tops (which should be concave). Then, it's on to wiping down the jars and labeling them for storage.

While you might be tired after an afternoon of canning, do not skip these important steps. It's easy to think "I'll do it later" when it comes to labeling. But I've found it's best to label the foods with the recipe name and date immediately after you finish canning when the information is fresh in my mind, and before I forget to do it.

As you get started in canning, it's also important to keep a notebook. Jot down your notes while the day is fresh in your mind. Did one jar fail to seal? Did you have any issues maintaining pressure? How long did it take for the pot to reach pressure? These notes are the beginning of your foundation of canning knowledge. Without detailed notes, it will take you much longer to develop your skills and master your own canning setup.

So, what's next? Clean jars should be stored upright, in neat rows, in a cool, dark place. You don't want the jars exposed to light, nor do you want them exposed to temperatures that fluctuate. In other words, while an outdoor shed or garage might be cool, dark, and the temperature never goes above 60°F (15.6°C) in the winter, it might fluctuate by 20°F to 30°F (11 to 17°C) some days or throughout a season. This is not an ideal environment for canned goods. Store them indoors in a pantry. Neat rows are essential so you can easily see that each jar looks the same as it did the day it was placed on the shelf. It's easier to spot a jar that looks different from the rest when they're aligned in a neat row.

If you find a white residue on your jars as you go to store them, don't panic. If it disappears when you wipe the jar but comes back when it dries, this is just a sign that your water has a high mineral content. Wiping it with a cloth dampened in a vinegar-water mixture will remove it.

As far as what to avoid when storing your jars, here are a few common mistakes to be aware of:

1. Do not tip and shake your jars from time to time to keep them evenly mixed. Let them settle and *only stir them after opening.*

2. Do not place jars with no labels on the shelf. Add the name of the food and date it was canned to each jar. If you're in a hurry, at least write that information on the lid with a marker!

3. Keep jars out of direct sunlight. If your pantry's light changes from season to season, double check to make sure there isn't a jar or two getting light for a couple hours a day.

4. Do not stack jars. This can keep you from seeing if a lid has loosened or become unsealed. If you need to fit more in the pantry, adjust your shelf height or install more shelves instead.

5. If you find an unsealed jar, do not try to save the food by reheating it. Your health is not worth a jar of food.

USE WHAT YOU CAN

If you enjoy cooking (and you probably do since you are reading this book), you will enjoy having shelves of canned goods based on your tastes and needs. When your basic foods are customized to your taste and ready at your fingertips, you can conveniently "shop" in your own store at home—with better quality and flavor than the grocery store. If you start planning meals to include at least one ingredient of your own, you will come to rely on your handiwork and see how that work is well worth the effort.

We have all seen beautiful photos of pantries bursting with rainbows of jars from floor to ceiling. I only wish my pantry was that colorful and full! The truth is, I can what my family will actually eat, and I run out of room before I run out of ideas.

You should also consider common serving sizes at your house. If you are a canning for just one or two people, it makes more sense to preserve your foods in pints (473 ml) and half pints (235 ml). A simple way to think about this is by looking at a can of vegetables from the grocery shelf. Do you use one can of beans when preparing a meal? If so, you can safely can a pint (473 ml) or half pint (235 ml) of beans.

Consider what your family likes to eat when selecting your canning recipes.

3 REASONS TO EAT FROM YOUR PANTRY

1. *Can for inspiration. I often go to the pantry, find a canned vegetable that catches my eye, and use that ingredient as a starting point for dinner. Alternatively, try the same exercise as forced inspiration: If you have way too many canned carrots beckoning, look for new recipes that will use up those carrots!*

2. *Can for every day and for rainy days. When I began canning, it was sometimes difficult to break out a jar I had worked so hard creating. You may find you hoard some of your more precious jars or favorite recipes. A great way around this is to compromise with yourself. If you find you have a favorite you're reluctant to use, save yourself just a jar or two for a special treat. This will let you work through the rest and ensure you don't end up with expired food, while also guaranteeing you have a jar or two of something special come February.*

3. *Can to save money. Utilize your pantry foods to save money. Were you about to run to the store because you have "nothing" on hand for dinner? What about all those canned tomatoes? Be resourceful about dinner, using mostly canned goods and grains you have on hand.*

SPOTTING PROBLEMS IN THE PANTRY

No matter how hard you try, occasionally a jar will go off. When this happens, it is critical that you do *not* try to salvage the food. Knowing the signs of spoilage and how to care for your canned goods is an essential part of pressure canning. Let's take a look at some things you might find in the pantry.

Sealed jars that don't stay sealed. First of all, your jars have to seal or they don't make it onto the shelves. Period. That said, a jar can unseal over time. Check your jars regularly and *if one becomes unsealed, discard it immediately.* If more than one seal fails from the same batch, go back to your notes from that canning day to try to figure what went wrong. You'll then know if that same thing happens again, you'll need to keep a very close eye on your jars.

Food fades in color. Over time, food can fade yet still be safe to eat. However, with that fading comes loss of nutrients. Fading food can occur due to exposure to light though. With exposure to sunlight also comes additional heat, which will decrease the shelf life of your food. Make sure you store food in a cool, dark place and use it within one year.

Foods that darken in color. If food floats to the top of the liquid in the jar, it may darken where it is exposed to air. This is not dangerous as the canning killed any harmful bacteria, but it is visually unappealing. It is important to cover the food with liquid before canning to try to avoid this; if you have food that breaks the surface of the liquid, you run the risk of darkened food.

Changes in food other than fading or darkening. Your food should not bubble, swell, shrivel, or become cloudy. If any of those things happens, discard the food. Bacteria can cause a variety of visible changes in your foods and it is never safe to try even a tiny taste if you see changes other than fading or darkening.

Mold in jars. *Mold is never safe* in your jars. You might see it grow on the contents of the jars, on the jar walls, or even on the underside of the lid. Do not try to remove the mold or think that heating it will help. Mold in jars is dangerous as it contains spores that become airborne when disturbed. When there is mold found in any can you should discard everything, including the jar and its contents.

WHERE DID ALL THE LIQUID GO?

When you remove your jars from the canner, sometimes there is not enough liquid left in the jars to cover the food. There are many potential reasons for this, but it's usually one of the most common causes to blame. Here are the top culprits for losing liquid during the canning process and tips on how to avoid them.

- **Jars that are too full or too tightly packed.** When food and liquid are boiled, they expand. If there is not enough headspace in the jar, liquid is forced out. Always follow the recipe guidelines for recommended headspace. More is not always better when it comes to canning!

- **Air bubbles are trapped in the canned food.** Trapped air bubbles can indicate the food was not canned properly. Always make sure to release air bubbles with a straight wooden or plastic utensil before topping up the jar to the specified level and sealing.

NOTE

Always leave the headspace recommended in the recipe so the food and liquid have room to expand under pressure.

- **Pressure fluctuations.** If pressure fluctuates during processing, liquid may be forced out of the jars. Control the pressure carefully and avoid frequent adjustments. If you experience a quick increase or decrease in pressure—even above the recommended recipe guideline for minimum pressure—make sure to check your jars carefully once they cool.

- **Pressure is released too rapidly.** A rapid release of pressure can also cause liquid to be forced out of the jars. This is one reason you should always allow your canner to cool to room temperature on its own. Never try to help it along by placing it in the fridge, freezer, or a bath of cool water.

WHY DID MY JARS BREAK?

It has happened to everyone who cans: The excitement of opening the canner quickly turns to shock as you are greeted with a mess of broken jars and wasted food. Even just one jar breaking can put a damper on a fun day of canning. Here are some of the most common reasons glass breaks in the canner and tips to prevent this from happening to you.

- **Reusing store product jars** instead of home canning jars is a surefire way to get a broken jar—or three—on canning day. Even if canning lids and rings fit the commercial jars, the glass may not be made to be reheated under pressure. This is why I recommend only using actual canning jars for your home canning.

- If a jar has been **damaged prior to canning**, it's probably going to crack under pressure. Inspecting each jar before you use it, making sure it has no chips or cracks, is crucial. Hold the jar up to the light and take your time during the inspection. The smallest crack is all it takes for the jar to break in the canner.

- Related to this last point, jars can be **damaged by metal objects**. Using metal spoons and other metal utensils to rearrange foods or release air bubbles can nick and weaken the jar. Even a small amount of damage to a canning jar can cause breakage once it's under pressure. It's important you don't damage the jars you've already inspected on canning day.

- If you place **jars in the canner without a rack**, they will not be stable during the canning process and they can break. Always use a rack when canning.

- **Hot jars** can crack if they are placed on a cold surface. In addition to saving your countertops, placing jars that come out of the canner onto a clean dish towel, away from drafts, will keep you from losing part of your batch due to breakage.

- When **hot jars are filled with cold water or cold jars are filled with hot food**, the glass can crack. Avoid this by keeping jars hot and only filling hot jars with hot food.

WHAT ARE THE MOST COMMON CANNING MISTAKES (AND HOW DO I AVOID THEM)?

All cooks make mistakes, but canners need to be precise and careful with their canning technique. There are common mistakes that many canners make, which could be, at the least, wasteful and, at the most, dangerous. Let's take a look at what to avoid and why.

- **Using outdated canning methods.** This is, perhaps, one of the most important things to avoid when canning. Just because your grandparents did something and survived doesn't mean you should do it as well. There's a reason today's safety standards differ from the standards decades ago. We have learned a great deal about safe canning and there's no reason not to follow the current canning guidelines.

- **Overpacking jars.** Perhaps the most common mistake beginning canners make is not leaving adequate headspace in the canning jars. Every recipe has proper headspace requirements and this requirement is essential for safe canning. Filling the jars beyond the recommended level means the food won't have room to expand while under pressure. The pressure on overfilled jars forces liquid out between the lid and rim and can keep the lid from sealing properly as the pressure returns to normal. Always fill jars leaving the correct amount of headspace.

- **Not adhering to proper pressure requirements and times.** While not following a recipe's instructions is not a common mistake canners make, some canners are not even aware when they are "breaking the rules." The length of time needed for the recipe is essential for heating the food to the center of the jar. If the pressure drops below the recommended level, it is not safe simply to resume the timer once you're back at pressures— yes, even if you were nearly done with a recipe! If the pressure drops below the recommended level, you must restart your timer to ensure safe canned food.

- **Interchanging ingredients in a recipe.** Recipes for pressure canning are designed with a length of cook time and pressure designed around the ingredients, both to properly heat them through and to take into account ingredient variables such as acidity. Do not change the recipe or you will risk your food being canned improperly, and spoilage can develop. The only changes you can make safely are to spices, such as oregano, thyme, etc.

- **Leaving screw bands on jars.** Leaving bands on jars can lead to stuck lids and can mask other issues—namely, it is hard to tell if the lid sealed properly if the edge of the seal is hidden by a band.

- **Starting with overripe foods.** Food that is pressure canned past its prime will result in recipes that have an unappealing color, texture, or flavor. If a food has started to decay, simply cutting out the visible "bad" spots may not be enough to remove all the decay. Your food must be as perfectly ripe as possible to get the best, and safest, results.

- **Overcooking recipes before canning.** Since foods are cooked at such high heat during the pressure canning process, if recipes are cooked too long before placing the food in the jars, the resulting food can become mushy. While there's no safety concern here, your family will have to eat their way through your mistake!

Chapter 2

TOMATOES AND SAUCES

The tomato was one of the most important crops in a farmer's wife's garden. She canned it whole or in pieces to use in later, winter-bound recipes; she canned it in the form of soups and sauces; she canned it as catsups and spicy condiments to serve along with roasts.

STEWED TOMATOES

METHOD: Pressure Canning

PROCESSING TIME: Pints (473 ml) 15 minutes; Quarts (946 ml) 20 minutes

PRESSURE: 10 Pounds (68.9 Kpa) Weighted Gauge, 11 Pounds (75.8 kPa) Dial Gauge

YIELD: About 3 pints (473 ml)

---

2 quarts (1.9 L) chopped tomatoes

¼ cup (38 g) chopped green bell peppers

¼ cup (40 g) chopped onions

2 teaspoons celery salt

2 teaspoons sugar

¼ teaspoon salt

1. Combine ingredients, cover, and cook 10 minutes, stirring often.

2. Pour hot into hot, sterilized pint (473 ml) or quart (946 ml) jars, leaving a ½-inch (1.3 cm) headspace.

3. Remove any air bubbles with a bubble freer (see below), wipe jar rims, and adjust lids.

4. Process pints (473 ml) for 15 minutes and quarts (946 ml) for 20 minutes.

5. With a jar lifter, remove the jars and place them on a clean dish towel away from any drafts. Allow to cool undisturbed for 12 to 24 hours and then check the seals. If any jars have not sealed properly, refrigerate them and use within 2 weeks. Label the remaining jars with the recipe name and date before storing.

—Adapted from the Clemson University Extension Service website

WHAT IS A BUBBLE FREER?

The bubble freer spatula is a long tool made of heat-resistant plastic that you use to remove air bubbles in a jar before sealing. You work the tool up and down the insides of the jar and around, releasing trapped bubbles.

TOMATOES—WHOLE, HALVED, AND DICED

Tomatoes, cut into halves or quarters as desired

METHOD: Boiling Water Bath Canning

PROCESSING TIME: Pints (473 ml)
40 minutes; Quarts (946 ml)
50 minutes

YIELD: Variable

---

3 pounds (1.4 kg) of tomatoes per quart (946 ml). Select tomatoes that are fresh and firm, not overripe. Cut into halves, quarters, or smaller chunks as desired.

Salt (optional)

Lemon juice

1. Wash and dip tomatoes in boiling water for 30 seconds. Plunge into cold water. Drain, peel, and core.

2. Add a teaspoon of salt (optional) and 2 tablespoons (28 ml) of lemon juice to each sterilized quart (946 ml) jar (for pint [473 ml] jars, add ½ teaspoon of salt and a tablespoon [15 ml] of lemon juice).

3. Using a funnel, fill hot, sterilized jars with tomatoes. Pack tomatoes down with a non-metal spoon or spatula. Top off with boiling water, leaving a ½-inch (1.3 cm) headspace. Remove any air bubbles with a rubber spatula or clean wooden chopstick.

4. Clean rims and any spills with sterile cloth. Secure lids and rings.

5. Place jars in a boiling water bath canner.

6. Return water to a boil and process 50 minutes for quarts (946 ml) and 40 minutes for pints (473 ml). Adjust for altitude if necessary (see Adjust for Altitude! on page 29).

7. Use a jar lifter to remove the jars and let cool undisturbed on a clean dish towel away from any drafts. Check the seals after 12 to 24 hours. Refrigerate any unsealed jars and use within 2 weeks. Label the remaining jars with the recipe name and date before storing.

STEWED TOMATOES II

Stewed tomatoes follow the same procedure as for whole and diced tomatoes except that extra flavor is added through the addition of celery, onions, and green bell peppers. This makes a great base for many sauces and recipes.

METHOD: Boiling Water Bath Canning

PROCESSING TIME: Pints (473 ml) 40 minutes; Quarts (946 ml) 50 minutes

YIELD: About 7 quarts (6.6 L)

---

24 cups (4.3 kg) diced tomatoes

2 cups (200 g) chopped celery

1 cup (160 g) chopped onion

1 cup (150 g) chopped green bell pepper

3 teaspoons (18 g) salt

NOTE: Do not add more onion, celery, or bell peppers than listed in this recipe unless you are using a pressure canner. It will make the pH balance less acidic and not feasible for boiling water bath canning.

1. Combine diced tomatoes and vegetables in a stainless steel or enamel pot and simmer for 10 minutes.

2. Add a teaspoon of salt and 2 tablespoons (28 ml) of lemon juice to each quart (946 ml); for pint (473 ml) jars, add ½ teaspoon of salt and a tablespoon (28 ml) of lemon juice.

3. Pack tomato mix into hot, sterilized jars, leaving a ½-inch (1.3 cm) headspace. Remove any air bubbles with a non-metal spatula or skewer.

4. Clean rims and any spills with sterile cloth. Secure lids and rings.

5. Place jars in a boiling water bath canner.

6. Return water to a boil and process 50 minutes for quarts (946 ml) and 40 minutes for pints (473 ml). Adjust for altitude if necessary (see Adjust for Altitude! on page 29).

7. Use a jar lifter to remove the jars and let cool undisturbed on a clean dish towel away from any drafts. Check the seals after 12 to 24 hours. Refrigerate any unsealed jars and use within 2 weeks. Label the remaining jars with the recipe name and date before storing.

TOMATO JUICE

Fresh, canned tomato and vegetable juice is one of my favorite breakfast treats in the winter. I also keep a jar at my office for a healthy afternoon pick-me-up.

METHOD: Boiling Water Bath Canning

PROCESSING TIME: Pints (473 ml) 40 minutes; Quarts (946 ml) 45 minutes

YIELD: About 7 pints (3.3 L)

---

24 cups (4.3 kg) fresh tomatoes, peeled, cored, and diced

2 cups (200 g) chopped celery

⅔ cup (110 g) chopped onion

3 tablespoons (39 g) sugar (to taste)

3 teaspoons (18 g) salt

1 teaspoon ground black pepper

Tabasco or other hot pepper sauce, to taste

Lemon juice

1. Combine all ingredients in a stainless steel or enamel pot and simmer, uncovered, for 25 minutes.

2. Force mixture through a food mill or process in a blender and strain through a cheesecloth-lined colander into a bowl.

3. Add 2 tablespoons (28 ml) of lemon juice to each quart (946 ml) jar; for pint (473 ml) jars, add a tablespoon (15 ml) of lemon juice.

4. Using a funnel, fill hot, sterilized jars with tomato juice, leaving a ½-inch (1.3 cm) headspace. Remove any air bubbles with a rubber spatula or skewer.

5. Clean rims and any spills with sterile cloth. Secure lids and rings.

6. Place jars on rack in canner with boiling water.

7. Once water returns to a boil, process 40 minutes for pints (473 ml) and 45 minutes for quarts (946 ml), adjusting for altitude if necessary (see Adjust for Altitude! on page 29).

8. Use a jar lifter to remove the jars and let cool undisturbed on a clean dish towel away from any drafts. Check the seals after 12 to 24 hours. Refrigerate any unsealed jars and use within 2 weeks. Label the remaining jars with the recipe name and date before storing.

TOMATO CATSUP I

METHOD: Boiling Water Bath Canning
PROCESSING TIME: 15 minutes
YIELD: 6 to 7 pints

---

24 pounds (10.9 kg) ripe tomatoes

3 cups (480 g) onions, chopped

¾ teaspoon cayenne pepper

4 teaspoons (8 g) whole cloves

2 sticks cinnamon, crushed into
small pieces under a knife handle

1½ teaspoons whole allspice
berries

2 tablespoons (13 g) celery seeds

3 cups (700 ml) vinegar, minimum
5 percent acidity

1½ cups (300 g) sugar

¼ cup (72 g) canning or
pickling salt

1. Wash tomatoes. Dip in boiling water for 30 to 60 seconds or until skins split. Then, dip in cold water, slip off skins, and remove cores. Quarter tomatoes and place in a 4-gallon (15.2 L) pot.

2. Add onions. Bring to boil and simmer 20 minutes, uncovered.

3. Combine spices in a spice bag. Place spices in a spice bag and vinegar in a 2-quart (1.9 L) saucepan. Bring to boil. Cover, turn off heat, and let stand for 20 minutes.

4. Remove spice bag from the vinegar and add the vinegar to the tomato mixture. Boil about 30 minutes.

5. Press boiled mixture through a food mill or sieve. Return to the pot. Add sugar and salt and boil gently, stirring frequently until volume is reduced by one-half or until mixture rounds up on spoon without separation.

6. Pour into hot, sterilized pint (473 ml) jars, leaving a ⅛-inch (3 mm) headspace.

7. Remove any air bubbles. Wipe jar rims. Adjust lids.

8. Process 15 minutes in a boiling water canner.

9. With a jar lifter, remove the jars and place them on a clean dish towel away from any drafts. Allow to cool undisturbed for 12 to 24 hours and then check the seals. If any jars have not sealed properly, refrigerate them and use within 2 weeks. Label the remaining jars with the recipe name and date before storing.

—Adapted from the National Center for Home Food Preservation (NCHFP) website

TOMATO CATSUP II

SEPTEMBER 1913

METHOD: Boiling Water Bath Canning
PROCESSING TIME: 15 minutes

___

24 pounds (10.9 g) tomatoes, strained

1 tablespoon (5 g) whole black peppercorns

1 tablespoon (6 g) whole cloves

2 sticks cinnamon

2 tablespoons (12 g) whole allspice berries

2⅔ pints (1.3 L) vinegar, minimum 5 percent acidity

1½ cups (300 g) sugar

¼ cup (72 g) canning or pickling salt

Follow directions for Tomato Catsup I, at left.

—*Adapted from the NCHFP website*

TOMATO CATSUP III

JUNE 1917

METHOD: Boiling Water Bath Canning
PROCESSING TIME: 15 minutes

___

4 pounds (1.8 kg) ripe tomatoes

3 cups (480 g) onion, chopped

1 teaspoon red pepper

3 bay leaves

1 lemon

1 teaspoon white pepper

1 teaspoon ground black pepper

2 teaspoons dry mustard

3 cups (700 ml) vinegar, minimum 5 percent acidity

¼ cup (72 g) canning or pickling salt

1½ cups (300 g) sugar

Follow directions for Tomato Catsup I, above, placing whole spices in spice bag and adding powdered spices and lemon as is.

—*Adapted from the NCHFP website*

SPICED TOMATOES I

JULY 1913

These two recipes for spiced tomatoes create two pungent sauces, not unlike the Tomato Catsup recipes on pages 70–71.

METHOD: Boiling Water Bath Canning

PROCESSING TIME: 15 minutes

YIELD: 6 to 7 pints

---

24 pounds (10.9 kg) ripe tomatoes

1¼ cups (285 g) brown sugar

4 teaspoons (8 g) whole cloves

4 teaspoons (8 g) whole allspice berries

2⅔ cups (635 ml) good vinegar, minimum 5 percent acidity

¼ cup (72 g) canning or pickling salt

Follow directions for preparing tomatoes from Tomato Catsup I, page 70. Add sugar, spices, and cinnamon and cook and process according to directions in Tomato Catsup I.

—Adapted from the NCHFP website

FRUITLESS PRESERVES

LULU G. PARKER

August 1910

With fruit so high and scarce this summer, the thrifty housewife may well turn to the vegetable garden for the wherewithall to fill her preserve jars. These tomato preserves are not mere substitutes; anyone who has tried them knows they are exceedingly "good eating."

Editor's note: The Farmer's Wife made Tomato Jam in the late summer of 1910 and Green Tomato Jam in the autumn of 1913 and similar recipes dozens of times over the years. Below are the recipes, for which no contemporary processing times exist. They should be stored in the refrigerator for immediate use.

SPICED GREEN TOMATOES

METHOD: Boiling Water Bath Canning

PROCESSING TIME: 15 minutes

YIELD: About 4 pints (1.9 L)

---

6 pounds (2.7 kg) small, whole green tomatoes, such as plum tomatoes

2 sticks cinnamon

1 tablespoon (6 g) whole cloves

9 cups (1.8 kg) sugar

1 tablespoon (6 g) whole allspice berries

1 pint (473 ml) cider vinegar, minimum 5 percent acidity

1 tablespoon (6 g) whole mace or ½ tablespoon ground

1. Wash, scald, and peel tomatoes.

2. Make a syrup of the sugar, vinegar, and spices. Drop the tomatoes into the syrup and boil until they become clear.

3. Pack into hot, sterilized pint (473 ml) jars, leaving a ½-inch (1.3 cm) headspace.

4. Strain syrup and pour over tomatoes with the syrup, again leaving a ½-inch (1.3 cm) headspace.

5. Remove any air bubbles and adjust headspace if needed. Wipe rims of jars with a dampened clean paper towel and seal.

6. Process 15 minutes in a boiling water bath.

7. With a jar lifter, remove the jars and place them on a clean dish towel away from any drafts. Allow to cool undisturbed for 12 to 24 hours and then check the seals. If any jars have not sealed properly, refrigerate them and use within 2 weeks. Label the remaining jars with the recipe name and date before storing.

—*Adapted from the NCHFP website*

TOMATO JAM

AUGUST 1910

1½ pounds (680 g) tomatoes

6 tablespoons (90 ml) bottled lemon juice

1-inch (2.5 cm) piece of fresh ginger

1. Peel and slice ripe tomatoes, put them with an equal weight of sugar, and boil an hour with 6 tablespoons (90 ml) of bottled lemon juice per every 1½ pounds (680 g) of tomatoes and an equal measure of water to fruit.

2. Tie ginger enough to flavor to taste (about 1-inch [2.5 cm] slice per 1½ pounds [680 g]) in a thin muslin bag and add to the jam before it is done, about 30 minutes.

3. When it passes the jelly test (see below), remove the ginger and skim.

4. Pack hot in hot, sterilized jars and store immediately in refrigerator, using up within a week.

GREEN TOMATO JAM

SEPTEMBER 1913

6 pounds (2.7 kg) green tomatoes

4 pounds (1.8 kg) sugar

1 cup (235 ml) water

2 ounces (55 g) grated fresh ginger

1. Slice tomatoes thin, mix with remaining ingredients, and simmer slowly for 3 hours.

2. Strain through a coarse strainer.

3. Pack hot in hot, sterilized jars, seal, and store immediately in refrigerator.

SHEET OR SPOON TEST: ALSO KNOWN AS THE JELLY TEST

Dip a cool, metal spoon into the boiling jelly mixture. Raise the spoon about 12 inches (30 cm) above the pan, out of the steam. Turn the spoon so the liquid runs off the side. When the mixture first starts to boil, the drops will be light and syrupy. As the syrup continues to boil, the drops will become heavier and will drop off the spoon two at a time. The jelly is done when the syrup forms two drops that flow together and sheet, or hang off, the edge of the spoon.

USING BOTTLED LEMON JUICE

When lemon or lime juice is listed in a recipe, you should use the bottled version rather than fresh unless specified. Yes, you read that right. I know this may come as a surprise, and frankly it's one of those things about canning that I personally find a bit challenging, but there is a very good reason for doing it this way. Bottled lemon juice and lime juice have a standard level of acidity, whereas the acidity levels of fresh lemons and fresh limes vary. Because acidity plays such an important role in jam making, it's necessary to add the proper amount, making bottled your safest option.

TOMATO SALSA

METHOD: Boiling Water Bath Canning

PROCESSING TIME: 35 minutes

YIELD: 5 pints (2.4 L)

---

10 cups (1.8 kg) tomatoes, peeled, cored, and diced

1 cup (150 g) chopped green bell pepper

2 cups (320 g) chopped onions

½ cup (72 g) chopped hot peppers (a mixture of banana and jalapeño peppers with seeds removed)

1. Add diced tomatoes to large, stainless steel or enamel pot and cook for 30 minutes until tomatoes are very soft and the large chunks are gone.

2. Using a large spoon or cup, remove excess liquid from the pot and then add remaining ingredients (except lemon juice).

3. Continue to cook at a low boil for 20 minutes, stirring frequently.

4. Using a funnel, fill hot, sterilized canning jars, leaving a ½-inch (1.3 cm) of headspace. Add a tablespoon (15 ml) of lemon juice to each jar. Remove any air bubbles with a rubber spatula or skewer.

5. Clean rims and any spills with sterile cloth. Secure lids and rings.

6. Process in a boiling water bath canner for 35 minutes, adjusting for altitude if necessary (see Adjust for Altitude! on page 29).

7. Use a jar lifter to remove the jars and let cool undisturbed on a clean dish towel away from any drafts. Check the seals after 12 to 24 hours. Refrigerate any unsealed jars and use within 2 weeks. Label the remaining jars with the recipe name and date before storing.

TOMATILLOS

When we lived in Nebraska, I grew both green and purple tomatillos for the farmers' market. Some customers had a little trepidation—after all, tomatillos are much less common than tomatoes in that part of the country. However, once I shared a few recipes for salsa verde and Mexican-inspired soups, people were hooked. Soon, I couldn't grow enough to keep up with demand! While it's true you can make and pressure can salsa (see Tomatillo Salsa on page 187), by canning the tomatillos as simply as possible, you'll have all options available when you crack open the jar.

METHOD: Pressure Canning

PROCESSING TIME: 10 minutes

PRESSURE: 10 Pounds (68.9 Kpa) Weighted Gauge, 11 Pounds (75.8 kPa) Dial Gauge

YIELD: 4 pints (1.9 L)

---

4 pounds (1.8 kg) fresh tomatillos, papery husks removed, washed and quartered

¼ cup (60 ml) freshly squeezed lemon juice (from about 2 lemons)

1. In large pot, combine the tomatillos with enough water to cover. Bring to boil over high heat and boil for 5 to 10 minutes until tender.

2. With a large spoon, carefully fill hot, sterilized jars with the tomatillos and some cooking water, leaving a ½-inch (1.3 cm) headspace.

3. Add 1 tablespoon (15 ml) of lemon juice to each jar.

4. Remove any air bubbles with a plastic or wooden utensil, adding more hot liquid as needed to maintain the proper ½-inch (1.3 cm) headspace.

5. Wipe the rims and seal the jars hand-tight with the 2-piece lids.

6. Carefully transfer the filled jars to the rack inside the pressure canner. Process the jars at the pressure listed above for 10 minutes.

7. Let the canner return to 0 pounds pressure (0.7 kPa). Wait 10 minutes more and then carefully open the canner lid according to the manufacturer's instructions.

8. With a jar lifter, remove the jars and place them on a clean dish towel away from any drafts. Allow to cool undisturbed for 12 to 24 hours and then check the seals. If any jars have not sealed properly, refrigerate them and use the tomatillos within 2 weeks. Label the remaining jars with the recipe name and date before storing.

Chapter 3

VEGETABLES

Home canning is a great way to enjoy summer vegetables and make quick meals. My favorite veggies to can are beets, beans, and succotash made from corn and lima beans. I also can a lot of cubed winter squash, which makes great soups and squash risotto! There are a number of vegetables that are not recommended for home canning. Broccoli and cauliflower become discolored and their strong flavors are unpleasantly intensified. Summer squash, zucchini, cabbage, and eggplant become mushy and off-flavored as well.

ASPARAGUS

METHOD: Pressure Canning

PROCESSING TIME: Pints (473 ml) 30 minutes;
Quarts (946 ml) 40 minutes

YIELD: 7 quarts (6.6 L)

---

24 pounds (10.9 kg) asparagus spears

1 teaspoon salt per jar (optional)

1. Wash and trim asparagus so spears can stand up in your jars.

2. Pack into hot, sterilized jars. Add a teaspoon of salt (optional). Fill jars with boiling water, making sure asparagus is fully submerged. Leave a 1-inch (2.5 cm) headspace.

3. Remove any air bubbles. Wipe rims and secure lids.

4. Process pints (473 ml) for 30 minutes and quarts (946 ml) for 40 minutes in pressure canner at pressure listed for your altitude and canner (see Adjust for Altitude! on page 29).

BEANS, GREEN & WAX

METHOD: Pressure Canning

PROCESSING TIME: 25 minutes

YIELD: 7 quarts (6.6 L)

---

14 pounds (6.4 kg) green or wax beans

1 teaspoon salt per jar (optional)

1. Wash and trim ends of beans. Snap into smaller pieces if desired.

2. Pack into hot, sterilized jars. Add a teaspoon of salt (optional). Fill jars with boiling water, covering beans. Leave a 1-inch (2.5 cm) headspace.

3. Remove any air bubbles. Wipe rims and secure lids.

4. Process pints (473 ml) and quarts (946 ml) for 25 minutes in pressure canner at pressure listed for your altitude and canner (see Adjust for Altitude! on page 29).

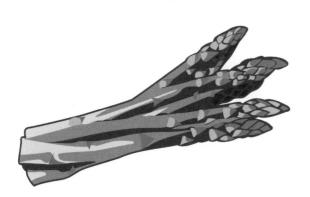

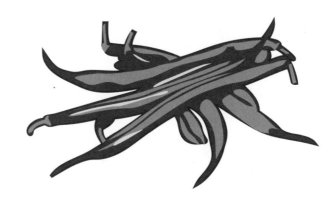

LIMA BEANS

METHOD: Pressure Canning

PROCESSING TIME: Pints (473 ml) 40 minutes;
Quarts (946 ml) 50 minutes

YIELD: 7 quarts (6.6 L)

---

30 pounds (13.6 kg) lima beans

1 teaspoon salt per jar (optional)

1. Wash and shell lima beans.

2. Pack into hot, sterilized jars. Add a teaspoon of salt (optional). Fill jars with boiling water, covering lima beans. Leave a 1-inch (2.5 cm) headspace.

3. Remove any air bubbles. Wipe rims and secure lids.

4. Process pints (473 ml) for 40 minutes and quarts (946 ml) for 50 minutes in pressure canner at pressure listed for your altitude and canner (see Adjust for Altitude! on page 29).

BEETS

METHOD: Pressure Canning

PROCESSING TIME: Pints (473 ml) 30 minutes;
Quarts (946 ml) 35 minutes

YIELD: 7 quarts (6.6 L)

---

21 pounds (9.5 kg) beets, tops removed

1 teaspoon salt per jar (optional)

1. Wash beets and boil for 20 minutes. Remove skins. Cut into cubes.

2. Pack into hot, sterilized jars. Add a teaspoon of salt (optional). Fill jars with boiling water, covering beets. Leave a 1-inch (2.5 cm) headspace.

3. Remove any air bubbles. Wipe rims and secure lids.

4. Process pints (473 ml) for 30 minutes and quarts (946 ml) for 35 minutes in pressure canner at pressure listed for your altitude and canner (see Adjust for Altitude! on page 29).

CARROTS

METHOD: Pressure Canning

PROCESSING TIME: Pints (473 ml) 25 minutes;
Quarts (946 ml) 30 minutes

YIELD: 7 quarts (6.6 L)

---

20 pounds (9.1 kg) carrots, tops removed

1 teaspoon salt per jar (optional)

1. Wash, peel, and slice carrots to desired size.

2. Pack into hot, sterilized jars. Add a teaspoon of salt (optional). Fill jars with boiling water, covering carrots. Leave a 1-inch (2.5 cm) headspace.

3. Remove any air bubbles. Wipe rims and secure lids.

4. Process pints (473 ml) for 25 minutes and quarts (946 ml) for 30 minutes in pressure canner at pressure listed for your altitude and canner (see Adjust for Altitude! on page 29).

CORN

METHOD: Pressure Canning

PROCESSING TIME: Pints (473 ml) 25 minutes;
Quarts (946 ml) 30 minutes

YIELD: 7 quarts (6.6 L)

---

30 pounds (13.6 kg) corn on the cob

1 teaspoon salt per jar (optional)

1. Husk corn, cook in boiling water for 3 minutes, and cut corn kernels off cobs.

2. Pack into hot, sterilized jars. Add a teaspoon of salt (optional). Fill jars with boiling water, covering corn kernels. Leave a 1-inch (2.5 cm) headspace.

3. Remove any air bubbles. Wipe rims and secure lids.

4. Process pints (473 ml) for 25 minutes and quarts (946 ml) for 30 minutes in pressure canner at pressure listed for your altitude and canner (see Adjust for Altitude! on page 29).

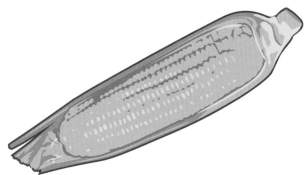

PEAS, SHELLED

METHOD: Pressure Canning
PROCESSING TIME: 40 minutes
YIELD: 9 pints (4.3 L)

---

20 pounds (9.1 kg) peas, shelled

1 teaspoon salt per jar (optional)

1. Wash peas.
2. Fill hot, sterilized jars with raw peas. Add a teaspoon of salt (optional). Fill jars with boiling water, covering peas. Leave a 1-inch (2.5 cm) headspace.
3. Remove any air bubbles. Wipe rims and secure lids.
4. Process pints (473 ml) and quarts (946 ml) for 40 minutes in pressure canner at pressure listed above for your altitude and canner (see Adjust for Altitude! on page 29).

PEPPERS

METHOD: Pressure Canning
PROCESSING TIME: 35 minutes
YIELD: 9 pints (4.3 L)

---

10 pounds (4.5 kg) peppers

½ teaspoon salt per jar (optional)

1. Blanch peppers in boiling water or blister in a broiler for 6 minutes. Place in a bowl and cover with plastic wrap or a tight-fitting plate. Let sit until cool and then remove skins. Cut to desired size.
2. Fill hot, sterilized jars with peppers. Add a ½ teaspoon of salt (optional). Fill jars with boiling water, covering peppers. Leave a 1-inch (2.5 cm) headspace.
3. Remove any air bubbles. Wipe rims and secure lids.
4. Process pints (473 ml) for 35 minutes in pressure canner at pressure listed for your altitude and canner (see Adjust for Altitude! on page 29).

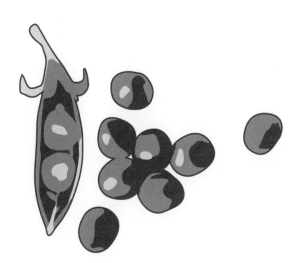

POTATOES

METHOD: Pressure Canning

PROCESSING TIME:
Pints (473 ml) 35 minutes;
Quarts (946 ml) 40 minutes

YIELD: 7 quarts (6.6 L)

---

20 pounds (9.1 kg) potatoes

Vitamin C (ascorbic acid) tablets, 500 mg (one tablet per gallon [3.8 L] of water)

1 teaspoon salt per jar (optional)

1. Wash and peel potatoes. Cut into ½- or 1-inch (1.3 or 2.5 cm) cubes.

   IMPORTANT: To prevent them from darkening, place the cubed potatoes in water with an ascorbic acid solution. The easiest way to do this is to crush six 500 mg Vitamin C tablets per gallon (3.8 L) of water (see Prevent Discoloration on page 85). Keep the potatoes submerged until you are ready to cook them. Otherwise, they'll turn a very unappetizing color of gray when canned and stored.

2. Transfer potatoes from ascorbic acid bath to boiling water and cook for 2 minutes.

3. Fill hot, sterilized jars with hot potatoes. Add a teaspoon of salt (optional). Fill jars with fresh boiling water, covering potatoes. Leave a 1-inch (2.5 cm) headspace.

4. Remove any air bubbles. Wipe rims and secure lids.

5. Process pints (473 ml) for 35 minutes and quarts (946 ml) for 40 minutes in pressure canner at pressure listed for your altitude and canner (see Adjust for Altitude! on page 29).

SQUASH (WINTER) AND PUMPKIN

Select winter squash and pumpkins with a hard rind. Do not use spaghetti squash or other varieties with stringy pulp. Smaller pumpkins meant for pies (as opposed to ones used for carving jack-o'-lanterns) produce better results.

METHOD: Pressure Canning

PROCESSING TIME:
Pints (473 ml) 55 minutes;
Quarts (946 ml) 90 minutes

YIELD: 7 quarts (6.6 L)

---

18 pounds (8.2 kg) hard winter squash or pumpkin

1. Wash squash/pumpkin, remove seeds, peel, and cut into 1-inch (2.5 cm) pieces.

2. Cook squash/pumpkin in boiling water for 2 minutes.

3. Pack hot, sterilized jars with cubes of squash/pumpkin. Fill jars with boiling water, covering squash/pumpkin. Leave a 1-inch (2.5 cm) headspace.

4. Remove any air bubbles. Wipe rims and secure lids.

5. Process pints (473 ml) for 55 minutes and quarts (946 ml) for 90 minutes in pressure canner at pressure listed for your altitude and canner (see Adjust for Altitude! on page 29).

IMPORTANT: Do not mash or purée squash/pumpkin prior to canning; the purée is too dense to reliably heat through. Keep the squash/pumpkin cubes intact for safe canning. To make purées or soups later, simply dump the canned squash/pumpkin cubes into a blender and mix for a few minutes.

PREVENT DISCOLORATION

Soak light-colored produce like apples, peaches, pears, nectarines, apricots, and potatoes in an ascorbic acid solution to keep from turning brown. Powdered ascorbic acid or crushed Vitamin C tablets are the best and easiest way to prevent produce from darkening. This is a simple, but important step. Here's how:

1. Crush three 500 mg Vitamin C (ascorbic acid) tablets into 2 quarts (1.9 L) of cold water and add fruit.

2. Soak for at least 2 minutes. Keep produce in solution until you're ready to use it.

CLASSIC VEGETABLE RECIPES

Canned vegetables can be so much more than the shriveled peas served in the school cafeteria. Home-canned vegetables are bright, plump, and full of natural flavor—without all the added salt and preservatives you find in factory-processed varieties.

Canning pairs perfectly with another of my favorite hobbies—gardening. I know that no matter how much I grow, I can preserve it all for a later date. This justifies my seed and plant collection! Not a gardener? No problem. If you are lucky enough to have a well-stocked farmers' market in your area, get to know the farmers who sell there. Tell them you're planning to can some of what you buy and ask what they like to put up. If you become a regular, some farmers will begin setting aside new vegetables for you to try canning—you're sure to learn a new recipe or two.

Buying local is the best strategy for procuring ingredients whenever possible. These farmers pick their produce at its peak ripeness and bring it directly to market. They do not have to pick underripe fruits and vegetables and ship them thousands of miles (kilometers), like traditional grocery store suppliers. You will have the best-quality food available in your area, and you'll be supporting your local economy. As an added bonus, your local farmers' market is usually less expensive than the grocery store.

Because there are so many options for canning vegetables, I selected recipes for this section that are classics in my pantry. They are great introductions to the joy of canning.

THE SWEETEST CANNED CORN

If summer to you means biting into a fresh ear of corn, you should be canning corn for a taste of summer come fall or winter. Just a bite of this canned sweet corn will make your taste buds very happy. Warning: It may make you want to fire up the grill in December! If you use good-quality corn, it remains plump and slightly crisp through the canning process. The secret to great canned corn is to can some of the sweetest corn you can find rather than adding sugar.

METHOD: Pressure Canning

PROCESSING TIME: 55 minutes

PRESSURE: 10 pounds (68.9 kPa) Weighted Gauge, 11 pounds (75.8 kPa) Dial Gauge

YIELD: 3 pints (1.4 L)

---

7 pounds (3.2 kg) fresh ears of corn, husks and silks removed

1½ teaspoons canning salt

1. Using a sharp knife, cut the corn kernels from the cobs. Cut about ¾ of the kernel to avoid cutting into the cob.

2. In a medium-size pot, bring at least 2 quarts (1.9 L) of water to a boil.

3. In a large pot over medium heat, combine the corn kernels with 1 cup (235 ml) of boiling water for each 2 cups (308 g) of corn. Bring the mixture to a simmer and cook for 5 minutes.

4. Using a slotted ladle or large slotted spoon, carefully ladle the corn evenly into hot, sterilized jars, leaving a bit more than 1 inch (2.5 cm) of headspace. Pour the hot cooking liquid over top, leaving a 1-inch (2.5 cm) headspace.

5. Add ½ teaspoon of salt to each pint (473 ml) jar.

6. Remove any air bubbles with a plastic or wooden utensil, adding more hot liquid as needed to maintain the proper 1-inch (2.5 cm) headspace.

7. Wipe the rims and seal the jars hand-tight with the 2-piece lids.

8. Carefully transfer the filled jars to the rack inside the pressure canner. Process the jars at the pressure listed above for 55 minutes.

9. Let the canner return to 0 pounds pressure (0.7 kPa). Wait 10 minutes more and then carefully open the canner lid according to the manufacturer's instructions.

10. With a jar lifter, remove the jars and place them on a clean dish towel away from any drafts. Allow to cool undisturbed for 12 to 24 hours and then check the seals. If any jars have not sealed properly, refrigerate them and use the corn within 2 weeks. Label the remaining jars with the recipe name and date before storing.

CREAMED CORN

You'd be forgiven for thinking there was actual cream in this creamed corn, yet this is the perfect side dish for vegans or even the base for a creamy vegan soup. It's rich yet lighter than dairy-filled creamed corn, thanks to the goodness of the natural corn "milk." Corn milk? Yes, and getting what I call corn milk is easy: After you blanch the corn and remove the kernels, run the back of your knife down the cob. You can even catch all the milk in the same bowl as the kernels as you go. It might just become your new cooking secret!

METHOD: Pressure Canning

PROCESSING TIME: 1 hour, 35 minutes

PRESSURE: 10 pounds (68.9 kPa) Weighted Gauge, 11 pounds (75.8 kPa) Dial Gauge

YIELD: 3 pints (1.4 L)

---

7 pounds (3.2 kg) fresh ears of corn, husks and silks removed

1½ teaspoons canning salt

1. In a large pot of boiling water (or more pots as needed) over high heat, blanch the corn on the cob for 4 minutes. Remove the corn and let the cobs cool enough to handle safely.

2. With a sharp knife, cut the corn kernels from the cobs. Cut about ¾ of the kernel to avoid cutting into the cob.

3. Run the back of your knife blade over the cob a second time to remove the corn "milk" and combine the "milk" with kernels.

4. In a large pot over high heat, combine the corn kernels with 1 cup (235 ml) of water for every 2 cups (308 g) corn–corn milk mixture. Bring the mixture to a boil.

5. In a separate pot over high heat, bring 2 quarts (1.9 L) water to a boil in case you need more hot liquid to top up your jars.

6. Using a slotted ladle or large slotted spoon, carefully ladle the corn evenly into hot, sterilized jars, leaving a bit more than 1 inch (2.5 cm) of headspace. Pour the boiling water over the top, as needed, leaving a 1-inch (2.5 cm) headspace.

7. Add ½ teaspoon of salt to each pint (473 ml) jar.

8. Remove any air bubbles with a plastic or wooden utensil, adding more boiling water as needed to maintain the proper 1-inch (2.5 cm) headspace.

9. Wipe the rims and seal the jars hand-tight with the 2-piece lids.

10. Carefully transfer the filled jars to the rack inside the pressure canner. Process the jars at the pressure listed above for 1 hour, 35 minutes.

11. Let the canner return to 0 pounds pressure (0.7 kPa). Wait 10 minutes more and then carefully open the canner lid according to the manufacturer's instructions.

12. With a jar lifter, remove the jars and place them on a clean dish towel away from any drafts. Allow to cool undisturbed for 12 to 24 hours and then check the seals. If any jars have not sealed properly, refrigerate them and use the corn within 2 weeks. Label the remaining jars with the recipe name and date before storing.

CORN RELISH

Corn relish is a versatile condiment. It can be used like creamed corn—for a pop of summery flavor in the deep of winter. However, it's also a summer classic, found at backyard barbecues across the country. At my house, we eat it on our burgers, mixed into chicken salad, and some even take an extra spoonful or two for a bite on the side!

METHOD: Pressure Canning

PROCESSING TIME: 20 minutes

PRESSURE: 10 pounds (68.9 kPa) Weighted Gauge, 11 pounds (75.8 kPa) Dial Gauge

YIELD: 6 pints (2.8 L)

---

16 to 20 fresh ears of corn, husks and silks removed

2 cups (320 g) chopped onion

1 cup (150 g) chopped green bell pepper

¾ cup (113 g) chopped red bell pepper

1½ cups (300 g) sugar

1 quart (946 ml) white or apple cider vinegar, minimum 5 percent acidity

1 tablespoon (9 g) dry mustard

1 tablespoon (11 g) mustard seeds

2 tablespoons (36 g) canning salt

1. With a sharp knife, cut the corn kernels from the ears until you have about 2 quarts (1.9 L) of kernels.

2. In large pot over high heat, combine the corn, onion, green and red bell peppers, sugar, vinegar, dry mustard, mustard seeds, and canning salt. Bring to a boil, stirring occasionally.

3. Once the mixture reaches a boil, stir it again, cover the pot, and simmer for 20 minutes. Continue stirring occasionally to prevent scorching.

4. Carefully ladle the corn mixture into hot, sterilized jars, leaving 1 inch (2.5 cm) of headspace. You should have enough relish to fill your jars and there is no recommended top-up liquid for this recipe.

5. Remove any air bubbles with a plastic or wooden utensil, adding more relish as needed to maintain the proper 1-inch (2.5 cm) headspace.

6. Wipe the rims and seal the jars hand-tight with the 2-piece lids.

7. Carefully transfer the filled jars to the rack inside the pressure canner. Process the jars at the pressure listed above for 20 minutes.

8. Let the canner return to 0 pounds pressure (0.7 kPa). Wait 10 minutes more and then carefully open the canner lid according to the manufacturer's instructions.

9. With a jar lifter, remove the jars and place them on a clean dish towel away from any drafts. Allow to cool undisturbed for 12 to 24 hours and then check the seals. If any jars have not sealed properly, refrigerate them and use the relish within 2 weeks. Label the remaining jars with the recipe name and date before storing.

PERFECTLY CANNED PEAS

Fresh peas are fun to pick and prepare. Stir-fry them, steam them, or snip the ends and eat 'em raw! However, almost nobody thinks of canning peas as the ideal way to treat these flavor-packed little morsels. I encourage you to get past the undeserved reputation of canned peas and try canning them at home. You'll soon find they're not mushy at all, and, in fact, pack nearly as much flavor as fresh peas. So, spread the word! Can those peas and share them with your friends.

METHOD: Pressure Canning

PROCESSING TIME: 40 minutes

PRESSURE: 10 pounds (68.9 kPa) Weighted Gauge, 11 pounds (75.8 kPa) Dial Gauge

YIELD: 3 pints (1.4 L)

---

7 pounds (3.2 kg) fresh peas in their pods, washed, and peas removed from the pods

1½ teaspoons canning salt

1. Place the peas in a large pot, cover them with water, and bring to a boil over high heat. Boil for 4 minutes or until they are bright green but not completely cooked.

2. Drain the peas over a large pot or bowl to reserve the cooking liquid. Pack the cooked peas loosely into hot, sterilized jars.

3. Pour the hot cooking liquid over the peas, leaving 1 inch (2.5 cm) of headspace.

4. Add ½ teaspoon of salt to each pint (473 ml) jar.

5. Remove any air bubbles with a plastic or wooden utensil, adding more hot cooking liquid as needed to maintain the proper 1-inch (2.5 cm) headspace.

6. Wipe the rims and seal the jars hand-tight with the 2-piece lids.

7. Carefully transfer the filled jars to the rack inside the pressure canner. Process the jars at the pressure listed above for 40 minutes.

8. Let the canner return to 0 pounds pressure (0.7 kPa). Wait 10 minutes more and then carefully open the canner lid according to the manufacturer's instructions.

9. With a jar lifter, remove the jars and place them on a clean dish towel away from any drafts. Allow to cool undisturbed for 12 to 24 hours and then check the seals. If any jars have not sealed properly, refrigerate them and use the peas within 2 weeks. Label the remaining jars with the recipe name and date before storing.

SPICY DILLY BEANS

Pickled green beans, also known as *dilly beans* in some circles, are a must-have for your pantry. They make a tangy component of bean salads, but they also work great as a condiment and as a unique topping for appetizers. Some even swear by them as a garnish for a Bloody Mary, used in place of the more traditional celery stalk. Mixing green and yellow beans adds a pop of color to the jars, but no matter the visual interest, these beans are tasty. You may not be able to make enough of them to last all year!

METHOD: Pressure Canning

PROCESSING TIME: 20 minutes

PRESSURE: 10 pounds (68.9 kPa) Weighted Gauge, 11 pounds (75.8 kPa) Dial Gauge

YIELD: 4 pints (1.9 L)

2½ cups (570 ml) distilled white vinegar, minimum 5% acidity

2½ cups (570 ml) water

¼ cup (72 g) canning salt

2½ pounds (1.1 kg) green beans, ends trimmed; measured and cut so they leave ¼ inch (6 mm) of headspace in the jars

4 garlic cloves, peeled

4 stems fresh dill, cut in half if tall

4 dried red chile peppers

1 teaspoon cayenne pepper

1 teaspoon dill seed

1. In a large pot over high heat, combine the vinegar, water, and salt. Bring the mixture to a boil and cook for 1 minute. Stir well while the mixture boils to make sure the salt dissolves. Reduce the heat to maintain a simmer and keep the liquid very hot while you continue to work.

2. Pack the beans upright in hot, sterilized jars, leaving ¼ inch (6 mm) of headspace. Cut the beans again, as needed, to leave the ¼-inch (6 mm) headspace.

3. In each jar, place 1 clove garlic, 1 dill sprig, 1 dried red chile pepper, ¼ teaspoon of cayenne pepper, and ¼ teaspoon of dill seed.

4. Carefully ladle the hot liquid over the beans, leaving ¼-inch (6 mm) of headspace.

5. Remove any air bubbles with a plastic or wooden utensil, adding more hot liquid as needed to maintain the proper ¼-inch (6 mm) headspace.

6. Wipe the rims and seal the jars hand-tight with the 2-piece lids.

7. Carefully transfer the filled jars to the rack inside the pressure canner. Process the jars at the pressure listed above for 20 minutes.

8. Let the canner return to 0 pounds pressure (0.7 kPa). Wait 10 minutes more and then carefully open the canner lid according to the manufacturer's instructions.

9. With a jar lifter, remove the jars and place them on a clean dish towel away from any drafts. Allow to cool undisturbed for 12 to 24 hours and then check the seals. If any jars have not sealed properly, refrigerate them and use the beans within 2 weeks. Label the remaining jars with the recipe name and date before storing.

GREEN BEANS

In my garden, I try to pick beans just as fast as they ripen. Fresh beans are the key to canning them and keeping a slight bite. If your beans have any bend, they will surely not be crisp after canning. While it is a dangerous mistake to switch ingredients in and out of canning recipes, for this one you have my permission to use any color string-type bean you wish. They all taste great! Use these beans as a last-minute addition to your favorite stir-fry or soup. They will add a burst of fresh flavor to any dish.

METHOD: Pressure Canning

PROCESSING TIME: 20 minutes

PRESSURE: 10 pounds (68.9 kPa) Weighted Gauge, 11 pounds (75.8 kPa) Dial Gauge

YIELD: 4 pints (1.9 L)

---

1 pound (455 g) green beans, ends trimmed and cut into 2-inch (5 cm) pieces

2 teaspoons canning salt

1. In a medium-size pot or kettle, bring 1 quart (946 ml) water to a boil.

2. While the water boils, pack the green beans into hot, sterilized jars as tightly as possible.

3. Pour the boiling water over the beans, leaving 1 inch (2.5 cm) of headspace.

4. Add ½ teaspoon of salt to each pint (473 ml) jar.

5. Remove any air bubbles with a plastic or wooden utensil, adding more boiling water as needed to maintain the proper 1-inch (2.5 cm) headspace.

6. Wipe the rims and seal the jars hand-tight with the 2-piece lids.

7. Carefully transfer the filled jars to the rack inside the pressure canner. Process the jars at the pressure listed above for 20 minutes.

8. Let the canner return to 0 pounds pressure (0.7 kPa). Wait 10 minutes more and then carefully open the canner lid according to the manufacturer's instructions.

9. With a jar lifter, remove the jars and place them on a clean dish towel away from any drafts. Allow to cool undisturbed for 12 to 24 hours and then check the seals. If any jars have not sealed properly, refrigerate them and use the green beans within 2 weeks. Label the remaining jars with the recipe name and date before storing.

SPICED PICKLED BEETS

If you're looking for a recipe that will make you famous with friends and family, look no further! While beets are healthy, they can sometimes be a tough sell to picky eaters or younger eaters who complain they "taste like dirt." This recipe is sure to change minds as the beets receive a treatment of sugar, spice, and everything nice. For those who already love beets, it will be hard to eat just one. Serve them as part of an appetizer spread and watch them disappear.

METHOD: Pressure Canning

PROCESSING TIME: 30 minutes

PRESSURE: 10 pounds (68.9 kPa) Weighted Gauge, 11 pounds (75.8 kPa) Dial Gauge

YIELD: 4 pints (1.9 L)

---

4 pounds (1.8 k) firm unblemished beets, washed, trimmed, leaving the root intact as well as about 2 inches (5 cm) of the stems

3 cups (480 g) thinly sliced white onion

2 cups (400 g) sugar

2½ cups (570 ml) distilled white vinegar, minimum 5% acidity

1½ cups (355 ml) water

1 teaspoon canning salt

2 tablespoons (12 g) whole-spice pickling mix, or a mix of 1 tablespoon (11 g) mustard seeds, 1 teaspoon whole allspice berries, 1 teaspoon whole cloves, and 3 cinnamon sticks

1. In a large pot, combine the beets with enough water to cover. Bring to a boil over high heat. Reduce the heat to low and simmer for about 20 minutes until fork-tender.

2. Drain the beets and run cold water over them to stop the cooking process. When cool enough to handle, use a sharp knife to remove the skins. The skins should easily come away from the flesh. Remove the stem and root at this point as well.

3. Slice the beets in ¼-inch (6 mm)-thick slices and place them in a large bowl. Set the beets aside.

4. Rinse the pot you cooked the beets in, place it over high heat, and combine the onion, sugar, vinegar, water, salt, and pickling mix in it. Bring the mixture to a boil. Reduce the heat to low and simmer for 5 minutes.

5. Add the beet slices to the hot mixture and simmer for 3 minutes more. Turn off the heat and remove the cinnamon sticks.

6. Carefully ladle the hot beet and onion mixture into hot, sterilized jars. Ladle the hot cooking liquid over the beets, leaving ½ inch (1.3 cm) of headspace.

7. Remove any air bubbles with a plastic or wooden utensil, adding more hot liquid as needed to maintain the proper ½-inch (1.3 cm) headspace.

8. Wipe the rims and seal the jars hand-tight with the 2-piece lids.

9. Carefully transfer the filled jars to the rack inside the pressure canner. Process the jars at the pressure listed above for 30 minutes.

10. Let the canner return to 0 pounds pressure (0.7 kPa). Wait 10 minutes more and then carefully open the canner lid according to the manufacturer's instructions.

11. With a jar lifter, remove the jars and place them on a clean dish towel away from any drafts. Allow to cool undisturbed for 12 to 24 hours and then check the seals. If any jars have not sealed properly, refrigerate them and use the beets within 2 weeks. Label the remaining jars with the recipe name and date before storing.

PICNIC-FRIENDLY BAKED BEANS

The problem with store-bought baked beans isn't the taste or the lack of variety. These days you can find maple baked beans, baked beans with thick-cut bacon, vegetarian baked beans—the list goes on! However, so many recipes contain questionable preservatives or flavor enhancers. Even the best recipes contain a large amount of sugar or other sweetener. You'll find this recipe makes beans with just the right amount of sweetness. The sauce is rich and the beans themselves still have some texture (something rarely said for store-bought baked beans). Serve alongside sandwiches and lemonade at your next picnic or plan an indoor "picnic" night in the middle of winter.

METHOD: Pressure Canning

PROCESSING TIME: 1 hour, 20 minutes

PRESSURE: 10 pounds (68.9 kPa) Weighted Gauge, 11 pounds (75.8 kPa) Dial Gauge

YIELD: 6 pints (2.8 L)

---

2 pounds (900 g) dried navy beans

6 quarts (5.7 L) water

½ pound (225 g) bacon, cut into small pieces

3 large onions, sliced

⅔ cup (150 g) packed brown sugar

4 teaspoons (24 g) salt

2 teaspoons dry mustard

⅓ cup (113 g) molasses

NOTE: This recipe requires soaking the beans for 12 hours before cooking and canning. You'll also need to bake the bean recipe for about 3 hours, so it's a good idea to soak the beans the night before you want to cook and can them.

1. The night before you want to can, place the beans into a large pot. Add 3 quarts (2.8 L) of water to cover the beans. Soak the beans, covered, for 12 hours.

2. Drain the beans and return them to the pot. Add the remaining 3 quarts (2.8 L) of water and bring the mixture to a boil over high heat. Reduce the heat to low and simmer the beans until soft and the skins begin to split, about 1½ to 2 hours. Drain the beans and reserve the cooking liquid.

3. Preheat the oven to 350°F (180°C, or gas mark 4).

4. Transfer the drained beans to a large baking dish and add the bacon and onions.

5. In large bowl, stir together the brown sugar, salt, dry mustard, and molasses. Add 4 cups (950 ml) of the reserved cooking liquid (add more water if needed to make 4 cups [950 ml]). Stir this sauce until it is well combined. Pour the sauce over the beans—but do not stir. Cover the dish with aluminum foil and bake for 3½ hours.

6. After 3½ hours, carefully ladle the bean into hot, sterilized jars, leaving 1 inch (2.5 cm) of headspace.

7. Remove any air bubbles with a plastic or wooden utensil, adding more beans as needed to maintain the proper 1-inch (2.5 cm) headspace.

8. Wipe the rims and seal the jars hand-tight with the 2-piece lids.

9. Carefully transfer the filled jars to the rack inside the pressure canner. Process the jars at the pressure listed above for 1 hour, 20 minutes.

10. Let the canner return to 0 pounds pressure (0.7 kPa). Wait 10 minutes more and then carefully open the canner lid according to the manufacturer's instructions.

11. With a jar lifter, remove the jars and place them on a clean dish towel away from any drafts. Allow to cool undisturbed for 12 to 24 hours and then check the seals. If any jars have not sealed properly, refrigerate them and use the baked beans within 2 weeks. Label the remaining jars with the recipe name and date before storing.

HEIRLOOM BEANS

Dried beans are practically magical. They are inexpensive and filling and can give a hearty boost to many recipes. You can even combine them with rice for a complete protein. If there's one downside they have, it's the time. Chances are, you reach much more for canned beans than dried on a daily basis—so why not can your own? While you can certainly use any dried beans you have on hand for this recipe, I recommend seeking out an heirloom bean to elevate this pantry staple. There are so many bean varieties you can order these days, and most are not available as canned beans in the grocery store! It is not necessary to add the salt pork or bacon, but it's a great way to infuse additional flavor into your beans and separate them from their store-bought counterparts. If you omit the salt pork or bacon, add a little salt, or not, depending on how you like to use your beans in recipes.

METHOD: Pressure Canning

PROCESSING TIME: 1 hour, 35 minutes

PRESSURE: 10 pounds (68.9 kPa) Weighted Gauge, 11 pounds (75.8 kPa) Dial Gauge

YIELD: 3 pints (1.4 L)

---

8 ounces (225 g) dried beans of choice

½ cup (75 g) cubed salt pork, or ¼ pound (115 g) good bacon, cut into bite-size pieces (optional; see headnote)

NOTE: Just like the Picnic-Friendly Baked Beans (page 96), these beans require an overnight (12 hour) soak before you're ready to cook and can.

1. The night before you want to can, place the beans in large pot and cover them with warm water. Soak the beans, covered, for 12 hours.

2. Drain the beans, return them to the pot, and cover them with fresh water. Cook over medium-high heat until they begin to boil. Stir and continue cooking the beans according to the package directions, but stop just short of cooking them all the way through.

3. Meanwhile, bring 1 quart (946 ml) of water to a boil in case you need more hot liquid to top up your jars. (Some beans absorb more water than others while cooking.)

4. Divide the salt pork or bacon evenly among the pint (473 ml) jars (if using).

5. Carefully ladle the hot beans into hot, sterilized jars. Pour the hot cooking liquid over the top, leaving 1 inch (2.5 cm) of headspace. If the cooking liquid does not go far enough, add the hot water to top up to the proper 1-inch (2.5 cm) headspace.

6. Remove any air bubbles with a plastic or wooden utensil, adding more hot liquid as needed to maintain the proper 1-inch (2.5 cm) headspace.

7. Wipe the rims and seal the jars hand-tight with the 2-piece lids.

8. Carefully transfer the filled jars to the rack inside the pressure canner. Process the jars at the pressure listed above for 1 hour, 35 minutes.

9. Let the canner return to 0 pounds pressure (0.7 kPa). Wait 10 minutes more and then carefully open the canner lid according to the manufacturer's instructions.

10. With a jar lifter, remove the jars and place them on a clean dish towel away from any drafts. Allow to cool undisturbed for 12 to 24 hours and then check the seals. If any jars have not sealed properly, refrigerate them and use the beans within 2 weeks. Label the remaining jars with the recipe name and date before storing.

LENTILS

Lentils are a popular base for healthy soup recipes. There are also many varieties of lentil salad, from Middle Eastern preparations to American classics. Unlike most beans, lentils do not need a long soak before cooking and that means there's no need to soak them before canning either. While lentils are one of the quicker legumes to cook from scratch, there's nothing as quick as cracking open a jar of your homemade canned lentils!

METHOD: Pressure Canning

PROCESSING TIME: 1 hour, 15 minutes

PRESSURE: 10 pounds (68.9 kPa) Weighted Gauge, 11 pounds (75.8 kPa) Dial Gauge

YIELD: 3 pints (1.4 L)

---

2 cups (384 g) dried lentils

4 cups (950 ml) Vegetable Broth (page 203) or store-bought broth

1 large onion, minced

1. Inspect the lentils carefully and remove any foreign objects, such as small stones. Place the lentils in a large pot and add the broth and onion. Bring the pot to a boil over high heat, reduce the heat, and simmer for about 5 minutes until the lentils are partially cooked.

2. Carefully ladle the lentils into hot, sterilized jars, filling each jar halfway. Ladle the hot cooking liquid over the lentils, leaving 1 inch (2.5 cm) of headspace in the jars.

3. Remove any air bubbles with a plastic or wooden utensil, adding more hot cooking liquid as needed to maintain the proper 1-inch (2.5 cm) headspace.

4. Wipe the rims and seal the jars hand-tight with the 2-piece lids.

5. Carefully transfer the filled jars to the rack inside the pressure canner. Process the jars at the pressure listed above for 1 hour, 15 minutes.

6. Let the canner return to 0 pounds pressure (0.7 kPa). Wait 10 minutes more and then carefully open the canner lid according to the manufacturer's instructions.

7. With a jar lifter, remove the jars and place them on a clean dish towel away from any drafts. Allow to cool undisturbed for 12 to 24 hours and then check the seals. If any jars have not sealed properly, refrigerate them and use the lentils within 2 weeks. Label the remaining jars with the recipe name and date before storing.

CANNED POTATOES

I know fall has arrived when the potato man comes down from Aroostook County to sell his potatoes by the 50 pound (22.7 kg) bag—50 pounds (22.7 kg)! I buy two bags, one for my shelves and one for dry storage. Canning potatoes is one concept that can take some getting used to, as they're not a popular product in most grocery stores. However, I think once you start canning them, you'll be converted. You can use the potatoes in nearly all the recipes you'd normally cook—except baked potatoes, of course! Having them precooked just means less time cooking dinner. Add them to soups and chowders or throw them on a sheet tray for roasting along with some quick-cooking vegetables. Since you just have to crisp the potatoes and not cook them from scratch, dinner is ready in no time.

METHOD: Pressure Canning

PROCESSING TIME: 35 minutes

PRESSURE: 10 pounds (68.9 kPa) Weighted Gauge, 11 pounds (75.8 kPa) Dial Gauge

YIELD: 6 pints (2.8 L)

---

3 pounds (1.4 kg) fresh potatoes, washed, peeled, and cut into ½-inch (1.3 cm) cubes

3 teaspoons (18 g) canning salt

1. In a large pot over high heat, bring 1 gallon (3.8 L) of water to a boil.

2. Place the potatoes into the boiling water. Return the water to a boil and cook for 2 minutes.

3. Using a large slotted spoon, pack the potatoes into hot, sterilized jars. Reserve the cooking liquid.

4. Add ½ teaspoon of salt to each jar.

5. Ladle the hot cooking liquid over the potatoes, leaving 1 inch (2.5 cm) of headspace.

6. Remove any air bubbles with a plastic or wooden utensil, adding more hot liquid as needed to maintain the proper 1-inch (2.5 cm) headspace.

7. Wipe the rims and seal the jars hand-tight with the 2-piece lids.

8. Carefully transfer the filled jars to the rack inside the pressure canner. Process the jars at the pressure listed above for 35 minutes.

9. Let the canner return to 0 pounds pressure (0.7 kPa). Wait 10 minutes more and then carefully open the canner lid according to the manufacturer's instructions.

10. With a jar lifter, remove the jars and place them on a clean dish towel away from any drafts. Allow to cool undisturbed for 12 to 24 hours and then check the seals. If any jars have not sealed properly, refrigerate them and use the potatoes within 2 weeks. Label the remaining jars with the recipe name and date before storing.

MIXED VEGETABLE MEDLEY

When I was a little girl, whenever my family had mixed vegetables, I picked out every piece of mushy carrot. Now that I make them myself, I make sure every vegetable is ripe so the whole mixture is delicious. I'm happy to say my kids don't leave any vegetable behind! One quick note: Make sure to wash and dice your vegetables to a uniform size before combining them to cook or they may not cook at the same speed. Beyond making for an easy out-of-the-jar side dish, mixed vegetables are great to have on hand for soups or as a topping for healthy grain bowls.

METHOD: Pressure Canning

PROCESSING TIME: 55 minutes

PRESSURE: 10 pounds (68.9 kPa) Weighted Gauge, 11 pounds (75.8 kPa) Dial Gauge

YIELD: 4 pints (1.9 L)

---

1 cup (180 g) chopped tomatoes

7 cups (weight will vary) total of a combination of the following, all cut to uniform sizes (see headnote):

Diced carrots (1-inch [2.5 cm] dice)

Sweet corn

Green beans, cut into 1-inch (2.5 cm) pieces

Diced zucchini (1-inch [2.5 cm] dice)

2 teaspoons canning salt

1. In a large pot, combine the tomatoes with the 7 cups (weight will vary) of vegetables you selected and add enough water to cover. Bring the mixture to a boil over high heat and boil for 5 minutes. Stir frequently to prevent any burning or sticking on the bottom of the pot.

2. Carefully ladle the vegetables evenly into hot, sterilized jars. Top with the hot cooking liquid, leaving 1 inch (2.5 cm) of headspace.

3. Add ½ teaspoon of salt to each jar.

4. Remove any air bubbles with a plastic or wooden utensil, adding more hot liquid as needed to maintain the proper 1-inch (2.5 cm) headspace.

5. Wipe the rims and seal the jars hand-tight with the 2-piece lids.

6. Carefully transfer the filled jars to the rack inside the pressure canner. Process the jars at the pressure listed above for 55 minutes.

7. Let the canner return to 0 pounds pressure (0.7 kPa). Wait 10 minutes more and then carefully open the canner lid according to the manufacturer's instructions.

8. With a jar lifter, remove the jars and place them on a clean dish towel away from any drafts. Allow to cool undisturbed for 12 to 24 hours and then check the seals. If any jars have not sealed properly, refrigerate them and use the vegetables within 2 weeks. Label the remaining jars with the recipe name and date before storing.

TASTE OF SUMMER CARROT STICKS

You might think canned carrot sticks would take away the fun of snapping into a fresh carrot, as you cook out some of the crunch. However, carrots take on a new flavor profile when canned. Cooked just enough to enhance the natural sweetness, canned carrot sticks are a healthy finger food whenever you need to mix up snack time.

METHOD: Pressure Canning

PROCESSING TIME: 25 minutes

PRESSURE: 10 pounds (68.9 kPa) Weighted Gauge, 11 pounds (75.8 kPa) Dial Gauge

YIELD: 3 pints (1.4 L)

---

6 pounds (2.7 kg) whole carrots, washed and peeled

1½ teaspoons canning salt

1. Cut the carrots into sticks very close to the same size, long enough to fit into the jars but still leave 1 inch (2.5 cm) of headspace.

2. Place the carrot sticks in a large saucepan and cover them with water. Bring to a boil over high heat, reduce the heat to a simmer, and cook for 5 minutes.

3. In another saucepan, bring a few cups (700 to 946 ml) of water to a boil as a reserve, if needed, to fill the jars to the proper headspace.

4. Tightly pack the carrots into hot, sterilized jars, leaving 1 inch (2.5 cm) of headspace.

5. Add ½ teaspoon of salt to each pint (473 ml) jar.

6. Ladle the hot cooking liquid over the carrots, leaving a 1-inch (2.5 cm) headspace.

7. Remove any air bubbles with a plastic or wooden utensil, adding the reserved hot water as needed to maintain the proper 1-inch (2.5 cm) headspace.

8. Wipe the rims and seal the jars hand-tight with the 2-piece lids.

9. Carefully transfer the filled jars to the rack inside the pressure canner. Process the jars at the pressure listed above for 25 minutes.

10. Let the canner return to 0 pounds pressure (0.7 kPa). Wait 10 minutes more and then carefully open the canner lid according to the manufacturer's instructions.

11. With a jar lifter, remove the jars and place them on a clean dish towel away from any drafts. Allow to cool undisturbed for 12 to 24 hours and then check the seals. If any jars have not sealed properly, refrigerate them and use the carrots within 2 weeks. Label the remaining jars with the recipe name and date before storing.

SWEET AND SPICY GINGER CARROT COINS

If you want a carrot recipe with some kick, you've come to the right place. In this recipe, the sweetness from brown sugar and orange juice marries with spicy ginger, making these carrots your new favorite finger food. I've also made this recipe with baby carrots instead of carrot coins with great results. They are fantastic for a party!

METHOD: Pressure Canning

PROCESSING TIME: 30 minutes

PRESSURE: 10 pounds (68.9 kPa) Weighted Gauge, 11 pounds (75.8 kPa) Dial Gauge

YIELD: 4 pints (1.9 L)

2½ pounds (1.1 kg) carrots, washed and peeled

2 cups (450 g) packed brown sugar

1 cup (235 ml) freshly squeezed orange juice (from 2 to 4 oranges)

2 cups (475 ml) water

2 pieces crystallized ginger (about 1 inch [2.5 cm] each), minced

1. Cut the carrots into 1⁄3-inch (8 mm)-thick coins or 1-inch (2.5 cm) chunks, unless you're using baby carrots, which you can process whole.

2. In a large saucepan over medium heat, combine the brown sugar, orange juice, water, and crystallized ginger. Cook until the sugar dissolves. Keep the syrup hot, stirring occasionally, as you continue to work. Reduce the heat if the mixture comes close to a simmer.

3. Pack the carrots tightly into hot, sterilized jars, leaving 1 inch (2.5 cm) of headspace.

4. Carefully ladle the hot syrup over the carrots. Leave 1 inch (2.5 cm) of headspace.

5. Remove any air bubbles with a plastic or wooden utensil, adding more hot syrup as needed to maintain the proper 1-inch (2.5 cm) headspace.

6. Wipe the rims and seal the jars hand-tight with the 2-piece lids.

7. Carefully transfer the filled jars to the rack inside the pressure canner. Process the jars at the pressure listed above for 30 minutes.

8. Let the canner return to 0 pounds pressure (0.7 kPa). Wait 10 minutes more and then carefully open the canner lid according to the manufacturer's instructions.

9. With a jar lifter, remove the jars and place them on a clean dish towel away from any drafts. Allow to cool undisturbed for 12 to 24 hours and then check the seals. If any jars have not sealed properly, refrigerate them and use the carrots within 2 weeks. Label the remaining jars with the recipe name and date before storing.

SPICY HOT PEPPER MIX

It seems as though every family has at least one eater who wants—no, needs—to turn the heat up. Yet, what constitutes spicy varies not only from person to person but also family to family. My family's "hot" might seem mild to you! The nice thing about this recipe is that it can be dialed up or down when it comes to heat. Make a batch of habaneros for the capsaicin hound in your house or seed jalapeño and serrano peppers from the garden for a milder mix. If your pepper mix turns out too hot, there's a way to soften the edge after processing. Chop some Taste of Summer Carrot Sticks (page 101) and mix them in a bowl with your peppers for a homemade riff on a classic taqueria condiment (Zanahorias en Escabeche).

METHOD: Pressure Canning

PROCESSING TIME: 15 minutes

PRESSURE: 10 pounds (68.9 kPa) Weighted Gauge, 11 pounds (75.8 kPa) Dial Gauge

YIELD: 3 pints (1.4 L)

---

3 quarts (2.8 L) assorted hot peppers

¾ cup (216 g) canning salt

5 cups (1.2 L) distilled white vinegar, minimum 5% acidity

1 cup (235 ml) water

¼ cup (50 g) sugar

2 or 3 garlic cloves, sliced

NOTE: You may want to start this recipe the night before, as you need 12 hours to soak the peppers before canning.

1. Wearing rubber gloves, wash the peppers and cut 2 slits lengthwise into each pepper.

2. In a very large bowl or large pot, combine the salt with 1 gallon (3.8 L) of water. Stir to dissolve the salt completely. Add the peppers and let sit for 12 hours.

3. Drain and rinse the peppers and pack them into hot, sterilized jars.

4. In a medium-size saucepan over medium heat, combine the vinegar, water, sugar, and garlic. Bring to a simmer and cook for 15 minutes. Remove and discard the garlic. Carefully pour the hot solution over the peppers, leaving a ½ inch (1.3 cm) of headspace.

5. Remove any air bubbles with a plastic or wooden utensil, adding more hot liquid as needed to maintain the proper ½-inch (1.3 cm) headspace.

6. Wipe the rims and seal the jars hand-tight with the 2-piece lids.

7. Carefully transfer the filled jars to the rack inside the pressure canner. Process the jars at the pressure listed above for 15 minutes.

8. Let the canner return to 0 pounds pressure (0.7 kPa). Wait 10 minutes more and then carefully open the canner lid according to the manufacturer's instructions.

9. With a jar lifter, remove the jars and place them on a clean dish towel away from any drafts. Allow to cool undisturbed for 12 to 24 hours and then check the seals. If any jars have not sealed properly, refrigerate them and use the peppers within 2 weeks. Label the remaining jars with the recipe name and date before storing.

Chapter 4

FRUIT PRESERVES AND CONSERVES

PRESERVES

Preserves are the most luxurious—perhaps even most decadent—of all the jelled goods. With whole, small fruits or uniform chunks of fruits, suspended in a jelled syrup, they straddle the line between a delicious but eminently functional jam and an elegant specialty dessert item. Preserves tend to have a slightly looser set than jams, and because of the relative translucence of the jelled syrup, incorporating additional colorful ingredients—thinly sliced lemon peel, for example—can add tremendously to the visual appeal of the preserve. Other specialty items, such as liqueurs, are excellent in preserves as well. Whether you prefer simple preserves, or preserves in a more glamorous form, there are many options to choose from in this section. And, either way, they're delicious.

SIMPLE CLASSIC: RASPBERRY PRESERVES

This simple, classic preserve highlights raspberries at their absolute best. Raspberries are so delicate that they tend to break apart when cooked, so this preserve is similar to jam in texture. Spread this delectable preserve on warm muffins with a bit of butter or enjoy it as a filling for thumbprints, turnovers, or other pastries!

METHOD: Boiling Water Bath Canning

PROCESSING TIME: 10 minutes

YIELD: 4 to 5 half-pint (235 ml) jars

2¼ pounds (1 kg) raspberries*

¼ cup (60 ml) water

2 teaspoons calcium water**

1½ cups (300 g) sugar

2 teaspoons Pomona's
   pectin powder

Not sure how much fruit to purchase? See Measuring Up! on page 33.

**For information on how to prepare calcium water, refer to page 30.*

1. Carefully pick through raspberries, removing stems and any damaged parts. Rinse raspberries only if necessary. Combine in a large saucepan with the ¼ cup (60 ml) of water. Bring to a boil over high heat, reduce heat, and simmer, covered, for 2 minutes or until raspberries release their juices, stirring occasionally and gently (don't worry if the berries break apart). Remove from heat.

2. Measure 4 cups (946 ml) of the cooked raspberries (saving any extra for another use) and return the measured quantity to the saucepan. Add calcium water and mix well.

3. In a separate bowl, combine sugar and pectin powder. Mix thoroughly and set aside.

4. Bring raspberry mixture back to a full boil over high heat. Slowly add the pectin-sugar mixture, stirring constantly. Continue to stir vigorously for 1 to 2 minutes to dissolve pectin while the preserves come back up to a boil. Once the preserves return to a full boil, remove the pan from the heat.

5. Ladle hot preserves into hot, sterilized jars, leaving ¼ inch (6 mm) of headspace. Remove trapped air bubbles, wipe rims with a damp cloth, put on lids and screw bands, and tighten to fingertip tight.

6. Lower filled jars into water bath canner. Place lid on canner, return to a rolling boil, and process for 10 minutes (adjusting for altitude if necessary; see Adjust for Altitude! on page 29).

7. Remove jars with a jar lifter and allow to cool undisturbed on a clean dish towel away from any drafts for 12 to 24 hours. Confirm that jars have sealed properly. Refrigerate any jars that have not sealed and use within 2 weeks. Label the remaining jars with the recipe name and date before storing.

CUSTOMIZE IT!

If you're looking for something new, try spicing it up! At the same time that you add the calcium water, add up to 1 teaspoon of ground ginger, cardamom, ground cloves, cinnamon, nutmeg, or allspice. Or, you can mix and match these spices—just be sure that the total spice quantity does not exceed 1 teaspoon.

SIMPLE CLASSIC: PEACH PRESERVES

Ripe, in-season, just-picked peaches say summer to me more than just about any fruit, and they're so naturally sweet and juicy that they need little else to really sing. This easy, classic preserve allows the luscious flavor of peaches to really shine through, showing them off at their simplest and most glorious. Try this preserve as a filling for *crostata* (an Italian baked tart) for a delightful treat!

METHOD: Boiling Water Bath Canning

PROCESSING TIME: 10 minutes

YIELD: 4 to 5 half-pint (235 ml) jars

2¾ pounds (1.2 kg) ripe peaches*

¼ cup (60 ml) water

¼ cup (60 ml) lemon juice

3½ teaspoons (17.5 ml) calcium water**

1 cup (200 g) sugar

2½ teaspoons (7.5 g) Pomona's pectin powder

Not sure how much fruit to purchase? See Measuring Up! on page 33.

**For information on how to prepare calcium water, refer to page 30.*

1. Peel and remove pits from peaches and then cut peaches into uniform-size pieces. (For more information, see How to Skin a Peach on page 145.)

2. Combine peaches and the ¼ cup (60 ml) of water in a saucepan. Bring to a boil over high heat, reduce heat, and simmer, covered, for 3 to 5 minutes or until fruit is soft (but still retains its shape), stirring occasionally. Remove from heat.

3. Measure 4 cups (946 ml) of the cooked mixture (saving any extra for another use) and return the measured quantity to the saucepan. Add lemon juice and calcium water and mix well.

4. In a separate bowl, combine sugar and pectin powder. Mix thoroughly and set aside.

5. Bring peach mixture to a full boil over high heat. Slowly add pectin-sugar mixture, stirring constantly. Continue to stir vigorously for 1 to 2 minutes to dissolve pectin while the preserves come back up to a boil. Once the preserves return to a full boil, remove the pan from the heat.

6. Ladle hot preserves into hot, sterilized jars, leaving ¼ inch (6 mm) of headspace. Remove trapped air bubbles, wipe rims with a damp cloth, put on lids and screw bands, and tighten to fingertip tight.

7. Lower filled jars into water bath canner. Place lid on canner, return to a rolling boil, and process for 10 minutes (adjusting for altitude if necessary; see Adjust for Altitude! on page 29).

8. Remove jars with a jar lifter and allow to cool undisturbed on a clean dish towel away from any drafts for 12 to 24 hours. Confirm that jars have sealed properly. Refrigerate any jars that have not sealed and use within 2 weeks. Label the remaining jars with the recipe name and date before storing.

CUSTOMIZE IT!

If you're looking for something new, try spicing it up! At the same time that you add the calcium water, add up to 1 teaspoon of ground ginger, cardamom, ground cloves, cinnamon, nutmeg, or allspice. Or, you can mix and match these spices—just be sure that the total spice quantity does not exceed 1 teaspoon.

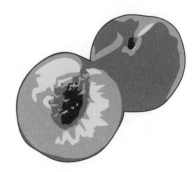

EVEN IT OUT!

Hot preserves that have not yet jelled have distinct solids (the fruit) and liquids (the syrup, which has not yet jelled). Because of this, when filling jars, it's easy to inadvertently put all the fruit in just a few of the jars, leaving a lot of extra fruit-less liquid. To avoid this, fill each jar with both solids and liquids, aiming for roughly the same amount of solids in each jar. Once you have all the jars filled, before putting the lids on, carefully move fruit and liquid in and out of jars as necessary, using a teaspoon, to even things out.

VANILLA-PLUM PRESERVES

Fresh, sweet, in-season plums have a wonderful depth and complexity, and the smooth richness of vanilla in this preserve really highlights this. For a luscious, visually stunning dessert, use these preserves layered with mascarpone cheese in a parfait!

METHOD: Boiling Water Bath Canning
PROCESSING TIME: 10 minutes
YIELD: 4 to 5 half-pint (235 ml) jars

2½ pounds (1.1 kg) ripe, sweet plums*

¼ cup (60 ml) water

1 vanilla bean

¼ cup (60 ml) lemon juice

3½ teaspoons (17.5 ml) calcium water**

1½ cups (300 g) sugar

2½ teaspoons (7.5 g) Pomona's pectin powder

Not sure how much fruit to purchase? See Measuring Up! on page 30.

**For information on how to prepare calcium water, refer to page 33.*

1. Rinse plums, remove stems, and slice in half. Remove pits and cut into uniform pieces. (For more information, see To Peel or Not to Peel? on page 129.)

2. Combine plums and the ¼ cup (60 ml) of water in a saucepan. Bring to a boil over high heat, reduce heat, and simmer, covered, for 4 to 6 minutes or until fruit is soft, stirring occasionally. Remove from heat.

3. Measure 4 cups (946 ml) of the cooked plums (saving any extra for another use) and return the measured quantity to the saucepan. Using a paring knife, slice the vanilla bean in half lengthwise and scrape out the seeds. Add the vanilla seeds and the bean pod itself to the plum mixture. Add lemon juice and calcium water and mix well.

4. In a separate bowl, combine sugar and pectin powder. Mix thoroughly and set aside.

5. Bring plum mixture back to a full boil over high heat. Slowly add pectin-sugar mixture, stirring constantly. Continue to stir vigorously for 1 to 2 minutes to dissolve pectin while the preserves come back up to a boil. Once the preserves return to a full boil, remove the pan from the heat. Using tongs, carefully remove the vanilla bean pod and discard.

6. Ladle hot preserves into hot, sterilized jars, leaving ¼ inch (6 mm) of headspace. Remove trapped air bubbles, wipe rims with a damp cloth, put on lids and screw bands, and tighten to fingertip tight.

7. Lower filled jars into water bath canner. Place lid on canner, return to a rolling boil, and process for 10 minutes (adjusting for altitude if necessary; see Adjust for Altitude! on page 29).

8. Remove jars with a jar lifter and allow to cool undisturbed on a clean dish towel away from any drafts for 12 to 24 hours. Confirm that jars have sealed properly. Refrigerate any jars that have not sealed and use within 2 weeks. Label the remaining jars with the recipe name and date before storing.

CUSTOMIZE IT!

If you prefer a less-processed sugar, such as turbinado (raw sugar), you can use that instead of regular white sugar. Just be sure to pulse it in a food processor a few times to make the granules fine enough that you'll be able to mix the pectin into the sugar effectively.

CHERRY-PORT PRESERVES

Combining luscious sweet cherry flavor with the depth and complexity of port wine, this gorgeous, deep-red preserve is just heavenly. It's a perfect addition to a special-occasion brunch and makes a wonderful gift. Or, spoon it on a slice of lemon pound cake and top with fresh whipped cream for a simple and elegant dessert.

METHOD: Boiling Water Bath Canning
PROCESSING TIME: 10 minutes
YIELD: 4 to 5 half-pint (235 ml) jars

1¾ pounds (795 g) sweet cherries*

½ cup (120 ml) water

¾ cup (175 ml) port wine

¼ cup (60 ml) lemon juice

2 teaspoons calcium water**

1 cup (200 g) sugar

1½ teaspoons Pomona's
   pectin powder

Not sure how much fruit to purchase? See Measuring Up! on page 30.

**For information on how to prepare calcium water, refer to page 33.*

1. Rinse cherries, remove stems, and then slice in half and remove pits. (For more information, see Painless Pitting on page 152.)

2. Combine cherry halves with the ½ cup (120 ml) of water in a saucepan. Bring to a boil over high heat, reduce heat, and simmer, covered, for 5 minutes, stirring occasionally. Remove from heat, add port wine, and mix well.

3. Measure 4 cups (946 ml) of the cherry mixture (saving any extra for another use) and return the measured quantity to the saucepan. Add lemon juice and calcium water and mix well.

4. In a separate bowl, combine sugar and pectin powder. Mix thoroughly and set aside.

5. Bring fruit mixture back to a full boil over high heat. Slowly add pectin-sugar mixture, stirring constantly. Continue to stir vigorously for 1 to 2 minutes to dissolve pectin while the preserves come back up to a boil. Once the mixture returns to a full boil, remove it from the heat.

6. Ladle hot preserves into hot, sterilized jars, leaving ¼ inch (6 mm) of headspace. Remove trapped air bubbles, wipe rims with a damp cloth, put on lids and screw bands, and tighten to fingertip tight.

7. Lower filled jars into water bath canner. Place lid on canner, return to a rolling boil, and process for 10 minutes (adjusting for altitude if necessary; see Adjust for Altitude! on page 29).

8. Remove jars with a jar lifter and allow to cool undisturbed on a clean dish towel away from any drafts for 12 to 24 hours. Confirm that jars have sealed properly. Refrigerate any jars that have not sealed and use within 2 weeks. Label the remaining jars with the recipe name and date before storing.

CUSTOMIZE IT!

Looking for something new? Try using lime juice in place of the lemon juice in this recipe.

LEMON-PEAR PRESERVES WITH CARDAMOM

In this delightful autumn preserve, sweet slices of pear are suspended in a subtly spiced, lemon-y jelled syrup. Its delightful fragrance is due in part to the lemon zest—the finely grated exterior part of the lemon. Zesting is easy to do: Leave the fruit whole and use a zester or a very fine grater to simply grate the outside peel of the fruit.

METHOD: Boiling Water Bath Canning

PROCESSING TIME: 10 minutes

YIELD: 4 to 5 half-pint (235 ml) jars

---

2 pounds (900 g) firm, ripe pears*

1¾ cups (410 ml) water

1 tablespoon (6 g) zest from a lemon

1 teaspoon ground cardamom

½ cup (120 ml) lemon juice

2 teaspoons calcium water**

1 cup (200 g) sugar

1½ teaspoons Pomona's pectin powder

*Not sure how much fruit to purchase? See Measuring Up! on page 33.

**For information on how to prepare calcium water, refer to page 30.

1. Peel and core pears. Quarter them lengthwise and then slice each quarter into a couple of smaller, uniform, lengthwise slices.

2. Combine sliced pears and 1¾ cups (410 ml) of water in a saucepan. Bring to a boil over high heat, reduce heat, and simmer, covered, for 3 to 5 minutes until fruit is soft (but still retains its shape), stirring occasionally. Remove from heat.

3. Measure 4 cups (946 ml) of the cooked pears (saving any extra for another use) and return the measured quantity to the saucepan. Add lemon zest, cardamom, lemon juice, and calcium water. Mix well.

4. In a separate bowl, combine sugar and pectin powder. Mix thoroughly and set aside.

5. Bring pear mixture to a full boil over high heat. Slowly add pectin-sugar mixture, stirring constantly. Continue to stir vigorously for 1 to 2 minutes to dissolve pectin while the preserves come back up to a boil. Once the preserves return to a full boil, remove the pan from the heat.

6. Ladle hot preserves into hot, sterilized jars, leaving ¼ inch (6 mm) of headspace.

7. Remove trapped air bubbles, wipe rims with a damp cloth, put on lids and screw bands, and tighten to fingertip tight.

8. Lower filled jars into water bath canner. Place lid on canner, return to a rolling boil, and process for 10 minutes (adjusting for altitude if necessary; see Adjust for Altitude! on page 29).

9. Remove jars with a jar lifter and allow to cool undisturbed on a clean dish towel away from any drafts for 12 to 24 hours. Confirm that jars have sealed properly. Refrigerate any jars that have not sealed and use within 2 weeks. Label the remaining jars with the recipe name and date before storing.

FRESH AND FIRM

For this recipe, be sure to use pears that are still quite firm, so the pear slices remain intact when cooked.

MANGO-GINGER PRESERVES

Mango and ginger is a common pairing in many Asian cuisines, and it makes sense—the unique heat and bite of ginger is a perfect counterpoint to the intense, sultry sweetness of a ripe mango. This recipe calls for crystallized ginger, a convenient alternative to fresh ginger, available at Asian markets and natural food stores. While the mangoes should be ripe, be sure to use ones that are still firm, so that they hold their shape in this preserve.

METHOD: Boiling Water Bath Canning
PROCESSING TIME: 10 minutes
YIELD: 4 to 5 half-pint (235 ml) jars

3½ pounds (1.6 kg) firm, ripe mangoes*

2 tablespoons (20 g) finely chopped crystallized ginger

½ cup (120 ml) lemon juice, divided

4 teaspoons (20 ml) calcium water**

1¼ cups (250 g) sugar

3 teaspoons (9 g) Pomona's pectin powder

Not sure how much fruit to purchase? See Measuring Up! on page 33.

**For information on how to prepare calcium water, refer to page 30.*

1. Peel, pit, and dice mangoes into uniform-size cubes. (For more information, see Mango Madness! on page 182.)

2. Combine mangoes in a saucepan with crystallized ginger and ¼ cup (60 ml) of the lemon juice. Bring to a boil over high heat, reduce heat, and simmer, covered, for 3 to 5 minutes until fruit is soft (but still retains its shape), stirring occasionally. Remove from heat.

3. Measure 4 cups (946 ml) of the cooked mango mixture (saving any extra for another use) and return the measured quantity to the saucepan. Add the remaining ¼ cup (60 ml) of lemon juice and the calcium water. Mix well.

4. In a separate bowl, combine sugar and pectin powder. Mix thoroughly and set aside.

5. Bring mango mixture back to a full boil over high heat. Slowly add pectin-sugar mixture, stirring constantly. Continue to stir vigorously for 1 to 2 minutes to dissolve pectin while the preserves come back up to a boil. Once the preserves return to a full boil, remove the pan from the heat.

6. Ladle hot preserves into hot, sterilized jars, leaving ¼ inch (6 mm) of headspace.

7. Remove trapped air bubbles, wipe rims with a damp cloth, put on lids and screw bands, and tighten to fingertip tight.

8. Lower filled jars into water bath canner. Place lid on canner, return to a rolling boil, and process for 10 minutes (adjusting for altitude if necessary; see Adjust for Altitude! on page 29).

9. Remove jars with a jar lifter and allow to cool undisturbed on a clean dish towel away from any drafts for 12 to 24 hours. Confirm that jars have sealed properly. Refrigerate any jars that have not sealed and use within 2 weeks. Label the remaining jars with the recipe name and date before storing.

SPICED GRAPE PRESERVES

Most of us are so accustomed to grapes being made into jelly that it's easy to forget that they can be put up in many other ways. This lightly spiced, dark purple preserve is a delightfully different way to enjoy grapes. It's a perfect, just-sweet-enough topping for yogurt and granola in a big bowl for breakfast.

METHOD: Boiling Water Bath Canning

PROCESSING TIME: 10 minutes

YIELD: 4 to 5 half-pint (235 ml) jars

2½ pounds (1.1 kg) sweet, seedless, purple or black grapes*

¼ cup (60 ml) orange juice

½ teaspoon ground cinnamon

¼ teaspoon ground cloves

¼ teaspoon ground ginger

¼ cup (60 ml) lemon juice

4 teaspoons (20 ml) calcium water**

¾ cup (150 g) sugar

3 teaspoons (9 g) Pomona's pectin powder

*Not sure how much fruit to purchase? See Measuring Up! on page 33.

**For information on how to prepare calcium water, refer to page 30.

1. Rinse grapes, remove stems, and slice grapes in half.

2. Combine grapes with orange juice in a saucepan. Bring to a boil over high heat, reduce heat, and simmer, covered, for 7 to 10 minutes or until fruit is soft, stirring occasionally. Remove from heat.

3. Measure 4 cups (946 ml) of the cooked mixture (saving any extra for another use) and return the measured quantity to the saucepan. Add cinnamon, ground cloves, ground ginger, lemon juice, and calcium water. Mix well.

4. In a separate bowl, combine sugar and pectin powder. Mix thoroughly and set aside.

5. Bring grape mixture back to a full boil over high heat. Slowly add pectin-sugar mixture, stirring constantly. Continue to stir vigorously for 1 to 2 minutes to dissolve pectin while the preserves come back up to a boil. Once the preserves return to a full boil, remove the pan from the heat.

6. Ladle hot preserves into hot, sterilized jars, leaving ¼ inch (6 mm) of headspace.

7. Remove trapped air bubbles, wipe rims with a damp cloth, put on lids and screw bands, and tighten to fingertip tight.

8. Lower filled jars into water bath canner. Place lid on canner, return to a rolling boil, and process for 10 minutes (adjusting for altitude if necessary; see Adjust for Altitude! on page 29).

9. Remove jars with a jar lifter and allow to cool undisturbed on a clean dish towel away from any drafts for 12 to 24 hours. Confirm that jars have sealed properly. Refrigerate any jars that have not sealed and use within 2 weeks. Label the remaining jars with the recipe name and date before storing.

CUSTOMIZE IT!

If you're looking for something new, why not try honey instead of sugar? In place of the sugar in this recipe, use ½ to 1 cup (170 to 340 g) of honey.

SHAPELY STRAWBERRIES

*Unlike jams, which usually require that you mash the fruit, when you're making preserves,
the idea is to keep individual pieces of fruit (or uniformly cut pieces of fruit) mostly whole
and intact. For strawberries, small or average-size berries are ideal, though larger berries
will work—simply slice them in half if they are too big. To help avoid mashing delicate fruit
unintentionally, use a wider saucepan so that fruit has room to spread out and cook evenly
without a lot of stirring. And when you do stir, stir with a back-and-forth motion, rather than
an up-and-down motion—this way you'll be less likely to crush the berries.*

STRAWBERRY-VANILLA PRESERVES

With ripe, in-season strawberries, combined with a smooth, exotic note of fresh vanilla, this preserve is nothing short of heavenly. It will add a bit of flair to the breakfast table (or bagel) of course, but it's also great in desserts—try it on top of a biscuit with a bit of whipped cream for a spectacular strawberry-vanilla shortcake! The berries in this preserve tend to float to the top during canning, so mix it up well before serving.

METHOD: Boiling Water Bath Canning

PROCESSING TIME: 10 minutes

YIELD: 4 to 5 half-pint (235 ml) jars

2¼ pounds (1 kg) strawberries*

½ cup (120 ml) water

1 vanilla bean

1½ teaspoons calcium water**

1¼ cups (250 g) sugar

1½ teaspoons Pomona's
  pectin powder

Not sure how much fruit to purchase? See Measuring Up! on page 33.

**For information on how to prepare calcium water, refer to page 30.*

1. Rinse strawberries and remove stems.

2. Combine strawberries and the ½ cup (120 ml) of water in a large saucepan. Using a paring knife, slice the vanilla bean in half lengthwise and scrape out the seeds. Add the vanilla seeds and the bean pod itself to the strawberries. Bring the mixture to a boil over high heat, reduce heat, and simmer, covered, for 3 to 4 minutes, stirring occasionally. Stir carefully—you don't want to crush the berries. Remove from heat.

3. Measure 4 cups (946 ml) of the cooked strawberry mixture (saving any extra for another use) and return the measured quantity to the saucepan. Add calcium water and mix well.

4. In a separate bowl, combine sugar and pectin powder. Mix thoroughly and set aside.

5. Bring strawberry mixture back to a full boil over high heat. Slowly add pectin-sugar mixture, stirring constantly. Continue to stir vigorously for 1 to 2 minutes to dissolve pectin while the preserves come back up to a boil. Once the preserves return to a full boil, remove the pan from the heat. Using tongs, carefully remove the vanilla bean pod from the preserves and discard.

6. Ladle hot preserves into hot, sterilized jars, leaving ¼ inch (6 mm) of headspace.

7. Remove trapped air bubbles, wipe rims with a damp cloth, put on lids and screw bands, and tighten to fingertip tight.

8. Lower filled jars into water bath canner. Place lid on canner, return to a rolling boil, and process for 10 minutes (adjusting for altitude if necessary; see Adjust for Altitude! on page 29).

9. Remove jars with a jar lifter and allow to cool undisturbed on a clean dish towel away from any drafts for 12 to 24 hours. Confirm that jars have sealed properly. Refrigerate any jars that have not sealed and use within 2 weeks. Label the remaining jars with the recipe name and date before storing.

GRATE THAT GINGER!

Using a paring knife or a vegetable peeler, slice the thin, brown skin off a chunk of fresh, firm ginger. Then, using a fine mesh grater, grate the ginger. Don't peel the whole root at once—continue to peel as you go along, so that you don't peel more than you need. Grating the ginger will create a good bit of juice; be sure to incorporate it into your measured quantity of grated ginger.

GINGERED LEMON-FIG PRESERVES

In this spectacular preserve, a touch of heat from the ginger and a little tartness from the lemons beautifully highlight the lushness of fresh, ripe figs. Try serving sandwiched between gingersnap cookies to accentuate its flavor profile. To ensure proper acidity levels, be sure to use commonly available, full-acid lemons such as Eureka or Lisbon lemons in this recipe.

METHOD: Boiling Water Bath Canning
PROCESSING TIME: 10 minutes
YIELD: 4 to 5 half-pint (235 ml) jars

---

2 pounds (900 g) ripe figs*

2 tablespoons (16 g) peeled, finely grated ginger

7 medium lemons, divided

4 teaspoons (20 ml) calcium water**

1¼ cups (250 g) sugar

3 teaspoons (9 g) Pomona's pectin powder

*Not sure how much fruit to purchase? See Measuring Up! on page 33.

**For information on how to prepare calcium water, refer to page 30.

1. Rinse figs, remove stems, and slice them in half lengthwise. (Cut them into smaller pieces if you prefer, or if you're working with large figs.) Combine figs in a saucepan with grated ginger.

2. Wash lemons thoroughly. Using a vegetable peeler, slice off long pieces of the exterior of some of the lemon peels, avoiding the inner white part. Then, using a chef's knife, slice these pieces into very thin strips about 1-inch (2.5 cm) long. Repeat this process until you have accumulated ¼ cup (24 g) of thin, 1-inch (2.5 cm) long strips. Add these strips to the fig mixture.

3. Slice lemons in half and squeeze out their juice, discarding the remaining peels. Divide the juice, setting aside ⅓ cup (80 ml) for later use. Add the remaining quantity to the fig mixture.

4. Bring the fig mixture to a boil over high heat, reduce heat, and simmer, covered, for 12 to 15 minutes or until lemon peels are soft, stirring occasionally. Remove from heat.

5. Measure 4 cups (946 ml) of the cooked fig mixture (saving any extra for another use) and return the measured quantity to the saucepan. Add the reserved ⅓ cup (80 ml) of lemon juice and calcium water and mix well.

6. In a separate bowl, combine sugar and pectin powder. Mix thoroughly and set aside.

7. Bring fig mixture back to a full boil over high heat. Slowly add pectin-sugar mixture, stirring constantly. Continue to stir vigorously for 1 to 2 minutes to dissolve pectin while the preserves come back up to a boil. Once the preserves return to a full boil, remove from heat.

8. Ladle hot preserves into hot, sterilized jars, leaving ¼ inch (6 mm) of headspace.

9. Remove trapped air bubbles, wipe rims with a damp cloth, put on lids and screw bands, and tighten to fingertip tight.

10. Lower filled jars into water bath canner. Place lid on canner, return to a rolling boil, and process for 10 minutes (adjusting for altitude if necessary; see Adjust for Altitude! on page 29).

11. Remove jars with a jar lifter and allow to cool undisturbed on a clean dish towel away from any drafts for 12 to 24 hours. Confirm that jars have sealed properly. Refrigerate any jars that have not sealed and use within 2 weeks. Label the remaining jars with the recipe name and date before storing.

CHOCOLATE-CHERRY PRESERVES

Chocolate and cherries were made for each other, and this preserve is proof. The combination of the two is insanely decadent. Be sure to use high-quality cocoa powder that is unsweetened and has no other added ingredients. Spoon this preserve on top of cheesecake for a stunning—and absolutely heavenly—dessert.

METHOD: Boiling Water Bath Canning

PROCESSING TIME: 10 minutes

YIELD: 4 to 5 half-pint (235 ml) jars

2½ pounds (1.1 kg) sweet cherries*

⅓ cup (27 g) sifted, unsweetened cocoa powder

½ cup (120 ml) water

¼ teaspoon cinnamon

1/8 teaspoon cayenne pepper

¼ cup (60 ml) lemon juice

3 teaspoons (15 ml) calcium water**

1¼ cups (250 g) sugar

2½ teaspoons (7.5 g) Pomona's pectin powder

*Not sure how much fruit to purchase? See Measuring Up! on page 33.

**For information on how to prepare calcium water, refer to page 30.

1. Rinse cherries, remove stems, and then slice in half and remove pits. (For more information, see Painless Pitting on page 152.)

2. Combine cherry halves with cocoa powder and the ½ cup (120 ml) of water in a saucepan. Bring to a boil over high heat, reduce heat, and simmer, covered, for 5 minutes, stirring occasionally. Remove from heat.

3. Measure 4 cups (946 ml) of the cooked mixture (saving any extra for another use) and return the measured quantity to the saucepan. Add cinnamon, cayenne pepper, lemon juice, and calcium water. Mix well.

4. In a separate bowl, combine sugar and pectin powder. Mix thoroughly and set aside.

5. Bring cherry mixture back to a full boil over high heat. Slowly add pectin-sugar mixture, stirring constantly. Continue to stir vigorously for 1 to 2 minutes to dissolve pectin while the preserves come back up to a boil. Once the mixture returns to a full boil, remove the pan from the heat.

6. Ladle hot preserves into hot, sterilized jars, leaving ¼ inch (6 mm) of headspace.

7. Remove trapped air bubbles, wipe rims with a damp cloth, put on lids and screw bands, and tighten to fingertip tight.

8. Lower filled jars into water bath canner. Place lid on canner, return to a rolling boil, and process for 10 minutes (adjusting for altitude if necessary; see Adjust for Altitude! on page 29).

9. Remove jars with a jar lifter and allow to cool undisturbed on a clean dish towel away from any drafts for 12 to 24 hours. Confirm that jars have sealed properly. Refrigerate any jars that have not sealed and use within 2 weeks. Label the remaining jars with the recipe name and date before storing.

CONSERVES

By definition, conserves contain an assortment of different ingredients, so they are much more varied than any of the other jelled goods. In addition to the primary fruit, conserves are studded with a variety of other ingredients, such as dried fruit, nuts, or vegetables, and they can be either sweet or savory. In their sweet form, conserves are similar to jams, but usually with an added dose of chewy or crunchy texture. Savory conserves are often deliciously unexpected. With the inclusion of onions, ginger, garlic, and other earthy spices, they are excellent as glazes on roasted or grilled meats and vegetables or as a condiment. This section contains a variety of conserves, both savory and sweet, so prepare yourself to enjoy some delicious—and perhaps unexpected—flavor combinations!

PEACH-PECAN-CHERRY CONSERVE

This luscious conserve makes me think of my maternal grandmother and her simple, self-sufficient life in rural Georgia. She and her neighbor shared the bounty of a beautiful old pecan tree, and after my grandmother died, her neighbor would mail a package of pecans picked from that tree to my mother every Christmas. These are the pecans I used when I created this recipe. Select peaches that are still somewhat firm so that the fruit will retain its shape when cooked.

METHOD: Boiling Water Bath Canning

PROCESSING TIME: 10 minutes

YIELD: 4 to 5 half-pint (235 ml) jars

---

2 pounds (900 g) ripe, firm peaches*

⅔ cup (107 g) dried cherries

½ cup (55 g) chopped pecans

1 cup (235 ml) water

¼ cup (60 ml) lemon juice

4 teaspoons (20 ml) calcium water**

¾ cup (150 g) sugar

3 teaspoons (9 g) Pomona's pectin powder

*Not sure how much fruit to purchase? See Measuring Up! on page 33.

**For information on how to prepare calcium water, refer to page 30.

1. Peel, remove pits, and dice peaches. (For more information, see How to Skin a Peach on page 145.)

2. Combine diced peaches in a saucepan with dried cherries, chopped pecans, and the 1 cup (235 ml) of water. Bring to a boil over high heat, reduce heat, and simmer, covered, for 5 to 10 minutes or until fruit is soft, stirring occasionally. Remove from heat.

3. Measure 4 cups (946 ml) of the cooked mixture (saving any extra for another use) and return the measured quantity to the saucepan. Add the lemon juice and calcium water and mix well.

4. In a separate bowl, combine sugar and pectin powder. Mix thoroughly and set aside.

5. Bring peach mixture back to a full boil over high heat. Slowly add pectin-sugar mixture, stirring constantly. Continue to stir vigorously for 1 to 2 minutes to dissolve pectin while the conserve comes back up to a boil. Once the conserve returns to a full boil, remove it from the heat.

6. Ladle hot conserve into hot, sterilized jars, leaving ¼ inch (6 mm) of headspace.

7. Remove trapped air bubbles, wipe rims with a damp cloth, put on lids and screw bands, and tighten to fingertip tight.

8. Lower filled jars into water bath canner. Place lid on canner, return to a rolling boil, and process for 10 minutes (adjusting for altitude if necessary; see Adjust for Altitude! on page 29).

9. Remove jars with a jar lifter and allow to cool undisturbed on a clean dish towel away from any drafts for 12 to 24 hours. Confirm that jars have sealed properly. Refrigerate any jars that have not sealed and use within 2 weeks. Label the remaining jars with the recipe name and date before storing.

CUSTOMIZE IT!

Looking for something new? Try using lime juice in place of the lemon juice in this recipe.

KEEP IT EQUAL

If you have too much fruit and need to get rid of some to meet the required 4-cup (946 ml) quantity, be sure that you remove solids and liquids equally. This is very important in maintaining both the proper consistency and proper acidity of the final product. Don't pour off the liquid—instead, remove extra solids and liquids from the measuring cup one spoonful at a time, making an effort to remove liquid spoonfuls and solid spoonfuls in roughly equal quantities.

SAVORY BLUEBERRY-GINGER CONSERVE

If you're looking for an alternative to cranberry sauce on your holiday table this fall and winter, give this gorgeous, savory conserve a try. With fresh ginger, orange peel, and other warm and earthy spices, it is a delicious, unexpected accompaniment to roasted meats and vegetables—and, of course, the lunches you make with the leftovers!

METHOD: Boiling Water Bath Canning
PROCESSING TIME: 10 minutes
YIELD: 4 to 5 half-pint (235 ml) jars

1½ pounds (680 g) blueberries*

¾ cup (120 g) diced onion

2 tablespoons (16 g) peeled, finely grated ginger (For more information, see Grate That Ginger! on page 118.)

¾ cup (175 ml) white vinegar, minimum 5 percent acidity

1 teaspoon mustard seeds

¼ teaspoon ground cinnamon

¼ teaspoon ground cloves

¼ teaspoon ground cardamom

½ teaspoon ground black pepper

½ teaspoon salt

2 medium oranges

2 tablespoons (28 ml) lemon juice

2 teaspoons calcium water**

1 cup (200 g) sugar

2 teaspoons Pomona's pectin powder

Not sure how much fruit to purchase? See Measuring Up! on page 33.

**For information on how to prepare calcium water, refer to page 30.*

1. Rinse the blueberries, remove stems, and combine in a large saucepan with onion, grated ginger, vinegar, mustard seeds, cinnamon, ground cloves, cardamom, black pepper, and salt.

2. Wash oranges thoroughly. Using a vegetable peeler, peel off some of the outer part of the orange peels, avoiding the inner white part, and chop finely. Repeat this process until you have accumulated 2 tablespoons (12 g) of finely chopped orange peel. Then, slice the oranges in half and squeeze out their juice. Add the 2 tablespoons (12 g) orange peel and the orange juice to the blueberry mixture and discard the remaining peels.

3. Bring blueberry mixture to a boil over high heat, reduce heat, and simmer, covered, for 15 minutes, stirring occasionally. Remove from heat.

4. Measure 4 cups (946 ml) of the cooked blueberry mixture (saving any extra for another use) and return the measured quantity to the saucepan. Add lemon juice and calcium water and mix well.

5. In a separate bowl, combine sugar and pectin powder. Mix thoroughly and set aside.

6. Bring the blueberry mixture back to a full boil over high heat. Slowly add pectin-sugar mixture, stirring constantly. Continue to stir vigorously for 1 to 2 minutes to dissolve pectin while the conserve comes back up to a boil. Once the conserve returns to a full boil, remove it from the heat.

7. Ladle hot conserve into hot, sterilized jars, leaving ¼ inch (6 mm) of headspace.

8. Remove trapped air bubbles, wipe rims with a damp cloth, put on lids and screw bands, and tighten to fingertip tight.

9. Lower filled jars into water bath canner. Place lid on canner, return to a rolling boil, and process for 10 minutes (adjusting for altitude if necessary; see Adjust for Altitude! on page 29).

10. Remove jars with a jar lifter and allow to cool undisturbed on a clean dish towel away from any drafts for 12 to 24 hours. Confirm that jars have sealed properly. Refrigerate any jars that have not sealed and use within 2 weeks. Label the remaining jars with the recipe name and date before storing.

SAVORY SPICED-MANGO CONSERVE

If you're a fan of chutney, give this conserve a try! Inspired by the classic Indian condiment, this conserve melds the sweetness of mangoes with the earthy, complex flavors of garlic, ginger, and a variety of other spices.

METHOD: Boiling Water Bath Canning
PROCESSING TIME: 10 minutes
YIELD: 4 to 5 half-pint (235 ml) jars

---

2 pounds (900 g) ripe, firm mangoes*

⅔ cup (110 g) diced onion

2 teaspoons peeled, finely grated ginger (For more information, see Grate That Ginger! on page 118.)

1 teaspoon minced garlic

¾ cup (175 ml) water

¾ cup (175 ml) white vinegar, minimum 5 percent acidity

½ cup (75 g) golden raisins (or dark raisins, if you prefer)

1½ teaspoons ground coriander

1 teaspoon mustard seeds

½ teaspoon ground cinnamon

½ teaspoon ground turmeric

¼ teaspoon ground cumin

1/8 teaspoon red pepper flakes

¼ teaspoon salt

3 tablespoons (45 ml) lemon juice

2 teaspoons calcium water**

1⅓ cups (267 g) sugar

2 teaspoons Pomona's pectin powder

Not sure how much fruit to purchase? See Measuring Up! on page 33.

**For information on how to prepare calcium water, refer to page 30.*

1. Peel, pit, and dice mangoes. (For more information, see Mango Madness! on page 182.)

2. In a saucepan, combine mangoes, onion, grated ginger, garlic, the ¾ cup (175 ml) of water, vinegar, raisins, coriander, mustard seeds, cinnamon, turmeric, cumin, red pepper flakes, and salt. Bring to a boil over high heat, reduce heat, and then simmer, covered, for 20 minutes, stirring occasionally. Remove from heat.

3. Measure 4 cups (946 ml) of the cooked mango mixture (saving any extra for another use) and return the measured quantity to the saucepan. Add the lemon juice and calcium water and mix well.

4. In a separate bowl, combine sugar and pectin powder. Mix thoroughly and set aside.

5. Bring the mango mixture back to a full boil over high heat. Slowly add sugar-pectin mixture, stirring constantly. Continue to stir vigorously for 1 to 2 minutes to dissolve pectin while the conserve comes back up to a boil. Once the conserve returns to a full boil, remove it from the heat.

6. Ladle hot conserve into hot, sterilized jars, leaving ¼ inch (6 mm) of headspace.

7. Remove trapped air bubbles, wipe rims with a damp cloth, put on lids and screw bands, and tighten to fingertip tight.

8. Lower filled jars into water bath canner. Place lid on canner, return to a rolling boil, and process for 10 minutes (adjusting for altitude if necessary; see Adjust for Altitude! on page 29).

9. Remove jars with a jar lifter and allow to cool undisturbed on a clean dish towel away from any drafts for 12 to 24 hours. Confirm that jars have sealed properly. Refrigerate any jars that have not sealed and use within 2 weeks. Label the remaining jars with the recipe name and date before storing.

CUSTOMIZE IT!

If you're looking for something new, try spicing it up! At the same time that you add the calcium water, add up to 1 teaspoon of ground ginger, cardamom, ground cloves, cinnamon, nutmeg, or allspice. Or, you can mix and match these spices—just be sure that the total spice quantity does not exceed 1 teaspoon.

HONEYED APRICOT-DATE-ALMOND CONSERVE

Inspired by some of the classic flavors of the Mediterranean and the Middle East, this rich, sweet conserve is a real treat. Swirl it into a steaming bowl of oatmeal, spoon it over a chilled bowl of coconut rice pudding, or enjoy it as a filling for crunchy, chewy cookie bars—no matter how you have it, it's simply delightful!

METHOD: Boiling Water Bath Canning
PROCESSING TIME: 10 minutes
YIELD: 4 to 5 half-pint (235 ml) jars

---

2 pounds (900 g) ripe apricots*

½ cup (90 g) finely chopped, dried dates

½ cup (46 g) sliced almonds

½ cup (120 ml) water

⅓ cup (80 ml) lemon juice

4 teaspoons (20 ml) calcium water**

½ cup (170 g) honey

3 teaspoons (9 g) Pomona's pectin powder

Not sure how much fruit to purchase? See Measuring Up! on page 33.

**For information on how to prepare calcium water, refer to page 30.*

1. Rinse apricots, remove stems, and then slice in half or pull apart. Remove pits and then dice apricots. (For more information, see To Peel or Not to Peel? See below.)

2. Combine diced apricots in a saucepan with chopped dates, sliced almonds, and the ½ cup (120 ml) of water. Bring to a boil over high heat, reduce heat, and simmer, covered, 5 to 10 minutes or until fruit is soft, stirring occasionally. Remove from heat.

3. Measure out 4 cups (946 ml) of the cooked mixture (saving any extra for another use) and return the measured quantity to the saucepan. Add the lemon juice and calcium water and mix well.

4. In a separate bowl, combine honey and pectin powder. Mix thoroughly and set aside.

5. Bring fruit mixture back to a full boil over high heat. Slowly add pectin-honey mixture, stirring constantly. Continue to stir vigorously for 1 to 2 minutes to dissolve pectin while the conserve comes back up to a boil. Once the conserve returns to a full boil, remove it from the heat.

6. Ladle hot conserve into hot, sterilized jars, leaving ¼ inch (6 mm) of headspace.

7. Remove trapped air bubbles, wipe rims with a damp cloth, put on lids and screw bands, and tighten to fingertip tight.

8. Lower filled jars into water bath canner. Place lid on canner, return to a rolling boil, and process for 10 minutes (adjusting for altitude if necessary; see Adjust for Altitude! on page 29).

9. Remove jars with a jar lifter and allow to cool undisturbed on a clean dish towel away from any drafts for 12 to 24 hours. Confirm that jars have sealed properly. Refrigerate any jars that have not sealed and use within 2 weeks. Label the remaining jars with the recipe name and date before storing.

TO PEEL OR NOT TO PEEL?

When it comes to plums and apricots, my answer to this question is always not to peel. Unlike peaches, plum and apricot skins take a bit of effort to remove. Fortunately, though, their skins are so delicate they seem to disappear when cooked, so they are almost imperceptible. And, if you slice the fruit into smaller pieces before mashing, the skins are even less noticeable. Some folks do choose to skin plums and apricots, but I prefer to leave the skins on.

CRYSTALLIZE IT!

This recipe calls for crystallized ginger—essentially, slices of fresh ginger that have been cooked and preserved with sugar. Crystallized ginger is easy and quick to chop, so it's very convenient in recipes. It's available at Asian markets and at many natural food stores.

PLUM-GINGER-ORANGE CONSERVE

The combination of orange, almond, and ginger melding with the sweet, rich tang of fresh plums makes this gorgeous purple conserve sing. Enjoy it atop shortcake cups, with a generous dollop of whipped cream—what a treat!

METHOD: Boiling Water Bath Canning

PROCESSING TIME: 10 minutes

YIELD: 4 to 5 half-pint (235 ml) jars

---

2 pounds (900 g) ripe,
   sweet plums*

1 tablespoon (10 g) finely
   chopped crystallized ginger

½ cup (46 g) sliced almonds

2 tablespoons (28 ml) orange
   liqueur (optional)

2 medium oranges, divided

¼ cup (60 ml) lemon juice

4 teaspoons (20 ml)
   calcium water**

1 cup (200 g) sugar

3 teaspoons (9 g) Pomona's
   pectin powder

Not sure how much fruit to purchase? See Measuring Up! on page 33.

**For information on how to prepare calcium water, refer to page 30.*

1. Rinse plums, remove stems, and slice in half. Remove pits and dice plums. (For more information, see To Peel or Not to Peel? on page 129.) Combine diced plums in a saucepan with crystallized ginger, sliced almonds, and orange liqueur if using.

2. Slice 1 of the oranges in half and squeeze out its juice, discarding seeds and the peel. Add the juice to the plum mixture.

3. Wash the remaining orange. Using a vegetable peeler, slice off pieces of the outer part of the peel and finely chop. Add 2 tablespoons (12 g) of the finely chopped peel to the plum mixture.

4. Remove the rest of the peel from the orange and discard the remaining peel. Remove and discard seeds, any extra white pith, and any especially fibrous parts of the membrane from the fruit. Finely chop the flesh of the fruit and then add to the plum mixture.

5. Bring fruit mixture to a boil over high heat, reduce heat, and simmer, covered, for 10 to 12 minutes or until the peel is soft, stirring occasionally. Remove from heat.

6. Measure 4 cups (946 ml) of the fruit mixture (saving any extra for another use) and return the measured quantity to the saucepan. Add the lemon juice and calcium water and mix well.

7. In a separate bowl, combine sugar and pectin powder. Mix and set aside.

8. Bring fruit mixture back to a full boil over high heat. Slowly add pectin-sugar mixture, stirring constantly. Continue to stir vigorously for 1 to 2 minutes to dissolve pectin while the conserve comes back up to a boil. Once the conserve returns to a full boil, remove from heat.

9. Ladle hot conserve into hot, sterilized jars, leaving ¼ inch (6 mm) of headspace.

10. Remove trapped air bubbles, wipe rims with a damp cloth, put on lids and screw bands, and tighten to fingertip tight.

11. Lower filled jars into water bath canner. Place lid on canner, return to a rolling boil, and process for 10 minutes (adjusting for altitude if necessary; see Adjust for Altitude! on page 29).

12. Remove jars with a jar lifter and allow to cool undisturbed on a clean dish towel away from any drafts for 12 to 24 hours. Confirm that jars have sealed properly. Refrigerate any jars that have not sealed and use within 2 weeks. Label the remaining jars with the recipe name and date before storing.

APPLE-RAISIN-WALNUT CONSERVE

I never tire of the combination of apples, raisins, and walnuts, along with a touch of autumnal spice, and this conserve is a wonderful way to enjoy the fresh, local apples that are abundant during fall. For a delicious, eye-catching fall or winter dessert, use this conserve as a filling for a lattice-top pie.

METHOD: Boiling Water Bath Canning
PROCESSING TIME: 10 minutes
YIELD: 4 to 5 half-pint (235 ml) jars

1½ pounds (680 g) hard,
   crisp apples*

½ cup (75 g) raisins

½ cup (60 g) chopped walnuts

½ teaspoon ground cinnamon

¼ teaspoon ground nutmeg

1/8 teaspoon ground cloves

1/8 teaspoon ground ginger

2¼ cups (530 ml) water

¼ cup (60 ml) lemon juice

4 teaspoons (20 ml)
   calcium water**

¾ cup (150 g) sugar

3 teaspoons (9 g) Pomona's
   pectin powder

*Not sure how much fruit to purchase?
See Measuring Up! on page 33.

**For information on how to prepare
calcium water, refer to page 30.

1. Peel apples, remove stems and cores, and dice. Combine diced apples in a saucepan with raisins, walnuts, cinnamon, nutmeg, ground cloves, ground ginger, and the 2¼ cups (530 ml) of water. Bring to a boil over high heat, reduce heat, and simmer, covered, for 5 to 10 minutes or until fruit is soft, stirring occasionally. Remove from heat.

2. Measure 4 cups (946 ml) of the cooked mixture (saving any extra for another use) and return the measured quantity to the saucepan. Add the lemon juice and calcium water and mix well.

3. In a separate bowl, combine sugar and pectin powder. Mix thoroughly and set aside.

4. Bring apple mixture back to a full boil over high heat. Slowly add pectin-sugar mixture, stirring constantly. Continue to stir vigorously for 1 to 2 minutes to dissolve pectin while the conserve comes back up to a boil. Once the conserve returns to a full boil, remove it from the heat.

5. Ladle hot conserve into hot, sterilized jars, leaving ¼ inch (6 mm) of headspace.

6. Remove trapped air bubbles, wipe rims with a damp cloth, put on lids and screw bands, and tighten to fingertip tight.

7. Lower filled jars into water bath canner. Place lid on canner, return to a rolling boil, and process for 10 minutes (adjusting for altitude if necessary; see Adjust for Altitude! on page 29).

8. Remove jars with a jar lifter and allow to cool undisturbed on a clean dish towel away from any drafts for 12 to 24 hours. Confirm that jars have sealed properly. Refrigerate any jars that have not sealed and use within 2 weeks. Label the remaining jars with the recipe name and date before storing.

GO FOR THE CRUNCH!

Use hard, crisp apples in this recipe so that the fruit will retain its shape when cooked—Granny Smiths work well.

Chapter 5

FRUIT JAMS AND JELLIES

FRUIT JAMS

Jams are the workhorses of jelled goods. Nothing more than mashed or chopped fruit that's been lightly sweetened and jelled by pectin, they are the simplest of all to make. Jams are incredibly practical and versatile, too—use them on peanut butter and jam sandwiches, in smoothies, in hot cereal, on toast, on yogurt, on granola, on ice cream, in cookies, and in pies . . . you get the idea. Jams are humble and unassuming and yet, extraordinarily delicious.

SIMPLE CLASSIC: BLUEBERRY JAM

Here in Maine, we're fortunate that blueberries are abundant in late summer, and I never tire of this classic way to enjoy them. Blueberries require very little prep, and this jam has few ingredients, so it's easy and quick to prepare, making it an excellent choice for new jam makers. A dollop of this luscious, deep blue jam on a muffin is scrumptious—or, try it on a cracker with some extra-sharp cheddar for an unexpected flavor treat.

METHOD: Boiling Water Bath Canning
PROCESSING TIME: 10 minutes
YIELD: 4 to 5 half-pint (235 ml) jars

2¼ pounds (1 kg) blueberries*

¼ cup (60 ml) lemon juice

2 teaspoons calcium water**

1 cup (200 g) sugar

2 teaspoons Pomona's
   pectin powder

Not sure how much fruit to purchase? See Measuring Up! on page 33.

**For information on how to prepare calcium water, refer to page 30.*

1. Rinse blueberries, remove stems, and mash in a large bowl.

2. Measure 4 cups (946 ml) of mashed blueberries (saving any extra for another use) and combine the measured quantity in a saucepan with lemon juice and calcium water. Mix well.

3. In a separate bowl, combine sugar and pectin powder. Mix thoroughly and set aside.

4. Bring blueberry mixture to a full boil over high heat. Slowly add pectin-sugar mixture, stirring constantly. Continue to stir vigorously for 1 to 2 minutes to dissolve pectin while the jam comes back up to a boil. Once the jam returns to a full boil, remove it from the heat.

5. Ladle hot jam into hot, sterilized jars, leaving ¼ inch (6 mm) of headspace.

6. Remove trapped air bubbles, wipe rims with a damp cloth, put on lids and screw bands, and tighten to fingertip tight.

7. Lower filled jars into water bath canner. Place lid on canner, return to a rolling boil, and process for 10 minutes (adjusting for altitude if necessary; see Adjust for Altitude! on page 29).

8. Remove jars with a jar lifter and allow to cool undisturbed on a clean dish towel away from any drafts for 12 to 24 hours. Confirm that jars have sealed properly. Refrigerate any jars that have not sealed and use within 2 weeks. Label the remaining jars with the recipe name and date before storing.

CUSTOMIZE IT!

If you're looking for something new, try spicing it up! At the same time that you add the calcium water, add up to 1 teaspoon of ground ginger, cardamom, ground cloves, cinnamon, nutmeg, or allspice. Or, you can mix and match these spices—just be sure that the total spice quantity does not exceed 1 teaspoon.

APRICOT ANGST

Trying to mash rock-hard apricots is really not a lot of fun, so be sure that your apricots are fully ripe and soft enough to mash before beginning. If they're not, however, simply place pitted, chopped apricots in a saucepan with ¼ cup (60 ml) of water (or slightly more if necessary). Simmer for 5 minutes to soften them and then mash. (There's no need to drain the water after cooking—simply mash the apricot mixture as is.)

SIMPLE CLASSIC: APRICOT JAM

Apricots fresh from the tree on a warm summer day are one of the world's true wonders. Well, perhaps that's overstating it a bit, but they certainly come close, in my mind anyway. This lovely little fruit tastes amazing unadorned, and this recipe is suitably simple, so it's ideal for beginning jam makers. Spread on a slice of pound cake or for a special treat, use it as a filling between layers of a cake!

METHOD: Boiling Water Bath Canning

PROCESSING TIME: 10 minutes

YIELD: 4 to 5 half-pint (235 ml) jars

2½ pounds (1.1 kg) fully ripe apricots*

¼ cup (60 ml) lemon juice

4 teaspoons (20 ml) calcium water**

1½ cups (300 g) sugar

3 teaspoons (9 g) Pomona's pectin powder

*Not sure how much fruit to purchase? See Measuring Up! on page 33.

**For information on how to prepare calcium water, refer to page 30.

1. Rinse apricots, remove stems, and then slice in half or pull apart. Remove pits, chop apricots into small pieces, and mash in a large bowl. (For more information, see To Peel or Not to Peel? on page 129.)

2. Measure 4 cups (946 ml) of mashed apricots (saving any extra for another use) and combine measured quantity in a saucepan with lemon juice and calcium water. Mix well.

3. In a separate bowl, combine sugar and pectin powder. Mix thoroughly and set aside.

4. Bring apricot mixture to a full boil over high heat. Slowly add pectin-sugar mixture, stirring constantly. Continue to stir vigorously for 1 to 2 minutes to dissolve pectin while the jam comes back up to a boil. Once the jam returns to a full boil, remove it from the heat.

5. Ladle hot jam into hot, sterilized jars, leaving ¼ inch (6 mm) of headspace.

6. Remove trapped air bubbles, wipe rims with a damp cloth, put on lids and screw bands, and tighten to fingertip tight.

7. Lower filled jars into water bath canner. Place lid on canner, return to a rolling boil, and process for 10 minutes (adjusting for altitude if necessary; see Adjust for Altitude! on page 29).

8. Remove jars with a jar lifter and allow to cool undisturbed on a clean dish towel away from any drafts for 12 to 24 hours. Confirm that jars have sealed properly. Refrigerate any jars that have not sealed and use within 2 weeks. Label the remaining jars with the recipe name and date before storing.

CUSTOMIZE IT!

If you're looking for something new, why not try different fruits? In place of or in combination with the apricot in this recipe, use sweet cherry, pear, mango, peach, fig, or sweet plum—or use a combination of any of these fruits.

SIMPLE CLASSIC: STRAWBERRY JAM

Classics are often classics for a reason, and this strawberry jam is a great example—when you're working with perfectly ripe, in-season fruit, you don't have to add much to make a spectacular jam. Use locally grown berries if you can, as their flavor and color will be richer and more vibrant than the grocery store variety. This is an excellent recipe to start with if you're new to jam making. For something different, try it warmed on top of pancakes—delicious!

METHOD: Boiling Water Bath Canning

PROCESSING TIME: 10 minutes

YIELD: 4 to 5 half-pint (235 ml) jars

2¼ pounds (1 kg) strawberries*

2 teaspoons calcium water**

1 cup (200 g) sugar

2 teaspoons Pomona's
   pectin powder

Not sure how much fruit to purchase? See Measuring Up! on page 33.

**For information on how to prepare calcium water, refer to page 30.*

1. Rinse strawberries, remove stems, and mash in a large bowl.

2. Measure 4 cups (946 ml) of mashed strawberries (saving any extra for another use) and combine the measured quantity in a saucepan with calcium water. Mix well.

3. In a separate bowl, combine sugar and pectin powder. Mix thoroughly and set aside.

4. Bring strawberry mixture to a full boil over high heat. Slowly add pectin-sugar mixture, stirring constantly. Continue to stir vigorously for 1 to 2 minutes to dissolve pectin while the jam comes back up to a boil. Once the jam returns to a full boil, remove it from the heat.

5. Ladle hot jam into hot, sterilized jars, leaving ¼ inch (6 mm) of headspace.

6. Remove trapped air bubbles, wipe rims with a damp cloth, put on lids and screw bands, and tighten to fingertip tight.

7. Lower filled jars into water bath canner. Place lid on canner, return to a rolling boil, and process for 10 minutes (adjusting for altitude if necessary; see Adjust for Altitude! on page 29).

8. Remove jars with a jar lifter and allow to cool undisturbed on a clean dish towel away from any drafts for 12 to 24 hours. Confirm that jars have sealed properly. Refrigerate any jars that have not sealed and use within 2 weeks. Label the remaining jars with the recipe name and date before storing.

CUSTOMIZE IT!

If you're looking for something new, why not try different fruits? In place of or in combination with the strawberry in this recipe, or in the All-Fruit Strawberry Jam (opposite) use kiwi, currant, raspberry, gooseberry, sour blackberry, sour cherry, sour plum, or canned pineapple—or use a combination of any of these fruits.

ALL-FRUIT STRAWBERRY JAM

I make this jam more than any other jam, hands down. My two young boys eat peanut butter and jam sandwiches nonstop it seems, and because I like to keep their sugar intake in check, this is my go-to choice. It's sweetened only with fruit juice concentrate, so it's about as close as you can get to just fruit in a jam, and it's loaded with fantastic, fresh strawberry flavor.

METHOD: Boiling Water Bath Canning

PROCESSING TIME: 10 minutes

YIELD: 4 half-pint (235 ml) jars

1¾ **pounds (800 g) strawberries***

2 **teaspoons calcium water****

1 **cup (235 ml) unsweetened white grape juice concentrate**

2 **teaspoons Pomona's pectin powder**

Not sure how much fruit to purchase? See Measuring Up! on page 33.

**For information on how to prepare calcium water, refer to page 30.*

1. Rinse strawberries, remove stems, and mash in a large bowl.

2. Measure 3 cups (700 ml) of mashed strawberries (saving any extra for another use) and combine the measured quantity in a saucepan with calcium water. Mix well.

3. In a separate pan, bring white grape juice concentrate to a boil. Carefully pour hot juice concentrate into a blender or food processor and then add pectin powder. Vent the lid and blend for 1 to 2 minutes, stopping to scrape down sides with a rubber spatula as needed, until powder is thoroughly dissolved. Set aside.

4. Bring strawberries to a full boil over high heat and then slowly add the pectin–juice concentrate mixture, stirring constantly. Continue to cook and stir jam for 1 minute as the jam comes back up to a boil. Once the jam returns to a full boil, remove it from the heat.

5. Ladle hot jam into hot, sterilized jars, leaving ¼ inch (6 mm) of headspace.

6. Remove trapped air bubbles, wipe rims with a damp cloth, put on lids and screw bands, and tighten to fingertip tight.

7. Lower filled jars into water bath canner. Place lid on canner, return to a rolling boil, and process for 10 minutes (adjusting for altitude if necessary; see Adjust for Altitude! on page 29).

8. Remove jars with a jar lifter and allow to cool undisturbed on a clean dish towel away from any drafts for 12 to 24 hours. Confirm that jars have sealed properly. Refrigerate any jars that have not sealed and use within 2 weeks. Label the remaining jars with the recipe name and date before storing.

STIR IT UP!

Strawberry jam often separates after canning, so be sure to mix it well before serving.

PERFECT PEACHES

This recipe requires mashed peaches, so be sure that your peaches are fully ripe and soft enough to mash. If they're not, however, simply place peeled, pitted, chopped peaches in a saucepan with ½ cup (120 ml) of water. Simmer for 5 minutes to soften them and then mash. (There is no need to drain the water after cooking—simply mash the peach mixture as is.)

ALL-FRUIT CHERRY-PEACH JAM

Cherries and peaches are so naturally sweet that they're especially suitable for an all-fruit jam. For the sweetest, most delicious jam, select peaches and cherries that are at peak ripeness and be sure to choose a sweet cherry variety—Bing cherries are a good option. This jam is so intensely fruity that you'll be hard-pressed not to eat it by the spoonful right out of the jar. It's also delicious swirled into a bowl of yogurt.

METHOD: Boiling Water Bath Canning
PROCESSING TIME: 10 minutes
YIELD: 4 half-pint (235 ml) jars

---

1 pound (455 g) fully ripe peaches*

1 pound (455 g) sweet cherries*

¼ cup (60 ml) lemon juice

4 teaspoons (20 ml)
calcium water**

1 cup (235 ml) unsweetened
apple juice concentrate

3 teaspoons (9 g) Pomona's
pectin powder

Not sure how much fruit to purchase? See Measuring Up! on page 33.

**For information on how to prepare calcium water, refer to page 30.*

1. Peel and remove pits from peaches and then mash the peaches in a large bowl. Set aside. (For more information, see How to Skin a Peac on page 145.)

2. Rinse cherries, remove stems, slice in half and remove pits, and then chop the cherries—by hand with a chef's knife or with a food processor. (For more information, see Painless Pitting on page 152.)

3. Combine the mashed peaches and the chopped cherries and mix well. Measure 3 cups (700 ml) of the fruit mixture (saving any extra for another use) and combine the measured quantity in a saucepan with lemon juice and calcium water. Mix well.

4. In a separate pan, bring apple juice concentrate to a boil. Carefully pour hot juice concentrate into a blender or food processor and then add pectin powder. Vent the lid and blend for 1 to 2 minutes, stopping to scrape down sides with a rubber spatula as needed, until powder is thoroughly dissolved. Set aside.

5. Bring cherry-peach mixture to a full boil over high heat and then slowly add the pectin–juice concentrate mixture, stirring constantly. Continue to cook and stir jam for 1 minute as the jam comes back up to a boil. Once the jam returns to a full boil, remove it from the heat.

6. Ladle hot jam into hot, sterilized jars, leaving ¼ inch (6 mm) of headspace.

7. Remove trapped air bubbles, wipe rims with a damp cloth, put on lids and screw bands, and tighten to fingertip tight.

8. Lower filled jars into water bath canner. Place lid on canner, return to a rolling boil, and process for 10 minutes (adjusting for altitude if necessary; see Adjust for Altitude! on page 29).

9. Remove jars with a jar lifter and allow to cool undisturbed on a clean dish towel away from any drafts for 12 to 24 hours. Confirm that jars have sealed properly. Refrigerate any jars that have not sealed and use within 2 weeks. Label the remaining jars with the recipe name and date before storing.

CUSTOMIZE IT!

If you're looking for something new, why not substitute some different fruits? In place of or in combination with the cherry and peach in this recipe, use pear, apricot, mango, fig, or sweet plum—or use a combination of any of these fruits.

HONEYED GINGER-PEACH JAM

The combination of ginger and peach is one of my favorites—the subtle heat of the ginger sets off the straight-ahead sweetness of fully ripe peaches just a bit, and the honey adds additional depth to this jam. Enjoy it with scones on a warm summer morning!

METHOD: Boiling Water Bath Canning
PROCESSING TIME: 10 minutes
YIELD: 4 to 5 half-pint (235 ml) jars

3¼ pounds (1.5 kg) fully ripe peaches* (For more information, see Perfect Peaches! on page 142.)

2 teaspoons peeled, finely grated ginger (For more information, see Grate That Ginger! on page 118.)

¼ cup (60 ml) lemon juice

4 teaspoons (20 ml) calcium water**

½ cup (170 g) honey

3 teaspoons (9 g) Pomona's pectin powder

Not sure how much fruit to purchase? See Measuring Up! on page 33.

**For information on how to prepare calcium water, refer to page 30.*

1. Peel and remove pits from peaches and then mash the peaches in a large bowl.

2. Measure 4 cups (946 ml) of mashed peaches (saving any extra for another use) and combine the measured quantity in a saucepan with grated ginger, lemon juice, and calcium water. Mix well.

3. In a separate bowl, combine honey and pectin powder. Mix thoroughly and set aside.

4. Bring peach mixture to a full boil over high heat. Slowly add pectin-honey mixture, stirring constantly. Continue to stir vigorously for 1 to 2 minutes to dissolve pectin while the jam comes back up to a boil. Once the jam returns to a full boil, remove it from the heat.

5. Ladle hot jam into hot, sterilized jars, leaving ¼ inch (6 mm) of headspace.

6. Remove trapped air bubbles, wipe rims with a damp cloth, put on lids and screw bands, and tighten to fingertip tight.

7. Lower filled jars into water bath canner. Place lid on canner, return to a rolling boil, and process for 10 minutes (adjusting for altitude if necessary; see Adjust for Altitude! on page 29).

8. Remove jars with a jar lifter and allow to cool undisturbed on a clean dish towel away from any drafts for 12 to 24 hours. Confirm that jars have sealed properly. Refrigerate any jars that have not sealed and use within 2 weeks. Label the remaining jars with the recipe name and date before storing.

HOW TO SKIN A PEACH

If you are dealing with a small quantity of fruit, slice off peach (or nectarine) skins with a paring knife (pitting and quartering the fruit first). However, if you're doubling the recipe and are working with a lot of fruit, you may want to blanch them to remove the skins instead. Simply drop peaches or nectarines one at a time into boiling water for about 30 to 60 seconds and then remove and immediately dunk in cold water. You should then be able to slip the skins right off.

PERFECT PEARS!

This recipe requires mashed pears, so be sure that your pears are fully ripe and soft enough to mash. If they're not, however, simply place peeled, cored, chopped pears in a saucepan with ½ cup (120 ml) of water. Simmer for 5 minutes to soften them and then mash. (There is no need to drain the water after cooking—simply mash the pear mixture as is.)

SPICED PEAR-CRANBERRY JAM

In my mind, pear and cranberry say autumn like few other fruits do, and with the addition of a few warming spices, I can't imagine a better jam to enjoy in cool weather and perhaps around the holidays. In this recipe, the cranberries are cooked whole, which gives this jam a toothsome, slightly chunky texture that I really enjoy. However, if you're not a fan of whole cranberries, feel free to coarsely chop them in your food processor before cooking them.

METHOD: Boiling Water Bath Canning

PROCESSING TIME: 10 minutes

YIELD: 4 to 5 half-pint (235 ml) jars

---

2 pounds (900 g) fully ripe pears*

1 bag (12 ounces, or 340 g) cranberries

¾ cup (175 ml) water

½ teaspoon ground cinnamon

¼ teaspoon ground nutmeg

¼ teaspoon ground ginger

¼ cup (60 ml) lemon juice

4 teaspoons (20 ml) calcium water**

1 cup (200 g) sugar

3 teaspoons (9 g) Pomona's pectin powder

Not sure how much fruit to purchase? See Measuring Up! on page 33.

**For information on how to prepare calcium water, refer to page 30.*

1. Peel and core pears and then mash pears in a large bowl. Set aside.

2. Rinse cranberries and then combine in a saucepan with the ¾ cup (175 ml) of water. Bring to a boil over high heat, reduce heat, and then simmer, covered, for 10 minutes or until fruit is soft and most cranberries have burst, stirring occasionally. Remove from heat and lightly mash cranberries.

3. Combine mashed cranberries and mashed pears and mix well. Measure 4 cups (946 ml) of the fruit mixture (saving any extra for another use) and return the measured quantity to the saucepan. Add cinnamon, nutmeg, ground ginger, lemon juice, and calcium water. Mix well.

4. In a separate bowl, combine sugar and pectin powder. Mix thoroughly and set aside.

5. Bring fruit mixture to a full boil over high heat. Slowly add the pectin-sugar mixture, stirring constantly. Continue to stir vigorously for 1 to 2 minutes to dissolve pectin while the jam comes back up to a boil. Once the jam returns to a full boil, remove it from the heat.

6. Ladle hot jam into hot, sterilized jars, leaving ¼ inch (6 mm) of headspace.

7. Remove trapped air bubbles, wipe rims with a damp cloth, put on lids and screw bands, and tighten to fingertip tight.

8. Lower filled jars into water bath canner. Place lid on canner, return to a rolling boil, and process for 10 minutes (adjusting for altitude if necessary; see Adjust for Altitude! on page 29).

9. Remove jars with a jar lifter and allow to cool undisturbed on a clean dish towel away from any drafts for 12 to 24 hours. Confirm that jars have sealed properly. Refrigerate any jars that have not sealed and use within 2 weeks. Label the remaining jars with the recipe name and date before storing.

STRAWBERRY-MANGO JAM

This delicious, pink jam is a perfect combination of the full-on, exotic sweetness of ripe mangoes, with the luscious, fragrant, slightly tart flavor of in-season, locally grown strawberries. I can't imagine a better jam to enjoy on muffins, outside, on a warm June morning.

METHOD: Boiling Water Bath Canning

PROCESSING TIME: 10 minutes

YIELD: 4 to 5 half-pint (235 ml) jars

---

1 pound (455 g) strawberries*

2 pounds (900 g) fully ripe mangoes*

2 tablespoons (28 ml) lemon juice

3 teaspoons (15 ml) calcium water**

1 cup (200 g) sugar

2½ teaspoons (7.5 g) Pomona's pectin powder

Not sure how much fruit to purchase? See Measuring Up! on page 33.

**For information on how to prepare calcium water, refer to page 30.*

1. Rinse strawberries, remove stems, and mash in a large bowl. Set aside.

2. Peel and pit mangoes and then mash in a large bowl.

3. Measure 2 cups (475 ml) of mashed mango and 2 cups (475 ml) of mashed strawberries (saving any extra for another use) and combine the measured quantities in a saucepan with lemon juice and calcium water. Mix well.

4. In a separate bowl, combine sugar and pectin powder. Mix thoroughly and set aside.

5. Bring fruit mixture to a full boil over high heat. Slowly add pectin-sugar mixture, stirring constantly. Continue to stir vigorously for 1 to 2 minutes to dissolve pectin while the jam comes back up to a boil. Once the jam returns to a full boil, remove it from the heat.

6. Ladle hot jam into hot, sterilized jars, leaving ¼ inch (6 mm) of headspace.

7. Remove trapped air bubbles, wipe rims with a damp cloth, put on lids and screw bands, and tighten to fingertip tight.

8. Lower filled jars into water bath canner. Place lid on canner, return to a rolling boil, and process for 10 minutes (adjusting for altitude if necessary; see Adjust for Altitude! on page 29).

9. Remove jars with a jar lifter and allow to cool undisturbed on a clean dish towel away from any drafts for 12 to 24 hours. Confirm that jars have sealed properly. Refrigerate any jars that have not sealed and use within 2 weeks. Label the remaining jars with the recipe name and date before storing.

DO THE MANGO MASH!

This recipe calls for mashed mangoes, so be sure that your mangoes are fully ripe and soft enough to mash. They'll also be much sweeter if they're fully ripe. If you simply can't wait for full ripeness, however, place peeled, pitted, chopped mango in a saucepan with ½ cup (120 ml) of water. Simmer for 5 minutes to soften and then mash mango by hand or purée in a food processor, being careful not to liquefy it. (There's no need to drain the water after cooking—simply mash or purée the mango mixture as is.)

APPLE-MAPLE JAM

Even though maple syrup is made in the spring, I tend to think of it as an autumn sort of flavor, and perhaps that's why I enjoy it so much paired with apples. This simple, homey, mildly spiced jam is delicious on toast, of course, but it also makes a great filling or topping for turnovers, croissants, mini-tarts, and other baked goods. For the best texture, use crisp, hard apples that will retain their shape when cooked—Granny Smiths are a good choice.

METHOD: Boiling Water Bath Canning

PROCESSING TIME: 10 minutes

YIELD: 4 to 5 half-pint (235 ml) jars

---

2 pounds (900 g) apples*

2 cups (473 ml) water

½ teaspoon ground cinnamon

⅓ cup (80 ml) lemon juice

4 teaspoons (20 ml) calcium water**

½ cup (120 ml) maple syrup

3 teaspoons (9 g) Pomona's pectin powder

*Not sure how much fruit to purchase? See Measuring Up! on page 33.

**For information on how to prepare calcium water, refer to page 30.

1. Peel apples, remove stems and cores, and dice.

2. Combine diced apples in a saucepan with the 2 cups (473 ml) of water. Bring to a boil over high heat, reduce heat, and then simmer, covered, for 5 to 10 minutes or until apples are soft, stirring occasionally. Remove from heat.

3. Measure 4 cups (946 ml) of cooked apples (saving any extra for another use) and return the measured quantity to the saucepan. Add cinnamon, lemon juice, and calcium water and mix well.

4. In a separate bowl, combine maple syrup and pectin powder. Mix thoroughly and set aside.

5. Bring apple mixture back to full boil over high heat. Slowly add pectin–maple syrup mixture, stirring constantly. Continue to stir vigorously for 1 to 2 minutes to dissolve pectin while the jam comes back up to a boil. Once the jam returns to a full boil, remove it from the heat.

6. Ladle hot jam into hot, sterilized jars, leaving ¼ inch (6 mm) of headspace.

7. Remove trapped air bubbles, wipe rims with a damp cloth, put on lids and screw bands, and tighten to fingertip tight.

8. Lower filled jars into water bath canner. Place lid on canner, return to a rolling boil, and process for 10 minutes (adjusting for altitude if necessary; see Adjust for Altitude! on page 29).

9. Remove jars with a jar lifter and allow to cool undisturbed on a clean dish towel away from any drafts for 12 to 24 hours. Confirm that jars have sealed properly. Refrigerate any jars that have not sealed and use within 2 weeks. Label the remaining jars with the recipe name and date before storing.

GO FOR THE REAL THING!

There is a lot of imitation maple syrup on grocery store shelves. Be sure to get the real thing. Check the label—what you're looking for is 100 percent pure maple syrup. It's a bit pricey, but it's so worth it!

PEAR-GINGER JAM

I never tire of ginger's subtle, unique heat, and because of its warmth, it's a perfect flavor for fall. In my mind, the pear is truly the queen of fall fruit, so the combination of the two is a natural—and an absolutely delicious one at that. For a scrumptious treat, try this earthy, mildly spiced jam slathered on waffles on a cool autumn morning!

METHOD: Boiling Water Bath Canning

PROCESSING TIME: 10 minutes

YIELD: 4 to 5 half-pint (235 ml) jars

3¼ pounds (1.5 kg) fully ripe pears* (For more information, see Perfect Pears! on page 146.)

1 tablespoon (8 g) peeled, finely grated ginger (For more information, see Grate That Ginger! on page 118.)

¼ cup (60 ml) lemon juice

4 teaspoons (20 ml) calcium water**

1¼ cups (250 g) sugar

3 teaspoons (9 g) Pomona's pectin powder

*Not sure how much fruit to purchase? See Measuring Up! on page 33.

**For information on how to prepare calcium water, refer to page 30.

1. Peel and core pears and then mash pears in a large bowl.

2. Measure 4 cups (946 ml) of mashed pear (saving any extra for another use) and combine the measured quantity in a saucepan with grated ginger, lemon juice, and calcium water. Mix well.

3. In a separate bowl, combine sugar and pectin powder. Mix thoroughly and set aside.

4. Bring fruit mixture to a full boil over high heat. Slowly add pectin-sugar mixture, stirring constantly. Continue to stir vigorously for 1 to 2 minutes to dissolve pectin while the jam returns to a boil. Once the jam returns to a full boil, remove it from the heat.

5. Ladle hot jam into hot, sterilized jars, leaving ¼ inch (6 mm) of headspace.

6. Remove trapped air bubbles, wipe rims with a damp cloth, put on lids and screw bands, and tighten to fingertip tight.

7. Lower filled jars into water bath canner. Place lid on canner, return to a rolling boil, and process for 10 minutes (adjusting for altitude if necessary; see Adjust for Altitude! on page 29).

8. Remove jars with a jar lifter and allow to cool undisturbed on a clean dish towel away from any drafts for 12 to 24 hours. Confirm that jars have sealed properly. Refrigerate any jars that have not sealed and use within 2 weeks. Label the remaining jars with the recipe name and date before storing.

CUSTOMIZE IT!

If you're looking for something a little different, why not try honey instead of sugar in this recipe? In place of the sugar, use ½ to 1 cup (170 to 340 g) of honey.

STRAWBERRY-PINEAPPLE JAM WITH HONEY

If you love strawberry jam but are looking for something just a little bit different, give this delightful jam a try. Pineapple adds a little bit of tropical flair, and honey adds an earthy twist. Canned pineapple makes this jam quick to make, and because the pineapple is so naturally sweet, very little extra sweetener is necessary, so the flavors of both fruits really shine through.

METHOD: Boiling Water Bath Canning

PROCESSING TIME: 10 minutes

YIELD: 4 to 5 half-pint (235 ml) jars

---

1 pound (455 g) strawberries*

1 can (20 ounces, or 560 g) crushed, unsweetened pineapple in its own juice

2 teaspoons calcium water**

⅓ cup (115 g) honey

2 teaspoons Pomona's pectin powder

Not sure how much fruit to purchase? See Measuring Up! on page 33.

**For information on how to prepare calcium water, refer to page 30.*

1. Rinse strawberries, remove stems, and mash in a large bowl. Add crushed pineapple (do not drain) and mix well to combine.

2. Measure 4 cups (946 ml) of the strawberry-pineapple mixture (saving any extra for another use) and combine the measured quantity in a saucepan with calcium water. Mix well.

3. In a separate bowl, combine honey and pectin powder. Mix thoroughly and set aside.

4. Bring strawberry-pineapple mixture to a full boil over high heat. Slowly add pectin-honey mixture, stirring constantly. Continue to stir vigorously for 1 to 2 minutes to dissolve pectin while the jam returns to a boil. Once the jam returns to a full boil, remove it from the heat.

5. Ladle hot jam into hot, sterilized jars, leaving ¼ inch (6 mm) of headspace.

6. Remove trapped air bubbles, wipe rims with a damp cloth, put on lids and screw bands, and tighten to fingertip tight.

7. Lower filled jars into water bath canner. Place lid on canner, return to a rolling boil, and process for 10 minutes (adjusting for altitude if necessary; see Adjust for Altitude! on page 29).

8. Remove jars with a jar lifter and allow to cool undisturbed on a clean dish towel away from any drafts for 12 to 24 hours. Confirm that jars have sealed properly. Refrigerate any jars that have not sealed and use within 2 weeks. Label the remaining jars with the recipe name and date before storing.

PAINLESS PITTING

Pitting cherries is really not hard, and it doesn't take that long. A cherry pitter (a handheld device that removes pits) is handy—and if you have one already, great—but it's certainly not necessary. All of the recipes in this book call for either cherry halves or chopped cherries, so simply slice cherries in half vertically with a paring knife and pick out the pit with your fingers. It's as easy as that!

SWEET CHERRY JAM

Adapted from a recipe by jam-maker Sally Gecks, this delightful, deep-red jam is a great option for cherry lovers who are keeping an eye on their sugar intake. It also makes a great on-the-go breakfast by layering it in a jar with some plain yogurt and granola. Be sure to use sweet cherries for this recipe—widely available Bing cherries are a great option. Unsweetened black cherry juice, sold in bottles, is available at most natural food stores.

METHOD: Boiling Water Bath Canning

PROCESSING TIME: 10 minutes

YIELD: 4 to 5 half-pint (235 ml) jars

---

2 pounds (900 g) sweet cherries*

1 cup (235 ml) unsweetened black cherry juice

¼ cup (60 ml) lemon juice

4 teaspoons (20 ml) calcium water**

⅓ cup (67 g) sugar

3 teaspoons (9 g) Pomona's pectin powder

Not sure how much fruit to purchase? See Measuring Up! on page 33.

**For information on how to prepare calcium water, refer to page 30.*

1. Rinse cherries, remove stems, slice in half, remove pits, and then chop the cherries—by hand with a chef's knife or with a food processor.

2. Combine chopped cherries and black cherry juice and mix well. Measure 4 cups (946 ml) of the cherry mixture (saving any extra for another use) and combine the measured quantity in a saucepan with lemon juice and calcium water. Mix well.

3. In a separate bowl, combine sugar and pectin powder. Mix thoroughly and set aside.

4. Bring fruit to a full boil over high heat. Slowly add sugar-pectin mixture, stirring constantly. Continue to stir vigorously for 1 to 2 minutes to dissolve pectin while the jam comes back up to a boil. Once the jam returns to a full boil, remove it from the heat.

5. Ladle hot jam into hot, sterilized jars, leaving ¼ inch (6 mm) of headspace.

6. Remove trapped air bubbles, wipe rims with a damp cloth, put on lids and screw bands, and tighten to fingertip tight.

7. Lower filled jars into water bath canner. Place lid on canner, return to a rolling boil, and process for 10 minutes (adjusting for altitude if necessary; see Adjust for Altitude! on page 29).

8. Remove jars with a jar lifter and allow to cool undisturbed on a clean dish towel away from any drafts for 12 to 24 hours. Confirm that jars have sealed properly. Refrigerate any jars that have not sealed and use within 2 weeks. Label the remaining jars with the recipe name and date before storing.

FRUIT JELLIES

Jellies are quite distinct from other pectin-jelled goods. Most jelled goods consist primarily of fruit that has been jelled, whereas jellies are the jelled *juice* of the fruit—or, in some cases, an infused liquid. Occasionally, a jelly will have something suspended in it—small pieces of pepper in a hot pepper jelly, for example—but generally speaking, jellies are smooth. Jellies can be intensely fruity and full-bodied but because they are made from juice or an infused liquid, harnessing the essence of an item, rather than the item itself, jellies can also be very refined. They lend themselves nicely to flavors derived from items you might not necessarily want to eat whole and that are perhaps a bit more subtle, such as flowers or herbs. There is quite a diverse selection of flavors that can be incorporated into jellies. I've tried to include a wide variety of flavors and flavor combinations in this section—as well as a few classics, of course.

CRANAPPLE JELLY

Cranberry and apple is a classic flavor combination, and this brilliant, translucent, bright-red jelly highlights these two spectacular fall fruits. The tartness of the cranberries offsets the sweetness of the apples beautifully in this jelly, which makes a delicious—and gorgeous—addition to a warm bowl of steel-cut oats or any autumn breakfast spread.

METHOD: Boiling Water Bath Canning

PROCESSING TIME: 10 minutes

YIELD: 4 to 5 half-pint (235 ml) jars

2¼ pounds (1 kg) apples*

1 bag (12 ounces, or 340 g) cranberries

3 cups (700 ml) water

¼ cup (60 ml) lemon juice

4 teaspoons (20 ml) calcium water**

1½ cups (300 g) sugar

4 teaspoons (12 g) Pomona's pectin powder

Not sure how much fruit to purchase? See Measuring Up! on page 33.

**For information on how to prepare calcium water, refer to page 30.*

1. Peel and core apples, if desired, and then chop. (For more information, see Pit and Peel … Or Not? on page 155.)

2. Rinse cranberries and then combine in a saucepan with chopped apples and the 3 cups (700 ml) of water. Bring to a boil over high heat, reduce heat, and simmer, covered, for 7 to 15 minutes or until fruit is soft, stirring occasionally. Remove from heat and mash the fruit.

3. Transfer mashed fruit to a damp jelly bag or layered cheesecloth, suspend over a bowl, and allow juice to drip until dripping stops—at least 2 hours. Discard fruit pulp or save for another use.

4. Measure 4 cups (946 ml) of the fruit juice (if you're short on juice, see Where's the Juice? On page 162 for more information) and combine in a saucepan with lemon juice and calcium water.

5. In a separate bowl, combine sugar and pectin powder. Mix thoroughly and set aside.

6. Bring fruit juice to a full boil over high heat and then slowly add pectin-sugar mixture, stirring constantly. Continue to stir vigorously for 1 to 2 minutes to dissolve pectin while the jelly comes back up to a boil. Once the jelly returns to a full boil, remove it from the heat.

7. Ladle hot jelly into hot, sterilized jars, leaving ¼ inch (6 mm) of headspace.

8. Remove trapped air bubbles, wipe rims with a damp cloth, put on lids and screw bands, and tighten to fingertip tight.

9. Lower filled jars into water bath canner. Place lid on canner, return to a rolling boil, and process for 10 minutes (adjusting for altitude if necessary; see Adjust for Altitude! on page 29).

10. Remove jars with a jar lifter and allow to cool undisturbed on a clean dish towel away from any drafts for 12 to 24 hours. Confirm that jars have sealed properly. Refrigerate any jars that have not sealed and use within 2 weeks. Label the remaining jars with the recipe name and date before storing.

PIT AND PEEL . . . OR NOT?

Because jelly making requires only the juice of the fruit, peeling, pitting, coring, and de-stemming are not essential. Skipping this step is certainly quicker, so the choice is yours. I prefer to remove pits, peels, cores, and stems, however, as it allows me to use the fruit pulp afterward for something else.

SIMPLE CLASSIC: APPLE JELLY

Apple jelly is a fall favorite, and it's a great way to use up extra apples during apple season. Even slightly soft apples that may have been hanging around for a while will work well for this recipe, as long as they are in good condition otherwise. With your pantry stocked, you'll be able to enjoy the lovely taste of apples in this delicate, golden jelly throughout the winter months! This is an easy recipe to start with if you're new to jelly making.

METHOD: Boiling Water Bath Canning

PROCESSING TIME: 10 minutes

YIELD: 4 to 5 half-pint (235 ml) jars

---

4 pounds (1.8 kg) apples*

4 cups (946 ml) water

¼ cup (60 ml) lemon juice

4 teaspoons (20 ml)
calcium water**

1 cup (200 g) sugar

4 teaspoons (12 g) Pomona's
pectin powder

*Not sure how much fruit to purchase?
See Measuring Up! on page 33.*

**For information on how to prepare
calcium water, refer to page 30.*

1. Peel and core apples, if desired, and then chop. (For more information, see Pit and Peel … or Not? on page 156.) Combine chopped apples in a saucepan with the 4 cups (946 ml) of water. Bring to a boil over high heat, reduce heat, and simmer, covered, for 7 to 15 minutes or until fruit is soft, stirring occasionally. Remove from heat and mash apples.

2. Transfer mashed fruit to a damp jelly bag or layered cheesecloth, suspend over a bowl, and allow juice to drip until dripping stops—at least 2 hours. Discard fruit pulp or save for another use.

3. Measure out 4 cups (946 ml) of the fruit juice (if you're short on juice, see Where's the Juice? on page 162 for more information) and combine in a saucepan with lemon juice and calcium water.

4. In a separate bowl, combine sugar and pectin powder. Mix thoroughly and set aside.

5. Bring juice to a full boil over high heat and then slowly add pectin-sugar mixture, stirring constantly. Continue to stir vigorously for 1 to 2 minutes to dissolve pectin while the jelly comes back up to a boil. Once the jelly returns to a full boil, remove it from the heat.

6. Ladle hot jelly into hot, sterilized jars, leaving ¼ inch (6 mm) of headspace.

7. Remove trapped air bubbles, wipe rims with a damp cloth, put on lids and screw bands, and tighten to fingertip tight.

8. Lower filled jars into water bath canner. Place lid on canner, return to a rolling boil, and process for 10 minutes (adjusting for altitude if necessary; see Adjust for Altitude! on page 29).

9. Remove jars with a jar lifter and allow to cool undisturbed on a clean dish towel away from any drafts for 12 to 24 hours. Confirm that jars have sealed properly. Refrigerate any jars that have not sealed and use within 2 weeks. Label the remaining jars with the recipe name and date before storing.

CUSTOMIZE IT!

If you're looking for something new, why not try honey instead of sugar? In place of the sugar in this recipe, use ½ to 1 cup (170 to 340 g) honey.

SIMPLE CLASSIC: RASPBERRY JELLY

This dramatic, deep-red jelly is the essence of raspberry, intensified in a jar, and it's nothing short of amazing. It's also an easy recipe to start with if you're new to jelly making. Raspberries are precious, and jelly requires a lot of them, but if you're a true raspberry lover, the results will be worth it. Spread it on a piece of pound cake, layer it with some fresh fruit and whipped cream, or turn it into a trifle if you're really feeling fancy.

METHOD: Boiling Water Bath Canning
PROCESSING TIME: 10 minutes
YIELD: 4 to 5 half-pint (235 ml) jars

---

4 pounds (1.8 kg) raspberries*

⅓ cup (80 ml) water

4 teaspoons (20 ml) calcium water**

1½ cups (300 g) sugar

4 teaspoons (12 g) Pomona's pectin powder

*Not sure how much fruit to purchase? See Measuring Up! on page 33.

**For information on how to prepare calcium water, refer to page 30.

1. Carefully pick through raspberries, removing stems and any damaged parts. Rinse raspberries only if necessary. Combine in a saucepan with the ⅓ cup (80 ml) of water. Bring to a boil over high heat, reduce heat, and simmer, covered, for 1 to 2 minutes, stirring occasionally. Remove from heat and mash raspberries. (For more information and an alternative, see Cook or Just Crush? on page 166.)

2. Transfer mashed fruit to a damp jelly bag or layered cheesecloth, suspend over a bowl, and allow juice to drip until dripping stops—at least 2 hours. Discard fruit pulp or save for another use.

3. Measure 4 cups (946 ml) of the juice (if you're short on juice, see Where's the Juice? on page 162 for more information) and combine in a saucepan with calcium water.

4. In a separate bowl, combine sugar and pectin powder. Mix thoroughly and set aside.

5. Bring the juice mixture to a full boil over high heat and then slowly add pectin-sugar mixture, stirring constantly. Continue to stir vigorously for 1 to 2 minutes to dissolve pectin while the jelly comes back up to a boil. Once the jelly returns to a full boil, remove it from the heat.

6. Ladle hot jelly into hot, sterilized jars, leaving ¼ inch (6 mm) of headspace.

7. Remove trapped air bubbles, wipe rims with a damp cloth, put on lids and screw bands, and tighten to fingertip tight.

8. Lower filled jars into water bath canner. Place lid on canner, return to a rolling boil, and process for 10 minutes (adjusting for altitude if necessary; see Adjust for Altitude! on page 29).

9. Remove jars with a jar lifter and allow to cool undisturbed on a clean dish towel away from any drafts for 12 to 24 hours. Confirm that jars have sealed properly. Refrigerate any jars that have not sealed and use within 2 weeks. Label the remaining jars with the recipe name and date before storing.

CUSTOMIZE IT!

If you're looking for something new, why not try different fruits? In place of or in combination with the raspberry in this recipe, use sour blackberry, currant, or strawberry—or use a combination of any of these fruits.

BLUEBERRY-VANILLA JELLY

A fresh vanilla bean adds a fragrant note of the exotic to just about any fruit, and this combination of blueberry and vanilla is one of my favorites. Try this luscious, deep-blue jelly slathered between the two layers of a cake for a spectacular, unexpected treat.

METHOD: Boiling Water Bath Canning
PROCESSING TIME: 10 minutes
YIELD: 4 to 5 half-pint (235 ml) jars

3½ pounds (1.6 kg) blueberries*

½ cup (120 ml) water

1 vanilla bean

¼ cup (60 ml) lemon juice

4 teaspoons (20 ml)
    calcium water**

1 cup (200 g) sugar

4 teaspoons (12 g) Pomona's
    pectin powder

Not sure how much fruit to purchase? See Measuring Up! on page 33.

**For information on how to prepare calcium water, refer to page 30.*

1. Rinse blueberries, remove stems, and combine in a saucepan with the ½ cup (120 ml) of water. Bring to a boil over high heat, reduce heat, and simmer, covered, for 3 to 5 minutes, stirring frequently. Remove from heat and mash the blueberries.

2. Transfer mashed fruit to a damp jelly bag or layered cheesecloth, suspend over a bowl, and allow juice to drip until dripping stops—at least 2 hours. Discard fruit pulp or save for another use.

3. Measure 4 cups (946 ml) of the fruit juice (if you're short on juice, see Where's the Juice? on page 162 for more information) and pour into a saucepan. Using a paring knife, slice the vanilla bean in half lengthwise and scrape out the seeds. Add the vanilla seeds and the vanilla bean pod itself to the juice, along with the lemon juice and calcium water. Mix well.

4. In a separate bowl, combine sugar and pectin powder. Mix thoroughly and set aside.

5. Bring the blueberry mixture to a full boil over high heat and then slowly add pectin-sugar mixture, stirring constantly. Continue to stir vigorously for 1 to 2 minutes to dissolve pectin while the jelly comes back up to a boil. Once the jelly returns to a full boil, remove it from the heat. Using tongs, carefully remove the vanilla bean pod and discard.

6. Ladle hot jelly into hot, sterilized jars, leaving ¼ inch (6 mm) of headspace.

7. Remove trapped air bubbles, wipe rims with a damp cloth, put on lids and screw bands, and tighten to fingertip tight.

8. Lower filled jars into water bath canner. Place lid on canner, return to a rolling boil, and process for 10 minutes (adjusting for altitude if necessary; see Adjust for Altitude! on page 29).

9. Remove jars with a jar lifter and allow to cool undisturbed on a clean dish towel away from any drafts for 12 to 24 hours. Confirm that jars have sealed properly. Refrigerate any jars that have not sealed and use within 2 weeks. Label the remaining jars with the recipe name and date before storing.

FROZEN EASE!

You can substitute frozen berries for the fresh, and if you don't have a lot of time, this is a good option. Simply cook the berries and then mash them as the recipe calls for.

WHERE'S THE JUICE?

What do you do if your jelly bag is done dripping, but you don't have enough juice? Slowly pour extra hot water— a very small amount at a time—onto the fruit pulp in the jelly bag, making sure it mixes with the fruit and drips out slowly, until you have the quantity of juice needed. Alternatively, you can dump the fruit pulp back in the pot with some extra water, cook for a few minutes, and then return the fruit to the jelly bag or cheesecloth to continue dripping until you have enough juice.

HONEYED PLUM-CARDAMOM JELLY

If you're lucky enough to have a plum tree (or have a friend who does!), and you have access to a good quantity of fresh plums in season, give this gorgeous, deep-purple jelly a try! Laced with the subtle, quietly complex flavor of cardamom, this jelly is a sophisticated accompaniment to scones at breakfast or afternoon tea.

METHOD: Boiling Water Bath Canning

PROCESSING TIME: 10 minutes

YIELD: 4 to 5 half-pint (235 ml) jars

---

4 pounds (1.8 kg) ripe,
   sweet plums*

1¼ cups (296 ml) water

1½ teaspoons ground cardamom

¼ cup (60 ml) lemon juice

5 teaspoons (25 ml)
   calcium water**

1 cup (340 g) honey

5 teaspoons (15 g) Pomona's
   pectin powder

Not sure how much fruit to purchase? See Measuring Up! on page 33.

**For information on how to prepare calcium water, refer to page 30.*

1. Rinse, remove pits, and quarter plums and then combine in a saucepan with the 1¼ cups (285 ml) of water. Bring to a boil over high heat, reduce heat, and simmer, covered, for 7 to 15 minutes or until fruit is soft, stirring occasionally. Remove from heat and mash plums.

2. Transfer mashed fruit to a damp jelly bag or layered cheesecloth, suspend over a bowl, and allow juice to drip until dripping stops—at least 2 hours. Discard fruit pulp or save for another use.

3. Measure 4 cups (946 ml) of the fruit juice (if you're short on juice, see Where's the Juice? on page 162 for more information) and combine in a saucepan with cardamom, lemon juice, and calcium water.

4. In a separate bowl, combine honey and pectin powder. Mix thoroughly and set aside.

5. Bring fruit juice to a full boil over high heat and then slowly add pectin-honey mixture, stirring constantly. Continue to stir vigorously for 1 to 2 minutes to dissolve pectin while the jelly comes back up to a boil. Once the jelly returns to a full boil, remove it from the heat.

6. Ladle hot jelly into hot, sterilized jars, leaving ¼ inch (6 mm) of headspace.

7. Remove trapped air bubbles, wipe rims with a damp cloth, put on lids and screw bands, and tighten to fingertip tight.

8. Lower filled jars into water bath canner. Place lid on canner, return to a rolling boil, and process for 10 minutes (adjusting for altitude if necessary; see Adjust for Altitude! on page 29).

9. Remove jars with a jar lifter and allow to cool undisturbed on a clean dish towel away from any drafts for 12 to 24 hours. Confirm that jars have sealed properly. Refrigerate any jars that have not sealed and use within 2 weeks. Label the remaining jars with the recipe name and date before storing.

ROSEMARY-WINE JELLY

This jelly calls for fresh herbs, and if you're fortunate enough to have a potted rosemary plant that you can bring indoors in the winter (as many herb-lovers do), you can make this jelly year-round. It makes a delicious glaze for roasted meats, and it is a perfect accompaniment to winter holiday meals and on other special occasions.

METHOD: Boiling Water Bath Canning
PROCESSING TIME: 10 minutes
YIELD: 4 to 5 half-pint (235 ml) jars

---

1 cup (27 g) coarsely chopped, firmly packed fresh rosemary leaves and stems

4¼ cups (1.1 L) dry white wine

½ cup (120 ml) white wine vinegar, minimum 5 percent acidity

4 teaspoons (20 ml) calcium water*

1 cup (200 g) sugar

4 teaspoons (12 g) Pomona's pectin powder

For information on how to prepare calcium water, refer to page 30.

1. Combine chopped fresh rosemary and the dry white wine in a saucepan and bring to a boil. Remove from heat, cover, and allow to steep for 20 minutes.

2. Using a fine mesh strainer or cheesecloth, drain the rosemary and discard, reserving the infused liquid.

3. Measure 4 cups (946 ml) of infused liquid (if necessary, add extra dry white wine to meet the required measurement) and return the measured quantity to the (clean) saucepan. Add vinegar and calcium water and mix well.

4. In a separate bowl, combine sugar and pectin powder. Mix thoroughly and set aside.

5. Bring infused liquid to a full boil over high heat. Slowly add pectin-sugar mixture, stirring constantly. Continue to stir vigorously for 1 to 2 minutes to dissolve pectin while the jelly comes back up to a boil. Once the jelly returns to a full boil, remove it from the heat.

6. Ladle hot jelly into hot, sterilized jars, leaving ¼ inch (6 mm) of headspace.

7. Remove trapped air bubbles, wipe rims with a damp cloth, put on lids and screw bands, and tighten to fingertip tight.

8. Lower filled jars into water bath canner. Place lid on canner, return to a rolling boil, and process for 10 minutes (adjusting for altitude if necessary; see Adjust for Altitude! on page 29).

9. Remove jars with a jar lifter and allow to cool undisturbed on a clean dish towel away from any drafts for 12 to 24 hours. Confirm that jars have sealed properly. Refrigerate any jars that have not sealed and use within 2 weeks. Label the remaining jars with the recipe name and date before storing.

TOUGH STUFF!

Mature rosemary plants often have tough stems that can be difficult to cut. Trying to chop these stems with a knife as you would other herbs can be an exercise in frustration. Instead, use scissors—they work beautifully!

COOK OR JUST CRUSH?

When you're dealing with juicy fruit such as strawberries, raspberries, or blackberries, it's not essential to cook your fruit with water before juicing them. You can simply mash fresh berries and then hang them in your jelly bag or cheesecloth to drip. It's your choice. I prefer to cook the berries first—with a tiny bit of water for just a couple of minutes—as I find it gets the juices flowing more easily.

STRAWBERRY-BALSAMIC JELLY

I adore the flavor combination of strawberry and balsamic, and this beautiful, dark-red jelly is particularly intriguing because, with just a small amount of balsamic vinegar, it straddles the line between a straight-ahead sweet jelly and a savory, more complex jelly. It's delicious atop scones at brunch, and it is equally good served with your favorite cheese in the evening as an appetizer.

METHOD: Boiling Water Bath Canning

PROCESSING TIME: 10 minutes

YIELD: 4 to 5 half-pint (235 ml) jars

---

4 pounds (1.8 kg) strawberries*

½ cup (120 ml) water

¼ cup (60 ml) balsamic vinegar, minimum 5 percent acidity

4 teaspoons (20 ml) calcium water**

1 cup (200 g) sugar

4 teaspoons (12 g) Pomona's pectin powder

Not sure how much fruit to purchase? See Measuring Up! on page 33.

**For information on how to prepare your calcium water, refer to page 30.*

1. Rinse strawberries and remove stems. Combine strawberries in a saucepan with the ½ cup (120 ml) of water and bring to a boil over high heat. Reduce heat and simmer, covered, for 2 to 4 minutes, stirring frequently. Remove from heat and mash strawberries. (Or, for an alternative method, see Cook or Just Crush? on page 166.)

2. Transfer mashed strawberries to a damp jelly bag or layered cheesecloth, suspend over a bowl, and allow juice to drip until it stops—at least 2 hours. Discard fruit pulp or save for another use.

3. Measure 4 cups (946 ml) of the strawberry juice (if you're short on juice, see Where's the Juice on page 162 for more information) and pour into a saucepan. Add balsamic vinegar and calcium water and mix well.

4. In a separate bowl, combine the sugar and the pectin powder. Mix thoroughly and set aside.

5. Bring the juice mixture to a full boil over high heat and then slowly add the pectin-sugar mixture, stirring constantly. Continue to stir vigorously for 1 to 2 minutes to thoroughly dissolve pectin as the jelly comes back up to a boil. Once the jelly returns to a full boil, remove it from the heat.

6. Ladle hot jelly into hot, sterilized jars, leaving ¼ inch (6 mm) of headspace.

7. Remove trapped air bubbles, wipe rims with a damp cloth, put on lids and screw bands, and tighten to fingertip tight.

8. Lower filled jars into water bath canner. Place lid on canner, return to a rolling boil, and process for 10 minutes (adjusting for altitude if necessary; see Adjust for Altitude! on page 29).

9. Remove jars with a jar lifter and allow to cool undisturbed on a clean dish towel away from any drafts for 12 to 24 hours. Confirm that jars have sealed properly. Refrigerate any jars that have not sealed and use within 2 weeks. Label the remaining jars with the recipe name and date before storing.

Chapter 6

MEATS

We raise our own meat here on the farm, so we know just how precious and valuable meat truly is. These days, we endeavor to make meat more of a supporting character in recipes than the main star. Yet, reducing the amount of meat you eat makes it even more important that the meat you use is of the best quality and flavor.

The same goes when buying meat. More of us than ever are paying attention to where our meat comes from, asking important questions of our producers. How were the animals raised? What were they fed? The answers have a very real impact on the quality of the meat you buy.

Since meat tends to be the most expensive item on any grocery list, avoiding waste is always important. Buying the proper amount for a canning recipe will help you stretch your dollars, as will having a canning recipe at the ready to take advantage of a sale at the grocery store.

Those new to canning may wonder why you should bother canning meat at all. Inferior canned meats, including heavily processed meat and fish, have given canned products a bad name. However, we need only look at gourmet foods and the foods of other countries to realize it doesn't have to be this way. Take, for example, some of the newer "canned" tunas on the market that come in pouches instead of cans. These packages often contain better quality tuna that has received better treatment during processing. Canned tuna can be delicious without drowning it in mayonnaise for tuna salad! Another example is the canned meat and fish in European countries, such as Spain and Portugal. It is not uncommon in a tapas bar to have something locally canned.

CAUTION

While most grocery stores are very good about reducing the price of meat well before a "best by" date, use caution when shopping sales. Even though the meat will be brought to a high temperature when pressure canning, there is no magical "undo" button for meat that is past its prime. Don't take the risk if you find meat with a bad date or that shows other signs it is past its prime. If you wouldn't grill it, don't can it.

When canning meat at home, you're sure to change minds as well. Canning meat locks in all the flavor. While it doesn't necessarily look appetizing or sound appetizing (a jar of juicy cherries will always conjure up a nicer mental image than a jar of juicy meat), the reality is that canned meat enhances recipes. And don't forget about canned recipes that contain meat, too. That's right, in this chapter we'll also make soups and stocks.

While these recipes will guide you in a similar manner as those in the other chapters in this book, this seems like a good place to run through a few general rules and best practices for canning meat and fish.

THE BASICS

When canning meat, your first task is to find the freshest meat. If you're used to shopping at the grocery store, you may need to talk to a local butcher about the signs of how to spot fresh meat from meat that's a few days old. Common signs of fresh meat include flesh that is firm but not too dry—it bounces back quickly when pressed with a finger. Meat should also not have any strong odors. That goes for fish as well—fishy smelling fish should never be canned. You will also need to confirm the meat hasn't been previously frozen. Frozen meat or fish will have an inferior texture when canned, even if thawed before canning.

Time will be your enemy from start to finish when canning meat. You want to move your meat through the canning cycle as soon as possible and that means getting it from butcher to jars quickly. Bacteria grow fast on meats and moving efficiently through the process is the only way to be safe. Only prepare enough meat for one canner's worth of jars at a time. Do not keep meat sitting at room temperature for too long at any time—including while you make the recipe.

If you do find you have too much meat to can all at once, keep it refrigerated at 32°F to 38°F (0°C to 3.3°C). Can it no later than the next day or use it for another recipe that doesn't require canning.

There are numerous ways to cut the meat, but, before you decide on that, you'll need to trim the meat well. Remove any bruising, fat, and silver skin you see. Fat can keep your jars from sealing well, and it can also develop a strong flavor with some types of meats. Fatty meats can also spoil more easily than lean meats. Don't worry about removing every speck, but do a thorough job trimming and you will appreciate the result.

Before you cut the meat, review your recipe. It will probably have a suggestion for how to process the meat; deviating greatly from that could make the recommended canning time unsafe. The other consideration is the meat itself. You may want to cut it with or against the grain.

The most common ways to cut meat for canning are into cubes or strips or grinding it. With cubed meat, the goal is to create those perfect bite-size pieces. Whether the meat will go in a soup recipe or be canned on its own, cutting the pieces as uniform as possible is key. Just like with vegetables or fruit, if you have pieces that are much smaller than the rest, they will overcook—and the big danger is letting a few large cubes slip through. If they don't hit the proper temperature at the center during canning, they can harbor harmful bacteria.

Cutting meat into strips is a common treatment for steaks or roasts. If you're cooking a recipe that calls for strips, I recommend cutting *against the grain* of the meat so the strips will fit in the jar lengthwise. Cutting against the grain will result in more tender pieces. Just as with cubed meat, cutting uniformly thick strips is key. Do not can any strips that are much thicker than what the recipe specifies.

Ground meat probably looks the least appetizing once canned, yet it's also the most useful type of meat in my pantry. Ground meat is family friendly and used in many comforting recipes, from red sauce to stroganoff. Having canned ground meat on hand also makes for an easy addition to casseroles and soups. Ground meat doesn't have to be beef either. Your butcher will happily grind fresh pork, chicken, or turkey. I recommend seasoning ground meat very lightly before canning. As you may use it in any number of recipes once you open the jar, if you have heavily seasoned beef, you may end up oversalting a sauce or stew.

You'll notice many recipes call for browning meat before canning. This step is key, as it's what makes your canned meat taste so much better than the "cooked in the can" variety. The browned layer goes through what is called the *Maillard reaction*, a complex interaction of sugars and amino acids that is only possible under high heat. Since you'll be fully cooking the meat when canning, the goal is usually just to create that browned layer, not cook the meat all the way through.

To make things easier when packing and unpacking jars, use wide-mouth jars when canning meat. Always leave the proper headspace as stated in the recipe and do not fill the jars too tightly. Also, while it might be tempting to thicken the canning liquid, resist the urge. You can always thicken it after you open the jars—it's a quick process to turn the thin canned sauce into a rich, thick gravy.

THINGS TO AVOID

Following are a few things to avoid when canning meat:

- **A water bath canner.** Canning meat and fish *must be done in a pressure canner.* All meats and seafood are low-acid foods and unsafe to can using a boiling water bath canner. You may have heard otherwise, but doing so is highly dangerous. It not only ruins expensive food, but can make you or your loved ones incredibly sick.

- **Thick sauces or gravies.** When canning meats, you cannot include a very thick gravy in the jar. Your meat will release its own juices and you can certainly thicken that juice when reheated, so *any gravy added to canned meats should be thin.* A good rule of thumb is to make any gravy-type liquid no thicker than tomato sauce in the jar. This allows good penetration of heat throughout the jar and into the center of each piece of meat.

- **Anything experimental.** When you can meat, it is important to follow proven recipes from reliable sources. It is no time to try new recipes or tweak the one you have. If needed, adjust the seasoning when it comes out of the jar.

CUBED PORK

We have a standing order with our butcher that I pick up each fall. He knows to call me the minute the meat is ready, as I want to get it home quickly to freeze or can. With pork, you have a good amount of leeway in the cuts you choose. As long as the meat is lean, you can cube it and can it according to the following recipe. I tend to can a variety of cuts in different base liquids to use throughout the year. Can pork in tomato juice for the beginning of a stew, in broth, or simply in salted water. The plainer the pork going in, the more versatile it is coming out—but you may find you like it best with the added flavor of broth. Whatever you choose, don't skip the browning! The flavor the pork picks up while browning can't be replicated by searing it after you can it.

METHOD: Pressure Canning

PROCESSING TIME: 1 hour, 15 minutes

PRESSURE: 10 pounds (68.9 kPa) Weighted Gauge, 11 pounds (75.8 kPa) Dial Gauge

YIELD: 4 pints (1.9 L)

---

3 pounds (1.4 kg) lean pork, trimmed of fat and cubed

1 quart (946 ml) water, tomato juice, or broth

1 teaspoon canning salt or 4 cubes of bouillon (optional)

1. In a large skillet over medium-high heat, lightly brown the pork, stirring, until it's between halfway and fully cooked. Remove the pork from the pan and set aside.

2. In a medium-size saucepan over medium-high heat, heat your liquid of choice until it reaches a boil.

3. Divide the pork evenly among hot, sterilized jars. Pour the hot liquid over the top, leaving 1 inch (2.5 cm) of headspace. If you'd like, add ¼ teaspoon salt or a bouillon cube to each jar.

4. Remove any air bubbles with a plastic or wooden utensil, adding more hot liquid as needed to maintain the proper 1-inch (2.5 cm) headspace.

5. Wipe the rims and seal the jars hand-tight with the 2-piece lids.

6. Carefully transfer the filled jars to the rack inside the pressure canner. Process the jars at the pressure listed above for 1 hour, 15 minutes.

7. Let the canner return to 0 pounds pressure (0.7 kPa). Wait 10 minutes more and then carefully open the canner lid according to the manufacturer's instructions.

8. With a jar lifter, remove the jars and place them on a clean dish towel away from any drafts. Allow to cool undisturbed for 12 to 24 hours and then check the seals. If any jars have not sealed properly, refrigerate them and use the pork within 1 week. Label the remaining jars with the recipe name and date before storing.

GROUND MEAT

Folks, this is it: the most useful (and some say the tastiest) protein in my pantry. It's always a family-wide disappointment when we run out of ground meat as I use homemade beef, pork, chicken, and turkey in a wide variety of recipes. You'll see every bit of flavor is kept in the jars during the canning process. With all that flavor, there's no need to oversalt the meat or your dish. In fact, adding too much salt is a classic mistake—salty meat added to a perfectly seasoned soup or sauce can ruin it. As with all meats, I recommend adjusting the seasonings only after cooking and canning safely.

METHOD: Pressure Canning

PROCESSING TIME: 1 hour, 15 minutes

PRESSURE: 10 pounds (68.9 kPa) Weighted Gauge, 11 pounds (75.8 kPa) Dial Gauge

YIELD: 4 pints (1.9 L)

---

4 pounds (1.8 kg) ground meat of choice

1 quart (946 ml) water, tomato juice, or broth

1 teaspoon canning salt or 4 cubes of bouillon (optional)

1. In a large skillet over medium-high heat and working in batches if necessary, fry the meat until it is lightly browned and about halfway cooked. Don't overload your pan trying to cook all the meat at once—the browning is crucial to this recipe.

2. In a medium-size saucepan over medium-high heat, heat your liquid of choice until it reaches a boil.

3. Divide the ground meat among hot, sterilized jars, packing it loosely. Pour the hot liquid into the hot jars over the meat, leaving 1 inch (2.5 cm) of headspace. If you'd like, add ¼ teaspoon salt or a bouillon cube to each jar.

4. Remove any air bubbles with a plastic or wooden utensil, adding more hot liquid as needed to maintain the proper 1-inch (2.5 cm) headspace.

5. Wipe the rims and seal the jars hand-tight with the 2-piece lids.

6. Carefully transfer the filled jars to the rack inside the pressure canner. Process the jars at the pressure listed above for 1 hour, 15 minutes.

7. Let the canner return to 0 pounds pressure (0.7 kPa). Wait 10 minutes more and then carefully open the canner lid according to the manufacturer's instructions.

8. With a jar lifter, remove the jars and place them on a clean dish towel away from any drafts. Allow to cool undisturbed for 12 to 24 hours and then check the seals. If any jars have not sealed properly, refrigerate them and use the meat within 1 week. Label the remaining jars with the recipe name and date before storing.

CANNED CHICKEN

Commercially made canned chicken must be one of the more dreadful canned meats. Chicken doesn't have the strong flavor of foods like tuna to cover the flavor imparted by the can. As if the producers wanted to make it worse, the quality of meat used for canned chicken is often not as high as chicken sold fresh. It may well be a blend of cuts, labeled as "with rib meat" or similar. Obviously, homemade canned chicken doesn't suffer from the same problems. You choose the cuts and quality and you process it in jars instead of cans. This chicken is ready straight from the can and not just for chicken salad. Try it in any recipe where you'd use a store-bought rotisserie chicken. My family is partial to wrapping it as chicken verde burritos.

METHOD: Pressure Canning

PROCESSING TIME: 1 hour, 15 minutes

PRESSURE: 10 pounds (68.9 kPa) Weighted Gauge, 11 pounds (75.8 kPa) Dial Gauge

YIELD: 4 pints (1.9 L)

---

4 pounds (1.8 kg) boneless, skinless chicken, trimmed of fat and cut into 1-inch (2.5 cm) cubes

1 teaspoon canning salt (optional)

1. Fill hot, sterilized jars loosely with the raw chicken, leaving 1¼ inches (3.1 cm) of headspace (see Note). Add ¼ tsp salt to each jar, if desired.

2. Wipe the rims and seal the jars hand-tight with the 2-piece lids.

3. Carefully transfer the filled jars to the rack inside the pressure canner. Process the jars at the pressure listed above for 1 hour, 15 minutes.

4. Let the canner return to 0 pounds pressure (0.7 kPa). Wait 10 minutes more and then carefully open the canner lid according to the manufacturer's instructions.

5. With a jar lifter, remove the jars and place them on a clean dish towel away from any drafts. Allow to cool undisturbed for 12 to 24 hours and then check the seals. If any jars have not sealed properly, refrigerate them and use the chicken within 1 week. Label the remaining jars with the recipe name and date before storing.

NOTE

Yes, the headspace for this recipe is more than 1 inch (2.5 cm), so there's a bit of extra room in the jars. The chicken will release its natural juices during cooking, so you will not need to add water before canning.

CANNED HADDOCK

Living on the coast, canning seafood and fish just makes sense. It's a "local" food, after all. Although I freeze much of it, having it ready to eat on the shelf provides another option. It's become a yearly tradition for my family to order haddock from a local fisherman and can it right after the catch. I use this mild-flavored fish like I would tuna: for fish burgers, in fish soup, and as the star of savory chowders. By keeping the flavoring plain when canning, it's easy to spice it up however I need to for a meal. I can dozens of jars, but there is no need to save so much of it if your family doesn't eat as much fish. If you can buy fresh fish in any quantity, try to save some for your shelf. It's wonderful!

METHOD: Pressure Canning

PROCESSING TIME: 1 hour, 40 minutes

PRESSURE: 10 pounds (68.9 kPa) Weighted Gauge, 11 pounds (75.8 kPa) Dial Gauge

YIELD: 6 pints (2.8 L)

---

12 pounds (5.4 kg) haddock, or similar freshwater fish fillets

6 teaspoons (36 g) canning salt

1. Make sure your fillets don't have any stray entrails, scales, or pieces of the head, tail, or fins. Cut the fish into pieces short enough to fit in the jars, keeping in mind the 1-inch (2.5 cm) required headspace. Cut the pieces as close as possible to uniform thickness. Fill the hot, sterilized jars with the fish, placing the pieces around the outside of the jar for a neater look and filling the center with the less than perfect pieces, leaving a 1-inch (2.5 cm) headspace.

2. Add 1 teaspoon of salt to each jar. Like canned chicken, you do not need to add any water to fill the jars.

3. Wipe the rims and seal the jars hand-tight with the 2-piece lids.

4. Carefully transfer the filled jars to the rack inside the pressure canner. Process the jars at the pressure listed above for 1 hour, 40 minutes.

5. Let the canner return to 0 pounds pressure (0.7 kPa). Wait 10 minutes more and then carefully open the canner lid according to the manufacturer's instructions.

6. With a jar lifter, remove the jars and place them on a clean dish towel away from any drafts. Allow to cool undisturbed for 12 to 24 hours and then check the seals. If any jars have not sealed properly, refrigerate them and use the fish within 1 week. Label the remaining jars with the recipe name and date before storing.

Chapter 7

SAUCES AND CONDIMENTS

They are the most versatile duo in your pantry. With just a little preparation and planning, the options for incorporating your sauces and condiments into your favorite dishes are almost unlimited. Whether you're in the mood for a kick from your favorite chutney or craving the sweetness of a rhubarb relish—or something in between—you'll find what you need amidst this fun and delicious collection.

CARROT AND DAIKON PICKLE

Bring a bit of Asian flair to your table with these simple pickles. Daikons (large, white Asian radishes) can be found at many farmers' markets and are becoming more popular in produce sections.

METHOD: Boiling Water Bath Canning
PROCESSING TIME: 15 minutes
YIELD: 3 pints (1.4 L)

---

1 pound (455 g) carrots, peeled and cut into matchsticks

3 pounds (1.4 kg) daikon radish, peeled and cut into matchsticks

4 teaspoons (20 g) kosher salt

1 cup (200 g) sugar, divided

2 cups (475 ml) rice vinegar, minimum 5 percent acidity

1 cup (235 ml) warm water

1. In a bowl, combine the carrots, daikon, salt, and a teaspoon of sugar. Let sit until the vegetables have wilted slightly and liquid pools at the bottom of the bowl, about 30 minutes. Drain vegetables; rinse and pat dry with paper towels. Transfer vegetables to a medium bowl.

2. In a saucepan, whisk together the remaining sugar, vinegar, and water. Bring to a boil and then simmer for 10 minutes.

3. Pack daikon radishes and carrots into hot, sterilized jars and cover with hot syrup, leaving a ½-inch (1.3 cm) headspace.

4. Remove any air bubbles. Wipe rims and secure lids.

5. Process half-pints (235 g) or pints (473 g) for 15 minutes in a boiling water bath canner, adjusting for altitude if necessary (see Adjust for Altitude! on page 29).

6. Use a jar lifter to remove the jars and let cool undisturbed on a clean dish towel away from any drafts. Check the seals after 12 to 24 hours. Refrigerate any unsealed jars and use within 2 weeks. Label the remaining jars with the recipe name and date before storing.

LEMONGRASS SYRUP

There are hundreds of ways to use this versatile syrup. Try ladling it over cakes or fruit salads or adding a tablespoon (15 ml) per glass to iced tea or lemonade.

METHOD: Boiling Water Bath Canning
PROCESSING TIME: 20 minutes
YIELD: 4 pints (1.9 L)

---

3 cups (600 g) sugar

3 cups (700 ml) water

3 cups (700 ml) white grape juice

8 lemongrass stalks (core only), sliced

4 lemongrass stalks (core only), cut to 3-inch (7.5 cm) pieces

1. In a saucepan, combine sugar, water, grape juice, and lemongrass slices and pieces. Simmer over medium heat for 10 minutes, stirring frequently.

2. Using tongs, remove lemongrass stalk pieces from syrup and place into hot, sterilized canning jars.

3. Strain syrup to remove lemongrass slices. Pour into jars, leaving a ½-inch (1.3 cm) headspace.

4. Remove any air bubbles. Wipe rims and secure lids.

5. Process for 20 minutes in a boiling water bath canner, adjusting for altitude if necessary (see Adjust for Altitude! on page 29).

6. Use a jar lifter to remove the jars and let cool undisturbed on a clean dish towel away from any drafts. Check the seals after 12 to 24 hours. Refrigerate any unsealed jars and use within 2 weeks. Label the remaining jars with the recipe name and date before storing.

Below are 3 fun cocktail ideas using lemongrass syrup.

LEMONGRASS MOJITO

In a cocktail shaker, combine 4 sprigs of fresh mint with a tablespoon (15 ml) of lemongrass syrup. Muddle mint and syrup (you can use the back of a spoon). Add a jigger (44 ml) of rum and ½ cup (4 cubes) of ice. Shake and pour all into a tall glass. Top with club soda. Garnish with a small stalk of lemongrass.

LEMONGRASS GIN FIZZ

In a cocktail shaker, mix a tablespoon (15 ml) of lemongrass syrup, ¼ teaspoon of lime juice, and a jigger (44 ml) of gin. Shake and pour into a cocktail glass. Top with either tonic water or ginger ale. Garnish with a lime wedge.

SIMPLE RUM SIPPER

In a highball, mix a tablespoon (15 ml) of lemongrass syrup with a jigger (44 ml) of rum and juice from a fresh lime. Add ice and top with club soda for a refreshing cocktail.

MANGO CHUTNEY

This makes a great side with many meals. We've toned down the spices in this recipe—if you like it fiery hot, simply add more cayenne pepper!

METHOD: Boiling Water Bath Canning
PROCESSING TIME: 15 minutes
YIELD: 8 half-pint (1.9 L) jars

---

9 pounds (4.1 kg) green mangoes, peeled, pitted, and sliced (see sidebar below)

1 cup (200 g) sugar

1 cup (235 ml) grape juice

2 cups (475 ml) cider vinegar, minimum 5 percent acidity

2 medium onions, chopped

2 red bell peppers, chopped

1 cup (145 g) raisins

1 tablespoon (18 g) salt

1½ teaspoons fresh ginger, finely chopped

¼ teaspoon cayenne pepper

1 teaspoon dry mustard

1 teaspoon ground cinnamon

1 tablespoon (7 g) ground cloves

2 garlic cloves, minced

Juice from 2 limes, plus zest

1. Place mango slices flat on a baking sheet. Sprinkle with 2 teaspoons of salt. Set aside for 8 to 12 hours (this removes the excess liquid).

2. Add sugar, grape juice, and vinegar to a saucepan or stockpot. Bring to a boil and then reduce to simmer.

3. Dice mangoes.

4. Add mangoes and remaining ingredients to saucepan or stockpot. Simmer for 30 to 45 minutes, stirring often.

5. Ladle into hot, sterilized half-pint (235 ml) jars, leaving a ¼-inch (6 mm) headspace.

6. Remove any air bubbles. Wipe rims and secure lids.

7. Process in a boiling water bath canner for 15 minutes, adjusting for altitude if necessary (see Adjust for Altitude! on page 29).

8. Use a jar lifter to remove the jars and let cool undisturbed on a clean dish towel away from any drafts. Check the seals after 12 to 24 hours. Refrigerate any unsealed jars and use within 2 weeks. Label the remaining jars with the recipe name and date before storing.

MANGO MADNESS!

Mangoes can be maddening if you don't know how to prepare them To cut up a mango with ease, hold the mango upright and starting from the top, slice down along one of the flat sides of the mango, cutting close along the flat side of the pit, slicing off as much flesh as possible. Then, repeat the process on the opposite flat side of the mango. Gently score the flesh of each of the sliced-off sides of the mango in a grid pattern and then push the skins inside out and carefully slice the mango cubes off the skins. Also, slice off and cut up any flesh remaining on the pit before discarding skins and pit.

NECTARINE-RASPBERRY PRESERVES

These preserves can be eaten alone or used to make a fruit crisp, pie, or bars.

METHOD: Boiling Water Bath Canning

PROCESSING TIME: Pints (473 ml)
30 minutes; Quarts (946 ml)
35 minutes

YIELD: 4 quarts (3.8 L)

---

10 pounds (4.5 kg) nectarines,
peeled and cut into bite-sized
pieces

1 quart (946 ml) plus 6 cups
(1.4 L) water, divided

3 Vitamin C tablets (500 mg each)

4 cups (946 ml) apple or white
grape juice

2 cups (475 ml) water

½ cup (100 g) sugar

3 pounds (1.4 kg) raspberries,
washed

1. Soak nectarines in a solution of 1 quart (946 ml) of water mixed with 3 crushed Vitamin C tablets for 2 to 3 minutes to prevent discoloration. Leave fruit in solution until ready to use.

2. Heat 6 cups (1.4 L) of water, apple or white grape juice, and sugar to a simmer. Add nectarines and cook for 5 minutes.

3. Use a slotted spoon to move nectarines from pan. Place in hot, sterilized quart (946 ml) jars. Add raspberries to jars. Fill with hot syrup. Add more boiling water if necessary, leaving a ½-inch (1.3 cm) headspace.

4. Remove any air bubbles. Wipe rims and secure lids.

5. Process in a boiling water bath canner: 30 minutes for pints (473 ml) and 35 minutes for quarts (946 ml), adjusting for altitude if necessary (see Adjust for Altitude! on page 29).

6. Use a jar lifter to remove the jars and let cool undisturbed on a clean dish towel away from any drafts. Check the seals after 12 to 24 hours. Refrigerate any unsealed jars and use within 2 weeks. Label the remaining jars with the recipe name and date before storing.

TOMATO TACO SAUCE

METHOD: Boiling Water Bath Canning

PROCESSING TIME: 20 minutes

YIELD: 7 pints (3.3 L)

---

20 pounds (9.1 kg) peeled, cored, finely chopped Roma tomatoes

2 garlic cloves, crushed

2½ cups (400 g) chopped onions

2 jalapeño peppers, seeded and chopped

2 long green chilis, seeded and chopped

1½ cups (355 ml) vinegar, minimum 5 percent acidity

1 tablespoon (18 g) salt

1½ tablespoons (9 g) ground black pepper

1 tablespoon (13 g) sugar

2 tablespoons (4 g) dried oregano

2 tablespoons (2 g) chopped cilantro

1 teaspoon ground cumin

1. Add all ingredients to a stockpot and cook at a simmer, stirring frequently until mixture thickens, about an hour.

   IMPORTANT: Do not add more onion or bell peppers than listed in this recipe unless you are using a pressure canner. These are low-acid vegetables and will reduce the acidity of the overall recipe to a level unsafe for boiling water bath canning. The added vinegar is also important to this and all salsa/hot sauce recipes for home canning. Vinegar increases the overall acidity of salsa and hot sauce recipes to ensure safe canning.

2. Purée in blender (be careful to only fill blender half full and use a towel to hold the lid down; hot liquids in blenders can be dangerous).

3. Fill sterilized pint jars (473 ml), leaving a ½-inch (1.3 cm) headspace.

4. Remove any air bubbles. Wipe rims and secure lids.

5. Process pints (473 ml) in a boiling water bath canner for 20 minutes, adjusting for altitude if necessary (see Adjust for Altitude! on page 29).

6. Use a jar lifter to remove the jars and let cool undisturbed on a clean dish towel away from any drafts. Check the seals after 12 to 24 hours. Refrigerate any unsealed jars and use within 2 weeks. Label the remaining jars with the recipe name and date before storing.

TACO SAUCE

Our version of Mexican night is pretty tame by most standards, but we love the slightly spicy taste of this recipe. Use it with the ground meat of your choice or get creative: I've found I can get as many vegetables as I want into my kids when I flavor them with this sauce. That said, it's not authentic. If you are a purist, be forewarned!

METHOD: Pressure Canning

PROCESSING TIME: 15 minutes

PRESSURE: 10 pounds (68.9 kPa) Weighted Gauge, 11 pounds (75.8 kPa) Dial Gauge

YIELD: 4 pints (1.9 L)

---

8 cups (1.4 kg) peeled, chopped, and drained tomatoes,

1 medium-size onion, chopped

1 cup (100 g) chopped scallion

½ cup (72 g) chopped seeded jalapeño peppers, or other green chile

4 garlic cloves, chopped

1 teaspoon salt

1 teaspoon chili powder

½ teaspoon ground cumin

1. In a saucepan over medium heat, combine the tomatoes, onion, scallion, jalapeños, garlic, salt, chili powder, and cumin. Stir to combine and bring to a simmer. Simmer for 30 minutes, stirring frequently.

2. Strain the sauce through a fine-mesh strainer and return it to the pan. Bring the sauce to a boil and cook for 5 minutes.

3. Carefully ladle the hot sauce into hot, sterilized jars, leaving 1 inch (2.5 cm) of headspace.

4. Remove any air bubbles with a plastic or wooden utensil, adding more hot sauce as needed to maintain the proper 1-inch (2.5 cm) headspace.

5. Wipe the rims and seal the jars hand-tight with the 2-piece lids.

6. Carefully transfer the filled jars to the rack inside the pressure canner. Process the jars at the pressure listed above for 15 minutes.

7. Let the canner return to 0 pounds pressure (0.7 kPa). Wait 10 minutes more and then carefully open the canner lid according to the manufacturer's instructions.

8. With a jar lifter, remove the jars and place them on a clean dish towel away from any drafts. Allow to cool undisturbed for 12 to 24 hours and then check the seals. If any jars have not sealed properly, refrigerate them and use the sauce within 2 weeks. Label the remaining jars with the recipe name and date before storing.

PEACH TOMATO SALSA

While I normally advocate only the freshest fruits and vegetables when canning, this salsa is an exception. It is a wonderful way to use peaches that aren't quite ripe. As with most fruit salsas, this is a great condiment not only for tacos, but for fish and chicken as well.

METHOD: Pressure Canning

PROCESSING TIME: 10 minutes

PRESSURE: 10 pounds (68.9 kPa) Weighted Gauge, 11 pounds (75.8 kPa) Dial Gauge

YIELD: 6 pints (2.8 L)

---

2 pounds (900 g) paste-type tomatoes, such as Roma

3 pounds (1.4 kg) peaches, chopped

2½ cups (400 g) chopped onion

2 cups (300 g) chopped green bell pepper

2 cups (300 g) chopped peeled apple

1 tablespoon (18 g) salt

1 teaspoon red pepper flakes

3¾ cups (845 g) packed light brown sugar

2¼ cups (535 ml) apple cider vinegar, minimum 5 percent acidity

¼ cup (25 g) pickling spice, tied in a muslin bag

1. Prepare an ice-water bath and bring a large saucepan of water to a boil.

2. Remove the tomato skins: Working 1 tomato at a time for best results, place the tomato into the boiling water for 1 minute. Transfer to the ice-water bath. The skins will split and peel off easily. Chop the peeled tomatoes.

3. Empty the pan and return it to medium-high heat. In it, combine the tomatoes, peaches, onion, green bell pepper, apple, salt, red pepper flakes, brown sugar, vinegar, and the muslin bag containing the pickling spices.

4. As the mixture starts to warm, stir to incorporate everything. Bring the mixture to a boil, stirring frequently to keep it from burning. Once the mixture boils, reduce the heat to low, and simmer for 30 minutes.

5. Remove and discard the muslin bag and turn off the heat.

6. Carefully ladle the salsa into hot, sterilized jars, leaving ½ inch (1.3 cm) of headspace.

7. Remove any air bubbles with a plastic or wooden utensil, adding more hot salsa as needed to maintain the proper ½-inch (1.3 cm) headspace.

8. Wipe the rims and seal the jars hand-tight with the 2-piece lids.

9. Carefully transfer the filled jars to the rack inside the pressure canner. Process the jars at the pressure listed above for 10 minutes.

10. Let the canner return to 0 pounds pressure (0.7 kPa). Wait 10 minutes more and then carefully open the canner lid according to the manufacturer's instructions.

11. With a jar lifter, remove the jars and place them on a clean dish towel away from any drafts. Allow to cool undisturbed for 12 to 24 hours and then check the seals. If any jars have not sealed properly, refrigerate them and use the salsa within 1 week. Label the remaining jars with the recipe name and date before storing.

TOMATILLO SALSA

For a change of pace, I like to make and serve this green, not-so-spicy salsa for everyday eating. If you're unfamiliar with tomatillo salsa, it is quite a departure from a classic red tomato salsa. The tomatillos have a unique flavor to start—tart, fruity, and slightly herbal. Throw in a good amount of vinegar and cilantro and you end up with a bright, fresh flavor. Use it as you would any salsa, as a dip or a topping for tacos. Or, try a recipe that features tomatillo salsa, such as enchiladas verde.

METHOD: Pressure Canning

PROCESSING TIME: 15 minutes

PRESSURE: 10 pounds (68.9 kPa) Weighted Gauge, 11 pounds (75.8 kPa) Dial Gauge

YIELD: 2 pints (946 ml)

---

2 pounds (900 g) tomatillos, cleaned, cored, and diced into small pieces

1 large onion, roughly chopped

4 large Anaheim chiles, seeded

4 garlic cloves, peeled

1 cup (235 ml) distilled white vinegar, minimum 5 percent acidity

¼ cup (60 ml) freshly squeezed lime juice (from about 2 limes)

2 tablespoons (2g) minced fresh cilantro leaves

2 teaspoons ground cumin

½ teaspoon canning salt

½ teaspoon red pepper flakes

1. Place the tomatillos in a large pot.

2. In a food processor, combine the onion, chiles, and garlic. Pulse a few times until the vegetables are broken into very small pieces. Add them to the tomatillos. Bring the mixture to a boil over high heat.

3. As the mixture starts to warm, add the vinegar, lime juice, cilantro, cumin, canning salt, and red pepper flakes. Stir well to incorporate the ingredients. Once the salsa boils, reduce the heat to low and simmer for 10 minutes.

4. Carefully ladle the hot salsa into hot, sterilized jars, leaving 1 inch (2.5 cm) of headspace.

5. Remove any air bubbles with a plastic or wooden utensil, adding more hot salsa as needed to maintain the proper 1-inch (2.5 cm) headspace.

6. Wipe the rims and seal the jars hand-tight with the 2-piece lids.

7. Carefully transfer the filled jars to the rack inside the pressure canner. Process the jars at the pressure listed above for 15 minutes.

8. Let the canner return to 0 pounds pressure (0.7 kPa). Wait 10 minutes more and then carefully open the canner lid according to the manufacturer's instructions.

9. With a jar lifter, remove the jars and place them on a clean dish towel away from any drafts. Allow to cool undisturbed for 12 to 24 hours and then check the seals. If any jars have not sealed properly, refrigerate them and use the salsa within 2 weeks. Label the remaining jars with the recipe name and date before storing.

GREEN TOMATO CHUTNEY

No matter how early I plant my tomatoes, I always end up with plenty that don't have a hint of red on them by first frost. I used to be upset by these stragglers until I found recipes like this that put green tomatoes to good use. Now, I'm actually quite happy if there are plenty of green tomatoes remaining at the end of gardening season.

METHOD: Pressure Canning

PROCESSING TIME: 10 minutes

PRESSURE: 10 pounds (68.9 kPa) Weighted Gauge, 11 pounds (75.8 kPa) Dial Gauge

YIELD: 4 pints (1.9 L)

---

10 paste-type tomatoes, such as Roma

2 onions, chopped

2 green bell peppers, seeded and chopped

2 garlic cloves, minced

2 chile peppers, such as Thai chiles, seeded and chopped (or include the seeds for more heat)

1 jalapeño pepper, seeded and chopped (or include the seeds for more heat)

¼ cup (60 ml) freshly squeezed lemon juice (from about 2 lemons)

1 tablespoon (18 g) salt

1 teaspoon freshly ground black pepper

2 tablespoons (2 g) chopped fresh cilantro leaves

1. Prepare an ice-water bath and bring a large pot of water to a boil.

2. Remove the tomato skins: Working 1 tomato at a time for best results, place the tomato into the boiling water for 1 minute. Transfer to the ice-water bath. The skins will split and peel off easily. Chop the peeled tomatoes.

3. Empty the pot and return it to medium-high heat. In it, combine the tomatoes, onions, green bell pepper, garlic, chile and jalapeño peppers, lemon juice, salt, black pepper, and cilantro. Stir to combine. Bring the mixture to a boil. Reduce the heat to low and simmer for 15 minutes, stirring frequently.

4. Carefully ladle the hot chutney into hot, sterilized jars, leaving ¾ inch (1.9 cm) of headspace.

5. Remove any air bubbles with a plastic or wooden utensil, adding more hot chutney as needed to maintain the proper ¾-inch (1.9 cm) headspace.

6. Wipe the rims and seal the jars hand-tight with the 2-piece lids.

7. Carefully transfer the filled jars to the rack inside the pressure canner. Process the jars at the pressure listed above for 10 minutes.

8. Let the canner return to 0 pounds pressure (0.7 kPa). Wait 10 minutes more and then carefully open the canner lid according to the manufacturer's instructions.

9. With a jar lifter, remove the jars and place them on a clean dish towel away from any drafts. Allow to cool undisturbed for 12 to 24 hours and then check the seals. If any jars have not sealed properly, refrigerate them and use the chutney within 2 weeks. Label the remaining jars with the recipe name and date before storing.

BARBECUE SAUCE

Every spring, we break out the grill long before the last snow. It must be funny to see us gathered around a smoking grill in our winter coats! With such a strong urge to grill, it's no surprise we use more barbecue sauce than the average family. I have to put up quite a bit so we don't run out.

Barbecue sauces vary by region and by personal preference, so I suppose I should tell you what our house sauce is like—it's thick but not too sweet, with just enough smoky flavor to enhance a good cut of meat. We usually wait until the food is cooked and add the sauce during the last minute or two. That way it flavors well, but the sugars in the sauce don't have a chance to burn.

METHOD: Pressure Canning

PROCESSING TIME: 15 minutes

PRESSURE: 10 pounds (68.9 kPa) Weighted Gauge, 11 pounds (75.8 kPa) Dial Gauge

YIELD: 2 pints (946 ml)

---

2 quarts (1.9 L) Roma tomatoes

1 cup (160 g) chopped onion

1 green bell pepper, seeded and chopped

1 hot pepper, such as jalapeño or serrano, seeded and minced

1 garlic clove, minced

½ cup (115 g) packed dark brown sugar

1½ teaspoons smoked paprika

1½ teaspoons salt

½ cup (120 ml) plus 2 tablespoons (28 ml) white or apple cider vinegar, minimum 5 percent acidity

1. Prepare an ice-water bath and bring a large saucepan of water to a boil.

2. Remove the tomato skins: Working 1 tomato at a time for best results, place the tomato into the boiling water for 1 minute. Transfer to the ice-water bath. The skins will split and peel off easily. Chop the peeled tomatoes.

3. In a large stockpot over medium heat, combine the chopped tomatoes, onion, green bell pepper, hot pepper, garlic, brown sugar, smoked paprika, salt, and vinegar. Cook for about 30 minutes until the vegetables are very soft.

4. Remove the pot from the heat and use an immersion blender or food mill to purée the sauce as much as possible. Strain the sauce through a fine-mesh to remove any large pieces. At this point, you should have a nice smooth sauce. Return the sauce to the heat and simmer until it has reduced by half, about 45 minutes.

5. Carefully ladle the hot barbecue sauce into hot, sterilized jars, leaving ½ inch (1.3 cm) of headspace.

6. Remove any air bubbles with a plastic or wooden utensil, adding more hot barbecue sauce as needed to maintain the proper ½-inch (1.3 cm) headspace.

7. Wipe the rims and seal the jars hand-tight with the 2-piece lids.

8. Carefully transfer the filled jars to the rack inside the pressure canner. Process the jars at the pressure listed above for 15 minutes.

9. Let the canner return to 0 pounds pressure (0.7 kPa). Wait 10 minutes more and then carefully open the canner lid according to the manufacturer's instructions.

10. With a jar lifter, remove the jars and place them on a clean dish towel away from any drafts. Allow to cool undisturbed for 12 to 24 hours and then check the seals. If any jars have not sealed properly, refrigerate them and use the barbecue sauce within 2 weeks. Label the remaining jars with the recipe name and date before storing.

TOMATO KETCHUP

Richer in tomato flavor and much less sweet, this is a reason to make french fries! Perhaps the most-used condiment on the farm, homemade ketchup isn't in the same category as the store-bought variety. If you have a picky eater or two who must have their favorite brand, you may not convert them.

METHOD: Pressure Canning

PROCESSING TIME: 10 minutes

PRESSURE: 10 pounds (68.9 kPa) Weighted Gauge, 11 pounds (75.8 kPa) Dial Gauge

YIELD: 4 pints (1.9 L)

---

13 pounds tomatoes, chopped

3 onions, chopped

4 cups (800 g) sugar

2 cups (475 ml) white or apple cider vinegar, 5%

3 teaspoons (18 g) salt

½ teaspoon ground cloves

½ teaspoon ground cinnamon

½ teaspoon dry mustard

½ teaspoon red pepper flakes

1. In a large stockpot over medium heat, combine the tomatoes and onions. Cook, stirring frequently, until the onions are soft.

2. Transfer the mixture to a cloth juice bag and hang above the pot or a large bowl. Let drain for 2 hours.

3. Meanwhile, prepare 4 pint jars and the canner: Clean the jars and prepare the 2-piece lids according to the manufacturer's guidelines. Keep the jars in hot but not boiling water until you're ready to use them. Prepare the canner by filling it with 2 to 3 inches (5 to 7.6 cm) of water and bringing it to a simmer, or according to your manufacturer's directions.

4. Run the drained pulp through a food mill or blend with an immersion blender to smooth out any seeds and skins. Return the smooth pulp mixture to the pot and place it over medium-high heat. Stir in the sugar, vinegar, salt, cloves, cinnamon, mustard, and red pepper flakes. Bring to a boil and boil for 10 minutes, stirring frequently.

5. Carefully ladle the hot ketchup into the hot jars, leaving ¾ inch (2 cm) of headspace.

6. Remove any air bubbles with a plastic or wooden utensil, adding more hot ketchup as needed to maintain the proper ¾-inch (2 cm) headspace.

7. Wipe the rims and seal the jars hand-tight with the 2-piece lids.

8. Carefully transfer the filled jars to the rack inside the pressure canner. Process the jars at the pressure listed above for 15 minutes.

9. Let the canner return to 0 pounds pressure. Wait 10 minutes more, then carefully open the canner lid according to the manufacturer's instructions.

10. With a jar lifter, remove the jars and place them on a clean dishtowel away from any drafts. Once the jars cool to room temperature, check the seals. If any jars have not sealed, refrigerate them and use the ketchup within 2 weeks.

PEPPER RELISH

AUGUST 1912

METHOD: Boiling Water Bath Canning
PROCESSING TIME: 5 minutes
YIELD: 9 half-pint (235 ml) jars

---

3 cups (450 g) red bell peppers, finely chopped

3 cups (450 g) green bell peppers, finely chopped

6 cups (960 g) onions, finely chopped

6 cups (1.4 L) vinegar, minimum 5 percent acidity

1½ cups (300 g) sugar

2 tablespoons (36 g) canning or pickling salt

1. Combine all together in a large pot and boil gently until thick and reduced by one-half.

2. Pack hot into hot, sterilized half-pint (235 ml) or pint (473 ml) jars, leaving ½ inch (1.3 cm) of headspace.

3. Remove any air bubbles. Wipe rims and secure lids.

4. Process for 5 minutes in a boiling water bath canner.

5. With a jar lifter, remove the jars and place them on a clean dish towel away from any drafts. Allow to cool undisturbed for 12 to 24 hours and then check the seals. If any jars have not sealed properly, refrigerate them and use within 2 weeks. Label the remaining jars with the recipe name and date before storing.

—*Adapted from the NCHFP website*

RHUBARB RELISH

JUNE 1938

This relish is delicious with meats.

¼ pound (55 g) raisins, chopped

½ pound (115 g) dates, chopped

3 cups (700 ml) vinegar, minimum 5 percent acidity

2 pounds (900 g) rhubarb

2 pounds (900 g) brown sugar

2 teaspoons ground ginger

1 tablespoon (18 g) canning or pickling salt

½ cup (60 g) walnuts, chopped

1. Cover raisins and dates with vinegar in a nonreactive bowl and let stand about an hour.
2. Wash rhubarb and cut in short lengths.
3. Combine raisin, date, and vinegar mixture with all ingredients except nuts.
4. Cook slowly until thick and clear—about 2 hours, stirring frequently.
5. Add nuts, cook 10 minutes longer.
6. Pack hot in hot, sterilized pint (473 ml) jars, seal, and store immediately in refrigerator.

—Mrs. D. C., Iowa

WILD GOOSEBERRY RELISH

AUGUST 1924

---

5 cups (750 g) wild gooseberries

1½ pounds (680 g) raisins

1 medium onion

3 tablespoons (54 g) salt

1 quart (946 ml) vinegar, minimum 5 percent acidity

1 cup (225 g) brown sugar

3 tablespoons (27 g) dry mustard

3 tablespoons (17 g) ground ginger

¼ teaspoon cayenne pepper

1 tablespoon (7 g) turmeric

1. Pick over, wash, and stem gooseberries.
2. Chop raisins and onion and add to gooseberries.
3. Place in kettle, add remaining ingredients, bring slowly to a boil, and simmer gently 45 minutes.
4. Strain through a coarse sieve.
5. Pack hot in hot, sterilized pint (473 ml) jars. Seal and store immediately in refrigerator.

GREEN TOMATO RELISH

SEPTEMBER 1913

METHOD: Boiling Water Bath Canning
PROCESSING TIME: 5 minutes
YIELD: 7 to 9 pints (3.3 to 4.3 L)

---

10 pounds (4.5 kg) small, hard green tomatoes

3 pounds (1.4 kg) mixed green and red bell pepper, diced

2 pounds (900 g) onions, diced

½ cup (144 g) canning or pickling salt

1 quart (946 ml) water

4 cups (800 g) sugar

1 quart (946 ml) cider vinegar, minimum 5 percent acidity

1 teaspoon each cinnamon, cloves, and mace in spice bag

⅓ cup (59 g) prepared yellow mustard

2 tablespoons (16 g) cornstarch

1. Wash tomatoes and chop fine.

2. Dissolve salt in water and pour over tomatoes in a large pot.

3. Bring to a boil, lower heat, and simmer 5 minutes.

4. Drain and return tomatoes to pot.

5. Add remaining ingredients, stir, and bring to a boil; lower heat and simmer 5 more minutes.

6. Discard spice bag and pack hot relish into hot, sterilized pint (473 ml) jars, leaving ½ inch (1.3 cm) of headspace.

7. Remove any air bubbles. Wipe the rims and secure lids.

8. Process for 5 minutes in a boiling water bath canner.

9. With a jar lifter, remove the jars and place them on a clean dish towel away from any drafts. Allow to cool undisturbed for 12 to 24 hours and then check the seals. If any jars have not sealed properly, refrigerate them and use within 2 weeks. Label the remaining jars with the recipe name and date before storing.

—Adapted from the NCHFP website

PICCALILLI

AUGUST 1932

METHOD: Boiling Water Bath Canning

PROCESSING TIME: 5 minutes

YIELD: 9 half-pint (235 ml) jars

---

6 cups (1.1 kg) green tomatoes, chopped

7½ cups (675 g) green cabbage, chopped

3 cups (450 g) red or green bell peppers, chopped

2¼ cups (360 g) onions, chopped

½ cup (144 g) canning or pickling salt

hot water

4½ cups (1.1 L) vinegar, minimum 5 percent acidity

3 cups (675 g) brown sugar

½ tablespoon mustard seeds

2 sticks cinnamon

½ tablespoon whole black peppercorns

¾ tablespoon whole cloves

¾ tablespoon whole allspice berries

1-inch (2.5 cm) piece fresh ginger

⅛ teaspoon cayenne pepper

1. Combine vegetables with salt in a large bowl and pour over hot water to cover. Let stand 12 hours.

2. Drain and squeeze dry in a clean kitchen towel.

3. Mix vinegar and sugar in a large kettle; add spices in spice bag and bring to a boil.

4. Add vegetables, return to boil, and boil gently for 30 minutes.

5. Discard spice bag. Pack hot into hot, sterilized half-pint (235 ml) jars, leaving ½ inch (1.3 cm) of headspace.

6. Pour over hot pickling liquid, again leaving ½ inch (1.3 cm) of headspace.

7. Remove any air bubbles. Wipe rims and secure lids.

8. Process for 5 minutes in a boiling water bath canner.

9. With a jar lifter, remove the jars and place them on a clean dish towel away from any drafts. Allow to cool undisturbed for 12 to 24 hours and then check the seals. If any jars have not sealed properly, refrigerate them and use within 2 weeks. Label the remaining jars with the recipe name and date before storing.

—Adapted from the NCHFP website

APPLE INDIAN CHUTNEY

SEPTEMBER 1935

This is a hot, delicious sauce.

6 pounds (2.7 kg) sour apples, peeled, cored, and chopped fine

2 lemons, chopped fine, peel and all, seeds removed

2 cups (290 g) raisins, chopped fine

2 hot green peppers

1 large onion, chopped

2 pounds (900 g) brown sugar

1 tablespoon (11 g) mustard seeds

1 tablespoon (6 g) ground ginger

½ tablespoon canning or pickling salt

3 cups (700 ml) vinegar, minimum 5 percent acidity

1. Mix apple with lemon to keep from turning dark.

2. Remove seeds from peppers and chop.

3. Combine all ingredients.

4. Bring to a boil and cook slowly until apples are tender.

5. Pack hot in hot, sterilized pint (473 ml) jars, seal, and store immediately in refrigerator.

Chapter 8

STOCKS, BROTHS, SOUPS, AND STEWS

Stocks and soups fill my pantry. They're great for saving lots of money and getting fast, healthy meals on the table in minutes. This section provides recipes for some of the basics and soups with more variations and different flavors.

CHICKEN OR BEEF STOCK

METHOD: Pressure Canning

PROCESSING TIME: Pints (473 ml)
20 minutes; Quarts (946 ml)
25 minutes

PRESSURE: Based on manufacturer's instructions and canning altitude

YIELD: 6 pints or 3 quarts (2.8 L)

---

3 pounds (1.4 kg) of chicken pieces or 6 pounds (2.7 kg) meaty beef bones

3 quarts (2.8 L) water

2 stalks celery, diced

2 onions, quartered

2 leeks (optional, but adds a nice flavor)

4 garlic cloves, chopped

12 whole black peppercorns

2 bay leaves

1½ tablespoons (27 g) salt

1. In a large stainless steel or enamel pot, combine all ingredients. Bring to a boil and then reduce heat and simmer for 2½ hours.

2. Remove chicken pieces or beef bones (reserve chicken for another use) and strain stock through a colander or sieve lined with cheesecloth.

3. Let cool and skim fat.

4. Return stock to a boil.

5. Ladle stock into hot, sterilized jars. Leave a 1-inch (2.5 cm) headspace.

6. Remove any air bubbles. Wipe rims and secure lids.

7. Process pints (473 ml) for 20 minutes and quarts (946 ml) for 25 minutes at pressure listed for your altitude and canner (see Adjust for Altitude! on page 29).

8. Use a jar lifter to remove the jars place them on a clean dish towel away from any drafts. Let cool undisturbed for 12 to 24 hours and then check the seals. Store any unsealed jars in the refrigerator and consume within 2 weeks. Label the remaining jars with the recipe name and date before storing.

VEGETABLE STOCK

METHOD: Pressure Canning

PROCESSING TIME: Pints (473 ml) 30 minutes; Quarts (946 ml) 35 minutes

PRESSURE: Based on manufacturer's instructions and canning altitude

YIELD: 8 pints or 4 quarts (3.8 L)

---

3 quarts (2.8 L) water

1 pound (455 g) carrots

4 stalks celery

2 onions

½ pound (225 g) mushrooms

1 red bell pepper

4 garlic cloves, sliced

3 bay leaves

1 teaspoon dried thyme

12 whole black peppercorns

½ pound (225 g) shallots (optional)

Other herbs as desired for more flavor

1. Chop vegetables (can be larger pieces).

2. In a large stainless steel or enamel pot, combine all ingredients. Bring to a boil and then reduce heat and simmer for 2½ hours. Uncover and continue to simmer for an additional hour.

3. Strain stock through a colander or sieve lined with cheesecloth.

4. Let cool and skim fat.

5. Return stock to a boil.

6. Ladle stock into hot jars. Leave a 1-inch (2.5 cm) headspace.

7. Remove any air bubbles. Wipe rims and secure lids.

8. Process pints (473 ml) for 30 minutes or quarts (946 ml) for 35 minutes at pressure listed for your altitude and canner (see Adjust for Altitude! on page 29).

9. Use a jar lifter to remove the jars place them on a clean dish towel away from any drafts. Let cool undisturbed for 12 to 24 hours and then check the seals. Store any unsealed jars in the refrigerator and consume within 2 weeks. Label the remaining jars with the recipe name and date before storing.

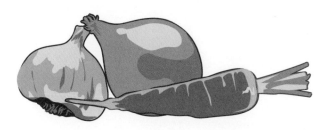

CHICKEN OR TURKEY BROTH

Both chicken and turkey soup are frequent menu items on our farm. Yet, I make this broth quite often because it's so useful beyond just the expected soups. A cup of broth with a pinch of cayenne pepper soothes even the worst cold. And my college-age children always ask for jars of it take back to their dorm rooms. I'm sure it ends up the base of many quick and easy dinners! Make your turkey broth after the holidays and get the most out of the bird—truly using every bit of it. For this recipe, make the broth the day before you can it so you can chill it and skim off the fat. You can use a 10 to 15 pound (4.5 to 6.8 kg) carcass for this or you can use cuts with meat. Just remove the meat and use it for something else after cooking instead of canning it.

METHOD: Pressure Canning

PROCESSING TIME: 20 minutes

PRESSURE: 10 pounds (68.9 kPa) Weighted Gauge, 11 pounds (75.8 kPa) Dial Gauge

YIELD: 8 pints (3.8 L)

---

3 pounds (1.4 kg) chicken or turkey pieces

1 gallon (3.8 L) water

2 celery stalks

2 onions, halved, skin on

15 whole black peppercorns

3 whole bay leaves

Salt to taste

1. In a large stockpot over high heat, combine the poultry pieces and water. Bring to a boil.

2. Add the celery, onions, peppercorns, bay leaves, and salt. Reduce the heat to low and simmer, covered, for 2 hours, stirring occasionally.

3. Strain the hot broth through a cheesecloth-lined colander or fine-mesh sieve. Chill overnight.

4. The next day, remove and discard the fat layer on top before proceeding with the recipe. Reheat the broth to boiling.

5. Carefully ladle the hot broth into hot, sterilized jars, leaving 1 inch (2.5 cm) of headspace.

6. Remove any air bubbles with a plastic or wooden utensil, adding more hot broth as needed to maintain the proper 1-inch (2.5 cm) headspace.

7. Wipe the rims and seal the jars hand-tight with the 2-piece lids.

8. Carefully transfer the filled jars to the rack inside the pressure canner. Process the jars at the pressure listed above for 20 minutes.

9. Let the canner return to 0 pounds pressure (0.7 kPa). Wait 10 minutes more and then carefully open the canner lid according to the manufacturer's instructions.

10. With a jar lifter, remove the jars and place them on a clean dish towel away from any drafts. Allow to cool undisturbed for 12 to 24 hours and then check the seals. If any jars have not sealed properly, refrigerate them and use the broth within 1 week. Label the remaining jars with the recipe name and date before storing.

BEEF BONE BROTH

Beef broth is perfect for those cold winter meals. It's a delicious treat on its own in a mug (just salt to taste) and is the ideal base for your favorite stew. Rather than shop for this recipe, I try to save all my beef bones in the freezer until I have enough for a batch of stock. The good news is, no bones are better than others for this recipe—save all of them! Be sure to remove any visible fat before freezing and store them in an airtight freezer bag. For this recipe, make the broth the day before you want to can it so you can chill it and skim off the fat. If you have a couple of days and a slow cooker, this recipe can be made that way as well. The flavor develops beautifully if cooked overnight.

METHOD: Pressure Canning

PROCESSING TIME: 25 minutes

PRESSURE: 10 pounds (68.9 kPa) Weighted Gauge, 11 pounds (75.8 kPa) Dial Gauge

YIELD: 8 pints (3.8 L)

---

3 pounds (1.4 kg) assorted beef bones

1 gallon (3.8 L) cold water

1 large yellow onion, halved, skin on

2 garlic cloves

Salt and ground black pepper to taste (optional)

1. In a large stockpot over high heat, combine the bones, cold water, onion, and garlic. Bring to a boil. Reduce the heat to low, cover the pot, and simmer for 4 hours. Alternatively, place all ingredients in a slow cooker set on low heat, cover the cooker, and cook for at least 8 hours or overnight.

2. Strain the broth through a cheesecloth-lined colander or fine-mesh sieve. Taste and season with salt or black pepper, if desired. Chill overnight.

3. The next day, remove and discard the fat layer on top before proceeding with the recipe. Reheat the broth to boiling.

4. Carefully ladle the hot broth into hot, sterilized jars, leaving 1 inch (2.5 cm) of headspace.

5. Remove any air bubbles with a plastic or wooden utensil, adding liquid as needed to maintain the proper 1-inch (2.5 cm) headspace.

6. Wipe the rims and seal the jars hand-tight with the 2-piece lids.

7. Carefully transfer the filled jars to the rack inside the pressure canner. Process the jars at the pressure listed above for 25 minutes.

8. Let the canner return to 0 pounds pressure (0.7 kPa). Wait 10 minutes more and then carefully open the canner lid according to the manufacturer's instructions.

9. With a jar lifter, remove the jars and place them on a clean dish towel away from any drafts. Allow to cool undisturbed for 12 to 24 hours and then check the seals. If any jars have not sealed properly, refrigerate them and use the broth within 1 week. Label the remaining jars with the recipe name and date before storing.

GARLIC BROTH

Broth is perhaps not the most glamorous of foods to can, but it is one of the nicest things to have on the shelf. Garlic broth is my little secret for restorative dishes. My favorite thing to do for a sick family member is to serve a mug of this with a few red pepper flakes floating in it. However, you can also use it in many recipes in place of Chicken or Turkey Broth (page 200). It's a great way to make your vegetable soups vegan without sacrificing the deep flavors that meat-based broths bring to a recipe.

METHOD: Pressure Canning

PROCESSING TIME: 20 minutes

PRESSURE: 10 pounds (68.9 kPa) Weighted Gauge, 11 pounds (75.8 kPa) Dial Gauge

YIELD: 8 pints (3.8 L)

---

20 garlic cloves, peeled

1 gallon (3.8 L) water

2 onions, halved, skin on

Salt and ground black pepper to taste

1. In a large stockpot over high heat, Combine the garlic and water. Bring to a boil.

2. Add the onions and reduce the heat to low. Simmer for 2 hours, stirring occasionally.

3. Carefully strain the hot broth through a cheesecloth-lined colander. Taste and season with salt and black pepper. Return the broth to the pot and heat over high heat until it boils. Turn off the heat.

4. Carefully ladle the hot broth into hot, sterilized jars, leaving 1 inch (2.5 cm) of headspace.

5. Remove any air bubbles with a plastic or wooden utensil, adding more hot broth as needed to maintain the proper 1-inch (2.5 cm) headspace.

6. Wipe the rims and seal the jars hand-tight with the 2-piece lids.

7. Carefully transfer the filled jars to the rack inside the pressure canner. Process the jars at the pressure listed above for 20 minutes.

8. Let the canner return to 0 pounds pressure (0.7 kPa). Wait 10 minutes more and then carefully open the canner lid according to the manufacturer's instructions.

9. With a jar lifter, remove the jars and place them on a clean dish towel away from any drafts. Allow to cool undisturbed for 12 to 24 hours and then check the seals. If any jars have not sealed properly, refrigerate them and use the broth within 1 week. Label the remaining jars with the recipe name and date before storing.

VEGETABLE BROTH

The following vegetable broth recipe is my base—but it's a bit different each time I make it when it comes to the pound and a half (680 g) of vegetables. That's because, just as with the Beef Bone Broth (page 201), the base is built on extras that I stash away. I keep a freezer bag in my freezer to add to throughout the month. I throw in leftover vegetables, like half an onion, the tops of carrots, and occasionally, extras from the farmers' market. When that bag is full, I empty it in a stockpot and cover everything with water. This mix of vegetables makes a wonderful broth for many recipes. Naturally, this recipe should be the foundation of your next vegetable stew, but don't stop there. Use this broth for bean soups or try it in a recipe in place of chicken broth.

METHOD: Pressure Canning

PROCESSING TIME: 20 minutes

PRESSURE: 10 pounds (68.9 kPa) Weighted Gauge, 11 pounds (75.8 kPa) Dial Gauge

YIELD: 4 pints (1.9 L)

---

2 quarts (1.9 L) water

1½ pounds (680 g) assorted vegetables

2 large carrots, peeled and halved

1 celery stalk

1 onion, halved, skin on

2 garlic cloves

3 whole bay leaves

Salt and ground black pepper to taste

1. In a large stockpot over high heat, combine all the ingredients and season with salt and black pepper. Bring to a boil. Reduce the heat to low and simmer for 2 hours, stirring occasionally.

2. Carefully strain the hot broth through a cheesecloth-lined colander. Return the broth to the pot and heat over high heat until it boils. Turn off the heat.

3. Carefully ladle the hot broth into hot, sterilized jars, leaving 1 inch (2.5 cm) of headspace.

4. Remove any air bubbles with a plastic or wooden utensil, adding more hot broth as needed to maintain the proper 1-inch (2.5 cm) headspace.

5. Wipe the rims and seal the jars hand-tight with the 2-piece lids.

6. Carefully transfer the filled jars to the rack inside the pressure canner. Process the jars at the pressure listed above for 20 minutes.

7. Let the canner return to 0 pounds pressure (0.7 kPa). Wait 10 minutes more and then carefully open the canner lid according to the manufacturer's instructions.

8. With a jar lifter, remove the jars and place them on a clean dish towel away from any drafts. Allow to cool undisturbed for 12 to 24 hours and then check the seals. If any jars have not sealed properly, refrigerate them and use the broth within 1 week. Label the remaining jars with the recipe name and date before storing.

KIDNEY BEAN SOUP

Canned bean soups are a lot like canned beans—they can get the job done, but it's hard to get excited about them. Worse even, canned soups often pack lots of sodium—perhaps making up for their shortcomings in texture or flavor! This soup is a clear upgrade and, even better, kid approved. One of my family's favorite meals is a combination of this soup with fresh-from-the-oven biscuits. I've also done some testing and this recipe holds up just fine if you want to omit the ham and use vegetable broth instead of a meat-based broth. As far as the salt goes, I recommend canning this recipe as is and allowing your family (or guests) to season with salt and black pepper when serving. The salt in the broth may well be enough for some.

METHOD: Pressure Canning

PROCESSING TIME: 1 hour

PRESSURE: 10 pounds (68.9 kPa) Weighted Gauge, 11 pounds (75.8 kPa) Dial Gauge

YIELD: 4 pints (1.9 L)

---

2 quarts (1.9 L) Chicken or Turkey Broth (page 200) or store-bought broth

1 cup (110 g) diced peeled potatoes

1 cup (154 g) fresh corn kernels

½ cup (50 g) sliced celery

½ large yellow onion, diced

1 garlic clove, thinly sliced

1 cup (150 g) cubed cooked ham

1 cup (256 g) canned and drained kidney beans

1. In a large stockpot over medium-high heat, combine the broth, potatoes, corn, celery, onion, and garlic. Cover the pot and heat until the mixture comes to a simmer.

2. Add the ham and kidney beans. Bring the mixture to a boil. Cook for 10 minutes.

3. Carefully ladle the hot soup into hot, sterilized jars, leaving 1 inch (2.5 cm) of headspace.

4. Wipe the rims and seal the jars hand-tight with the 2-piece lids.

5. Carefully transfer the filled jars to the rack inside the pressure canner. Process the jars at the pressure listed above for 1 hour.

6. Let the canner return to 0 pounds pressure (0.7 kPa). Wait 10 minutes more and then carefully open the canner lid according to the manufacturer's instructions.

7. With a jar lifter, remove the jars and place them on a clean dish towel away from any drafts. Allow to cool undisturbed for 12 to 24 hours and then check the seals. If any jars have not sealed properly, refrigerate them and use the soup within 2 weeks. Label the remaining jars with the recipe name and date before storing.

VEGETABLE SOUP

It's a mystery to me why many children who avoid vegetables come dinnertime will eat a full bowl of vegetable soup. Who am I to argue? I'm always happy to find a way to make sure my kids eat the vegetables I put in front of them. This soup is a personal favorite. It's what I reach for to pack a thermos for lunch when I'm headed out for the day. It's hearty and filling on its own, but you can make it more of a meal with a thick slice of buttered bread. One important note: Make sure you use chickpeas or another bean that has been precooked—don't use dried beans in this recipe!

METHOD: Pressure Canning

PROCESSING TIME: 1 hour

PRESSURE: 10 pounds (68.9 kPa) Weighted Gauge, 11 pounds (75.8 kPa) Dial Gauge

YIELD: 3 pints (1.4 L)

---

1 pint (473 ml) canned tomatoes

2 cups (475 ml) water

1 cup (164 g) canned corn

1 cup (240 g) canned and drained chickpeas, or other cooked bean

3 carrots, sliced

1½ pounds (680 g) potatoes, peeled and cubed

1 medium-size onion, chopped

½ cup (50 g) chopped celery

2 garlic cloves, minced

Salt and ground black pepper to taste

1 teaspoon dried Italian seasoning

1. In a large heavy stockpot over high heat, combine the tomatoes, water, corn, chickpeas, carrots, potatoes, onion, celery, and garlic. Season with salt and black pepper. Stir to combine and bring to a boil. Reduce the heat to a simmer and stir in the Italian seasoning. Simmer the soup for 10 minutes.

2. Increase the heat and bring the soup to a boil again.

3. Carefully ladle the hot soup into hot, sterilized jars, leaving 1 inch (2.5 cm) of headspace.

4. Remove any air bubbles with a plastic or wooden utensil, adding more hot soup as needed to maintain the proper 1-inch (2.5 cm) headspace.

5. Wipe the rims and seal the jars hand-tight with the 2-piece lids.

6. Carefully transfer the filled jars to the rack inside the pressure canner. Process the jars at the pressure listed above for 1 hour.

7. Let the canner return to 0 pounds pressure (0.7 kPa). Wait 10 minutes more and then carefully open the canner lid according to the manufacturer's instructions.

8. With a jar lifter, remove the jars and place them on a clean dish towel away from any drafts. Allow to cool undisturbed for 12 to 24 hours and then check the seals. If any jars have not sealed properly, refrigerate them and use the soup within 2 weeks. Label the remaining jars with the recipe name and date before storing.

THANKSGIVING TURKEY SOUP

This soup tastes like Thanksgiving in a jar. I often use the turkey bones from the big day to make the broth and throw in a little of the leftover turkey from our meal. Since I brine my turkey the night before, the meat starts out moist. I experimented by adding the cranberries one year and now I do it every time. Try it and you'll see—they seem to pull the whole recipe together.

METHOD: Pressure Canning

PROCESSING TIME: 1 hour

PRESSURE: 10 pounds (68.9 kPa) Weighted Gauge, 11 pounds (75.8 kPa) Dial Gauge

YIELD: 4 pints (1.9 L)

---

2 quarts (1.9 L) Chicken or Turkey Broth (page 200), or store-bought broth

½ cup (50 g) sliced celery

½ cup (61 g) sliced carrot

½ large yellow onion, chopped

1 cup (154 g) fresh or (164 g) canned and drained corn

½ cup (55 g) chopped fresh cranberries

1 cup (140 g) shredded cooked turkey

1 cup (177 g) Great Northern beans, cooked and drained

1 fresh sage leaf, or ½ teaspoon dried sage

Salt and ground black pepper to taste

1. In a large stockpot over medium-high heat, combine the broth, celery, carrot, onion, corn, and cranberries. Cover the pot and bring to a simmer.

2. Add the turkey, beans, and sage. Season with salt and black pepper. Continue cooking until the soup comes to a boil.

3. Carefully ladle the hot soup into hot, sterilized jars, leaving 1 inch (2.5 cm) of headspace.

4. Remove any air bubbles with a plastic or wooden utensil, adding more hot soup as needed to maintain the proper 1-inch (2.5 cm) headspace.

5. Wipe the rims and seal the jars hand-tight with the 2-piece lids.

6. Carefully transfer the filled jars to the rack inside the pressure canner. Process the jars at the pressure listed above for 1 hour.

7. Let the canner return to 0 pounds pressure (0.7 kPa). Wait 10 minutes more and then carefully open the canner lid according to the manufacturer's instructions.

8. With a jar lifter, remove the jars and place them on a clean dish towel away from any drafts. Allow to cool undisturbed for 12 to 24 hours and then check the seals. If any jars have not sealed properly, refrigerate them and use the soup within 1 week. Label the remaining jars with the recipe name and date before storing.

PRESSURE CANNING SOUPS

There is nothing like a comforting bowl of soup after a long day at work, as the perfect lunch, or when you don't feel well. Like most foods, home-canned soups taste better than store-bought cans—and you can leave out the questionable preservatives.

Making soups for canning is almost the same as making them to serve immediately for dinner. There are just a few simple rules to follow to be sure your soups are canned safely.

1. Do not add starches such as noodles and rice to your canned soups. These foods become mushy and fall apart during the canning process. Even if the soups look good after the jars come out of the canner, reheating the soup will result in a breakdown of the starches and an undesirable mushy texture. Add the rice or noodles to the soup after you crack the jar to serve it.

2. When canning soups, add more broth than you would when making it on the stovetop. I fill my jars one-fourth of the way with vegetables and meat and the rest of the way with broth.

3. Cooled soup may thicken slightly in the jar when using homemade meat broths. If this happens, it's completely normal. Once you reheat the soup, it will quickly thin again.

4. Some ingredients do not belong in canned soups as they become so strong in flavor they overwhelm the recipe—broccoli, cabbage, and brussels sprouts all taste too intense after canning, in my opinion. If you want to experiment with these ingredients, use less than you normally would so they don't overpower your recipe.

5. When adding dried beans to your soups, cook them before adding to the recipe. Dry beans absorb quite a bit of moisture and will absorb too much broth.

MEXICAN CHICKEN SOUP

Slightly spicy, this soup is just right with a piece of fresh cornbread. I love serving it with a dollop of sour cream as well. Make it as spicy as you like. My family falls into the "medium heat" category, but the base recipe here is as mild as the taco seasoning you use. To spice it up, leave in some or all of the jalapeño seeds and add a few dashes of hot sauce when serving.

METHOD: Pressure Canning

PROCESSING TIME: 1 hour

PRESSURE: 10 pounds (68.9 kPa) Weighted Gauge, 11 pounds (75.8 kPa) Dial Gauge

YIELD: 4 pints (1.9 L)

---

2 quarts (1.9 L) Chicken or Turkey Broth (page 200), or store-bought broth

½ cup (50 g) sliced celery

½ large yellow onion, chopped

2 garlic cloves, sliced

1 cup (180 g) diced tomatoes

1 cup (154 g) fresh or (164 g) canned and drained corn

1 jalapeño pepper, seeded and minced

1 cup (140 g) shredded cooked chicken

1 cup (240 g) canned and drained black beans

2 teaspoons taco seasoning

Salt to taste

1. In a large stockpot over medium-high heat, combine the broth, celery, onion, garlic, tomatoes, corn, and jalapeño. Cover the pot and bring to a simmer.

2. Stir in the chicken, black beans, and taco seasoning. Taste and add salt, if desired. Continue to heat the broth to a boil.

3. Carefully ladle the hot soup into hot, sterilized jars, leaving 1 inch (2.5 cm) of headspace.

4. Remove any air bubbles with a plastic or wooden utensil, adding more hot soup as needed to maintain the proper 1-inch (2.5 cm) headspace.

5. Wipe the rims and seal the jars hand-tight with the 2-piece lids.

6. Carefully transfer the filled jars to the rack inside the pressure canner. Process the jars at the pressure listed above for 1 hour.

7. Let the canner return to 0 pounds pressure (0.7 kPa). Wait 10 minutes more and then carefully open the canner lid according to the manufacturer's instructions.

8. With a jar lifter, remove the jars and place them on a clean dish towel away from any drafts. Allow to cool undisturbed for 12 to 24 hours and then check the seals. If any jars have not sealed properly, refrigerate them and use the soup within 1 week. Label the remaining jars with the recipe name and date before storing.

CHICKEN AND CHICKPEA SOUP

I first started canning my own soup when I realized how much better the homemade versions of my childhood soups tasted. It's also a convenient meal: a pint (473 ml) of chicken soup and a couple of grilled sandwiches make for a filling meal in minutes. It saves me time and money for months if I can a few dozen jars for the winter. You may substitute your favorite vegetables in this recipe, but do *not* add any starch, such as rice or noodles. Starches break down during the canning process.

METHOD: Pressure Canning

PROCESSING TIME: 1 hour

PRESSURE: 10 pounds (68.9 kPa) Weighted Gauge, 11 pounds (75.8 kPa) Dial Gauge

YIELD: 6 pints (2.8 L)

1½ quarts (1.4 L) Chicken or Turkey Broth (page 200), or store-bought broth

2 cups (328 g) canned and drained corn kernels

1 cup (160 g) chopped onion

1 cup (122 g) sliced carrot

1 cup (100 g) sliced celery

1 cup (150 g) fresh or (130 g) frozen peas

1 cup (240 g) canned and drained chickpeas

1 whole bay leaf

2 fresh sage leaves, crumbled

Salt and ground black pepper to taste

2 cups (280 g) chopped cooked chicken

1. In a large stockpot over medium-high heat, combine the broth, corn, onion, carrot, celery, peas, chickpeas, bay leaf, and sage. Season with salt and black pepper. Bring the soup to a simmer. Taste and adjust the seasonings, as you like. Remove the bay leaf.

2. Using a funnel to keep the rims clean, divide the chicken evenly among hot, sterilized jars, filling them about one-fourth full.

3. Carefully pour the hot soup over the chicken and fill the jars, leaving 1 inch (2.5 cm) of headspace.

4. Remove any air bubbles with a plastic or wooden utensil, adding liquid as needed to maintain the proper 1-inch (2.5 cm) headspace.

5. Wipe the rims and seal the jars hand-tight with the 2-piece lids.

6. Carefully transfer the filled jars to the rack inside the pressure canner. Process the jars at the pressure listed above for 1 hour.

7. Let the canner return to 0 pounds pressure (0.7 kPa). Wait 10 minutes more and then carefully open the canner lid according to the manufacturer's instructions.

8. With a jar lifter, remove the jars and place them on a clean dish towel away from any drafts. Allow to cool undisturbed for 12 to 24 hours and then check the seals. If any jars have not sealed properly, refrigerate them and use the soup within 1 week. Label the remaining jars with the recipe name and date before storing.

BEEF SOUP WITH LENTILS

Beef soup with lentils is a go-to dish when I want to get my kids to eat some beans. This is the heartiest soup I make, which makes it perfect after a long day of sledding or climbing around the beach during low tide in winter. It's filling on its own but I recommend serving it with a thick slice of homemade bread on the side.

METHOD: Pressure Canning

PROCESSING TIME: 1 hour

PRESSURE: 10 pounds (68.9 kPa) Weighted Gauge, 11 pounds (75.8 kPa) Dial Gauge

YIELD: 4 pints (1.9 L)

---

2 quarts (1.9 L) broth of your choice

1 cup (100 g) peeled and cubed potato

½ cup (50 g) sliced celery

½ large yellow onion, chopped

½ cup (61 g) sliced carrot

½ cup (154 g) fresh or (164 g) canned and drained corn

1 cup (150 g) shredded cooked beef

1 cup (198 g) lentils, cooked and drained

1 bay leaf

Salt and ground black pepper to taste

1. In a large stockpot over medium-high heat, combine the broth, potato, celery, onion, carrot, and corn. Cover the pot and bring to a simmer.

2. Add the beef, lentils, and bay leaf. Season with salt and black pepper. Continue cooking until the soup comes to a boil. Remove the bay leaf.

3. Carefully ladle the hot soup into hot, sterilized jars, leaving 1 inch (2.5 cm) of headspace.

4. Remove any air bubbles with a plastic or wooden utensil, adding more hot soup as needed to maintain the proper 1-inch (2.5 cm) headspace.

5. Wipe the rims and seal the jars hand-tight with the 2-piece lids.

6. Carefully transfer the filled jars to the rack inside the pressure canner. Process the jars at the pressure listed above for 1 hour.

7. Let the canner return to 0 pounds pressure (0.7 kPa). Wait 10 minutes more and then carefully open the canner lid according to the manufacturer's instructions.

8. With a jar lifter, remove the jars and place them on a clean dish towel away from any drafts. Allow to cool undisturbed for 12 to 24 hours and then check the seals. If any jars have not sealed properly, refrigerate them and use the soup within 1 week. Label the remaining jars with the recipe name and date before storing.

TRADITIONAL CHICKEN SOUP

METHOD: Pressure Canning

PROCESSING TIME: Pints (473 ml) 75 minutes; Quarts (946 ml) 90 minutes

YIELD: 6 pints or 3 quarts (2.8 L)

---

2 cups (280 g) diced chicken

3 quarts (2.8 L) chicken stock (see recipe for Chicken Stock on page 198)

2 stalks celery, diced

3 carrots, diced

1 large onion, diced

1 teaspoon dried tarragon (or other herb if preferred)

1 tablespoon (18 g) salt

1 teaspoon freshly ground black pepper

1. In a large stainless steel or enamel pot, combine all ingredients. Bring to a boil and then reduce heat and simmer for 30 minutes.

2. Ladle soup into hot, sterilized jars. Leave a 1-inch (2.5 cm) headspace.

3. Remove any air bubbles. Wipe rims and secure lids.

4. Process pints (473 ml) for 75 minutes or quarts (946 ml) for 90 minutes at pressure listed for your altitude and canner (see Adjust for Altitude! on page 29).

5. Use a jar lifter to remove the jars and let cool undisturbed on a clean dish towel away from any drafts. Check the seals after 12 to 24 hours. Refrigerate any unsealed jars and use within 2 weeks. Label the remaining jars with the recipe name and date before storing.

NOTE

Do NOT can chicken soup with noodles. When you're ready to eat chicken noodle soup, pour canned broth and vegetables into a pan and add the noodles. Cook until noodles are tender.

CREAMY SQUASH SOUP

METHOD: Pressure Canning

PROCESSING TIME: Pints (473 ml)
55 minutes; Quarts (946 ml)
90 minute

YIELD: about 5 quarts (4.7 L)

2½ pounds (1.1 kg) potatoes
(red or other boiling potatoes)

2 quarts (1.9 L) water

3 Vitamin C tablets (300 mg each)

5 pounds (2.3 kg) butternut squash,
peeled and cut into ½-inch
(1.3 cm) cubes

3 onions, chopped

5 carrots, cut into ½-inch
(1.3 cm) cubes

5 celery stalks, cut into ½-inch
(1.3 cm) cubes

Boiling water

1. Peel and cut potatoes into ½-inch (1.3 cm) cubes. To prevent darkening, soak in an ascorbic acid solution of three 500 mg Vitamin C tablets crushed into 2 quarts (1.9 L) of water.

2. Boil squash and potato cubes for two minutes.

3. Pack squash, potatoes, onions, carrots, and celery into jars. Do not mash!

4. Cover with boiling water, leaving a 1-inch (2.5 cm) headspace.

5. Remove any air bubbles. Wipe rims and secure lids.

6. Process pints (473 ml) for 55 minutes and quarts (946 ml) for 90 minutes at pressure listed for your altitude and canner (see Adjust for Altitude! on page 29).

7. Use a jar lifter to remove the jars and let cool undisturbed on a clean dish towel away from any drafts. Check the seals after 12 to 24 hours. Refrigerate any unsealed jars and use within 2 weeks. Label the remaining jars with the recipe name and date before storing.

8. When you're ready to eat, drain squash/vegetable mixture. Add it to a blender with a cup (235 ml) of milk, cream, or water per quart (946 ml) of canned vegetables (more or less, depending on how thick you like your soup). Pour into a pan and heat. Add additional spices at this time according to your taste. Curry or ginger adds great flavor.

LENTIL AND KIELBASA SOUP

This is a hearty meal in a bowl!

METHOD: Pressure Canning
PROCESSING TIME: 90 minutes
YIELD: 5 quarts (4.7 L)

2½ cups (480 g) dried lentils, rinsed

1½ pounds (680 g) kielbasa (smoked sausage), sliced into ½-inch (1.3 cm) pieces

2 large onions, chopped

5 carrots, chopped

7 garlic cloves, chopped

6 pounds (2.7 kg) tomatoes, peeled, seeded, and chopped

¼ cup (5 g) dried parsley

1½ tablespoons (11 g) ground cumin

2½ tablespoons (18 g) paprika

1 tablespoon (18 g) salt

5 cups (1.2 L) chicken or vegetable stock

2 teaspoons ground black pepper

1. Add lentils and 8 cups (1.9 L) of water to a stockpot. Bring to a boil and boil for 2 minutes. Set aside to soak for an hour.

2. Drain lentils. Add 8 cups (1.9 L) of fresh water, return to a boil, and then strain, reserving lentil water. Transfer lentils to hot, sterilized quart jars (946 ml), filling each jar a quarter full.

3. Add remaining ingredients and lentil water to a stockpot and simmer for 15 minutes.

4. Divide vegetables and kielbasa into hot, sterilized jars. Top off with soup liquid, leaving a 1-inch (2.5 cm) headspace. If necessary, add additional boiling water to jars to fill.

5. Remove any air bubbles. Wipe rims and secure lids.

6. Process in a pressure canner for 90 minutes at pressure listed for your altitude and canner (see Adjust for Altitude! on page 29).

7. Use a jar lifter to remove the jars and let cool undisturbed on a clean dish towel away from any drafts. Check the seals after 12 to 24 hours. Refrigerate any unsealed jars and use within 2 weeks. Label the remaining jars with the recipe name and date before storing.

MASOOR DAL SOUP

METHOD: Pressure Canning

PROCESSING TIME: Pints (473 ml) 75 minutes; Quarts (946 ml) 90 minutes

YIELD: 5 pints (2.4 L)

2½ cups (480 g) dried split red lentils

1 medium yellow onion, chopped

3 carrots, sliced

2 garlic cloves, minced

½ cup (120 ml) water

6 cups (1.4 L) chicken or vegetable stock

1 lemon, sliced and seeded

1 tablespoon (6 g) curry powder (Use a good quality.)

1 teaspoon freshly grated ginger

2 bay leaves

1. Add lentils and 8 cups (1.9 L) of water to a stockpot. Bring to a boil and boil for 2 minutes. Set aside to soak for an hour.

2. Drain lentils. Add 8 cups (1.9 L) of fresh water, return to a boil, and then strain, reserving lentil water. Transfer lentils to hot, quart-sized (946 ml) sterilized jars, filling each jar halfway.

3. Add onions, carrot, and garlic to stockpot with ½ cup (120 ml) of water. Cook for 3 minutes.

4. Add stock, 4 cups (946 ml) of reserved lentil water, lemon, and spices to pot. Bring to a boil. Cover, reduce heat, and cook for 15 minutes. Add tomatoes and cook for 5 minutes. Remove lemon slices and bay leaves.

5. Ladle soup broth over lentils in canning jars, leaving a 1-inch (2.5 cm) headspace.

6. Remove any air bubbles. Wipe rims and secure lids.

7. Process pints (473 ml) for 75 minutes and quarts (946 ml) for 90 minutes at pressure listed for your altitude and canner (see Adjust for Altitude! on page 29).

8. Use a jar lifter to remove the jars and let cool undisturbed on a clean dish towel away from any drafts. Check the seals after 12 to 24 hours. Refrigerate any unsealed jars and use within 2 weeks. Label the remaining jars with the recipe name and date before storing.

9. To serve, heat and garnish with fresh cilantro and a pinch of garam masala.

ROPA VIEJA

This is a flavorful beef stew popular in Cuban cuisine.

METHOD: Pressure Canning
PROCESSING TIME: 90 minutes
YIELD: 4 quarts (3.8 L)

---

2 pounds (900 g) skirt or
   flank steak, cut into 4-inch
   (10 cm) chunks

8 cups (1.9 L) water

2 carrots, chopped

1 onion, chopped

2 stalks celery, chopped

1 bay leaf

6 garlic cloves

2 teaspoons dried oregano

2 teaspoons ground cumin

2 teaspoons salt

1 teaspoon whole black
   peppercorns

2 green bell peppers, cut into strips

2 red bell peppers, cut into strips

2 yellow bell peppers, cut into strips

1 red onion, cut into ¼-inch
   (6 mm) strips

1½ pounds (680 g) tomatoes,
   skinned, seeded, and chopped

1 teaspoon ground black pepper

1. Combine beef, water, carrots, onion, celery, bay leaf, 3 garlic cloves (crushed), a teaspoon of oregano, a teaspoon of cumin, a teaspoon of salt, and peppercorns in a large stockpot and bring to a simmer. Simmer 30 minutes.

2. Transfer meat onto a large plate. Shred into bite-sized pieces.

3. Pour soup liquid through a strainer into a bowl. Discard solids. Return liquid to pot. Bring to a boil. Simmer 30 minutes until liquid is reduced by half. Add bell peppers, red onion, tomatoes, 3 garlic cloves (minced), a teaspoon of oregano, a teaspoon of cumin, a teaspoon of salt, and a teaspoon of black pepper. Simmer 10 minutes.

4. Divide meat evenly among hot, sterilized jars, filling each jar a third full. Using a slotted spoon, divide vegetables among jars. Ladle liquid into jars, filling to leave a 1-inch (2.5 cm) of headspace (use boiling water if you need extra liquid).

5. Remove any air bubbles. Wipe rims and secure lids.

6. Process quarts (946 ml) for 90 minutes in a pressure canner at pressure listed for your altitude and canner (see Adjust for Altitude! on page 29).

7. Use a jar lifter to remove the jars and let cool undisturbed on a clean dish towel away from any drafts. Check the seals after 12 to 24 hours. Refrigerate any unsealed jars and use within 2 weeks. Label the remaining jars with the recipe name and date before storing.

TEX-MEX VEGETARIAN CHILI

METHOD: Pressure Canning or Boiling Water Bath Canning (variation at end of recipe)

PROCESSING TIME:

Pressure Canning: Pints (473 ml) 75 minutes; Quarts (946 ml) 90 minutes

Boiling Water Bath Canning: Pints (473 ml) 50 minutes

YIELD: 5 pints (2.4 L)

---

1 cup (184 g) dried kidney beans

4 cups (946 ml) water

2½ pounds (1.1 kg) tomatoes, halved

1 onion, quartered

3 garlic cloves

½ green bell pepper, chopped

¼ jalapeño pepper

1½ teaspoons ground cumin

2 teaspoons paprika

½ teaspoon dried thyme

½ teaspoon dried sage

1 teaspoon dried oregano

1 teaspoon hot sauce

5 tablespoons (75 ml) lemon juice

1. Boil kidney beans in 4 cups (946 ml) of water for 2 minutes. Remove from heat and let set for an hour or overnight. Rinse beans and simmer in 4 cups (946 ml) of fresh water for 30 minutes.

2. Arrange tomatoes, onion, garlic, green bell pepper, and jalapeño in one layer on baking sheet. Broil 2 inches (5 cm) from heat, turning frequently with tongs until skins start to char, about 10 to 15 minutes. Cool and remove skins and seeds from tomatoes and peppers.

3. Add roasted vegetables, spices, and hot sauce to a stockpot. Cook at a simmer for 10 minutes.

4. Divide beans evenly among hot, sterilized canning jars. Ladle vegetable mixture into jars, leaving a ½-inch (1.3 cm) headspace. Top each pint (473 ml) with a tablespoon (15 ml) of lemon juice.

5. Remove any air bubbles. Wipe rims and secure lids.

6. Process pints (473 ml) for 75 minutes or quarts (946 ml) for 90 minutes in a pressure canner, at pressure listed for your altitude and canner (see Adjust for Altitude! on page 29).

7. Use a jar lifter to remove the jars and let cool undisturbed on a clean dish towel away from any drafts. Check the seals after 12 to 24 hours. Refrigerate any unsealed jars and use within 2 weeks. Label the remaining jars with the recipe name and date before storing.

8. To serve, heat chili. Mix a teaspoon of cornmeal with a tablespoon (15 ml) of water. Stir mixture into a pint (473 ml) of chili. Serve topped with shredded cheese.

VARIATION

To can this recipe using the Boiling Water Bath Canning (see page 28), omit the beans and simply add canned or rehydrated beans when serving the chili. Process pints (473 ml) for 50 minutes, adjusting for altitude.

TOM YUM GAI

Tom Yum is one of the most famous Thai dishes, served widely in Thailand, Burma, Singapore, and Indonesia. This recipe is characterized by hot and sour flavors, and the ingredients can easily be found at specialty and Asian markets.

METHOD: Pressure Canning

PROCESSING TIME: 90 minutes

YIELD: 4 to 5 quarts (3.8 to 4.7 L)

---

10 cups (2.4 L) chicken stock

6 cups (1.5 L) water

1-inch (2.5 cm) piece of galangal or ginger, sliced thin

5 kaffir lime leaves (available at ethnic markets—in a pinch, substitute lime zest)

3 stalks of lemongrass, cut into 1-inch (2.5 cm) pieces

2 tablespoons (32 g) hot chili paste

5 small Thai or Serrano chilis, left whole

6 tablespoons (90 ml) fish sauce

9 tablespoons (135 ml) fresh lime juice

6 shallots, thinly sliced

3 Roma tomatoes, skinned, seeded, and chopped

1 cup (122 g) carrots, sliced

1 pound (455 g) chicken breast, cut into strips 1 inch (2.5 cm) wide and 2 inches (5 cm) long

1. Bring stock and water to a boil in a stockpot. Add all ingredients. Simmer for 20 minutes.

2. Divide evenly among hot, sterilized quart jars (946 ml), adding one whole chili per jar (make sure chili is intact—if it breaks open, the soup will become quite hot). Top with boiling water if necessary, leaving a 1-inch (2.5 cm) headspace.

3. Remove any air bubbles. Wipe rims and secure lids.

4. Process for 90 minutes, adjusting for altitude if necessary (see Adjust for Altitude! on page 29).

5. Use a jar lifter to remove the jars and let cool undisturbed on a clean dish towel away from any drafts. Check the seals after 12 to 24 hours. Refrigerate any unsealed jars and use within 2 weeks. Label the remaining jars with the recipe name and date before storing.

6. To serve, heat and top with cilantro leaves. Canned straw mushrooms may also be added.

INDEX